IN
MEMORIAM

A Scots guardsman giving a wounded German prisoner a drink, August 1918.

IN
MEMORIAM

REMEMBERING THE GREAT WAR

IN ASSOCIATION WITH THE
IMPERIAL WAR MUSEUM

ROBIN CROSS

1 3 5 7 9 10 8 6 4 2

Published in 2008 by Ebury Press, an imprint of Ebury Publishing

A Random House Group Company

Text © Robin Cross 2008

Photographs © The Imperial War Museum 2008
www.iwm.org.uk

Foreword © Ian Hislop 2008

Introduction © Malcolm Brown 2008

The Random House Group Limited Reg. No. 954009

Addresses for companies within the Random House Group can be found at
www.randomhouse.co.uk

A CIP catalogue record for this book is available from the British Library

The Random House Group Limited supports The Forest Stewardship Council (FSC),
the leading international forest certification organisation. All our titles that are printed on
Greenpeace approved FSC certified paper carry the FSC logo. Our paper procurement policy
can be found at www.rbooks.co.uk/environment

To buy books by your favourite authors and register for offers visit www.rbooks.co.uk

Designed by Two Associates

Printed and bound in Italy by Printer Trento, Sri

ISBN 978-0-09-192530-7

CONTENTS

ACKNOWLEDGEMENTS

Robin Cross would like to thank the following for their assistance in the preparation of this book: the picture researcher Elaine Willis, Malcolm Brown and the staff of the Imperial War Museum, including Angela Godwin, Elizabeth Bowers, Abigail Ratcliffe, Madeleine James, Kate Clements, Cressida Finch, Tony Richards, Martin Boswell, Glyn Biesty, the staff of the Photograph Archive and Department of Art and, in particular, Terry Charman, who read the manuscript.

The author and publishers have made all reasonable efforts to contact the copyright holders for permission, and apologise for any omissions or errors in the form of credit given. They would like to thank the following for permission to reproduce copyright material:

The Barbara Levy Agency on behalf of the Estate of George Sassoon for the lines quoted from "Memorial Tablet, 1918" (page 86) and "Counter Attack" (page 245) by Siegfried Sassoon, from *Collected Poems*.

FOREWORD

"You're obsessed with the First World War," said one of my friends. "How can you not be?" I replied. Perhaps this is partly because I had spent much of my life ignoring the war and had failed even to find out about my own grandfather's service in the trenches. Yet once I knew the details, courtesy of the BBC's *Who Do You Think You Are?* series – that he had fought in the Highland Light Infantry, that he and his brother had joined up in the ranks after university because they thought they would get to the front line quicker, that he had gone over the top in the mist wearing a kilt with lice in the seams, that he was lucky to have survived the battle at all – I became fascinated by the war and realised that my grandfather was just one of millions of ordinary people caught up in the most extraordinary events.

I then made a series of television documentaries about the First World War called *Not Forgotten*. I was originally going to put a question mark at the end of the title because although I wanted to believe that the sacrifice of those who took part in the war was "not forgotten", I was not entirely convinced, and I thought that telling some of their individual stories might jog the national memory a bit.

I realise, of course, that I am just the latest in a long line of more distinguished and more dedicated attempts to say "lest we forget" which goes right back to the war itself – and which starts with the Imperial War Museum. Even before the war had ended, plans were being made to ensure that its casualties would be remembered. Architects and artists worked on designing dignified cemeteries and memorials, poets on devising lasting inscriptions. We still have these extraordinary public reminders of the war, and some of my work uses them as a starting point for remembering the lives of some of those names carved in stone.

But the country also has another legacy, planned at the same time, that has proved even more valuable – the Imperial War Museum itself. Sir Alfred Mond said of the Museum that it was "not conceived as a monument of military glory but rather as a record of toil and sacrifice". And so it has proved with its extraordinary collection not just of artefacts, but of first-hand accounts of those who took part in the conflict. Every First World War researcher ends up in the Museum's huge collection of documents, diaries and letters. Like all the other documentary makers, I have repeatedly turned up asking for their help finding material about Victoria Cross winners, or front-line vicars, or shell-shock victims, or black officers, or women ambulance drivers, or conscientious objectors or just ordinary soldiers. And I have always been amazed at what they have.

With the ninetieth anniversary of the end of the Great War it seems entirely appropriate for the Museum to show the public some of this remarkable material in a specially commemorative exhibition and book. The exhibition is confidently titled *In Memoriam*, and as long as there is an opportunity for current and future generations to engage with these vivid and moving accounts of the war, then it will probably be true to say that the lives of those that toiled and sacrificed are Not Forgotten. Without a question mark.

INTRODUCTION
A WAR OF LASTING MEMORY

Any book about a war must deal with battles, campaigns and political issues. These are essential parts of the fabric of every major conflict, particularly, as in the case of the First World War, one which caused so much upheaval and changed the world in so many ways, so that nothing was ever the same again. Yet a war is not an abstract phenomenon, or a mindless force of nature. Basically, it is the sum total of the experiences of individuals: those individual experiences, however, set against the background of great events way beyond their control.

Wars, inevitably, deal in the mass: populations of millions, armies of many thousands, statistics that seem to defy comprehension. Yet every single unit in such myriad figures is a person, whether man, woman or child. We know that more than 17,000 British soldiers perished on a summer's day in Picardy in 1916 on the first day of the Battle of the Somme, while another 40,000 were wounded or went missing. But every one of those who looked out across no man's land towards the German lines on that bright July morning hoped he would be brave enough to face the ordeal confronting him, hoped too that he would come safely through, while perhaps secretly fearing he might not.

Consider the photograph (opposite) of Captain Charlie May, of the 22nd Battalion, The Manchester Regiment, also known as the 7th Manchester Pals. Shortly before the start of the Somme battle he had written, in the diary-letter he composed over many weeks for his wife and young daughter:

Opposite Captain Charles Campbell "Charlie" May, 22nd Battalion, The Manchester Regiment, killed in action 1 July 1916, aged 27.

"I do not want to die. If it be that I am to go, I am ready. But the thought that I may never see you or our darling baby again turns my bowels to water. I cannot think of it with even a semblance of equanimity."

CAPTAIN CHARLIE MAY, 22ND BATTALION, MANCHESTER REGIMENT

G. Wynspeare Herbe[
Lanca[

He wrote the final sentences of his letter on the morning of the battle, less than two hours before zero hour. Aware that the week-long bombardment by the artillery was meant to have destroyed all life in the German front line, so that the British advance might be unopposed, he noted that the enemy's machine guns, far from being silenced, were still firing. He wrote: "I trust they will not claim too many of our lads before the day is over."

Before the sun was properly up, only minutes after the offensive began, Charlie May became one of the "lads" whom those machine guns claimed. There were 57,000 casualties between a summer dawn and dusk: here is one man whose story personalises that huge, incomprehensible mass.

I am the son of a soldier who served in that war. I was brought up under its shadow and lived through the Second World War as a child and teenager. Again, there were the massed figures, indeed on a far larger scale.

Thinking back over the last ninety and more years, so much of it spent in conflict or coping with the consequences of conflict, and seeking for some meaningful metaphor, or even straw, to clutch at, I find my memory jogged by not a fact, but a fiction, a film which had an immense impact on people of my generation. *The Third Man*, made in the late 1940s, was set in a bleak, bomb-shattered Cold War Vienna, with as its central character a profiteer-cum-gangster named Harry Lime, charismatically played by the late great Orson Welles. As he and his pre-war school friend Holly Martins soar above the city's seedy Prater area in the cabin of a giant Ferris wheel, the people on the ground below become a pattern of slowly swirling black dots. Looking down on them contemptuously, Harry Lime puts to his friend the serious, searching question: "Would you really feel any pity if one of those dots stopped moving for ever?" From that viewpoint, you see exactly what he meant – what difference would it make if one of those dots was 'taken out', 'liquidated', suddenly ceased to exist? Yet each one of those insignificant dots represented a living, breathing human being.

Most of my writings about the First World War have focused on the black dots: on the stories of individual participants, whether soldiers, sailors, airmen, nurses, munition workers, or just ordinary civilians, as interpreted through their diaries, letters or memoirs. The already quoted Captain May was one of those dots, one among hundreds. But I find something special, even haunting, about images of the black dots en masse, especially, for example, those taken in the autumn of 1918 by the Canadian official war photographer David McClellan (opposite).

Opposite Battle of the St Quentin Canal: Brigadier General J V Campbell VC CMG congratulating soldiers of the 137th (Staffordshire) Brigade, 46th (North Midland) Division, on their successful crossing of the Canal on 29 September 1918.

11

Above A file of men of the East Yorkshire Regiment picking their way around shell craters in newly won ground at Frezenburg, Battle of Passchendaele, 5 September 1917. *Opposite* Members of 'B' Company, 1st Battalion, The Scots Guards, in a front-line trench, October 1915.

I find a similar resonance in the striking silhouette photographs which were the speciality of the British war photographer Ernest Brooks, such as his image (above) of soldiers picking their way through shell craters in the Ypres salient in September 1917, halfway through the five-month offensive now generally known by the name of the, by then, totally destroyed Belgian village where the campaign ended, Passchendaele. They appear as abstract shapes against the sky, a mix of Tommies with rifle and pack and, probably, an officer or two, but we are always aware that each shape is a man, with his hopes and fears, his loved ones back home, his knowledge of his vulnerability to the hazards of shot and shell.

By contrast, I find something fascinating, and challenging, in the close-up image of the soldiers in a trench also reproduced here (opposite), a photograph of men of the 1st Battalion, The Scots Guards in a front-line trench somewhere on the Western Front, in 1915.

One Tommy in particular seems to fix his gaze on us, looking searchingly into our eyes all these decades later, as though he were asking, on behalf of himself and his comrades: "What do you think of us? Were we fools or dupes, or were we heroes? Did we make the world a better place, or a worse one? Should we be remembered, or should we be forgotten?"

Whatever the answers to such questions, and there are few easy ones, we can surely claim one thing as certain: this is a war we have not forgotten, and will not forget. It is far too fixed in the general consciousness for that. Significantly, the process of memorialisation began long before the fighting stopped. Already the military cemeteries, which would lay their unmistakable footprint across former battle zones, were being constructed, in due course to be followed by the building of such notable memorials as the Menin Gate at Ypres or the Memorial to the Missing of the Somme, inevitably producing places of pilgrimage and thereby initiating a culture that continues unabated to this day. The Imperial War Museum was itself a wartime creation, resulting from the recognition that the conflict in progress was of such importance that it required a focus of permanent memory. Its actual address might have shifted over the years – at one time it was based at Crystal Palace but fortunately had moved elsewhere long before that famous architectural phenomenon went up in flames in 1936, by which date the Museum had just arrived at its present home in Lambeth – but its commemorative role has remained unchanged and indeed grown markedly in public recognition and awareness in recent times.

After the guns fell silent and the pace of coping with consequences of the war quickened, the fact of the deaths of so many men whose bodies could not be found led directly to a totally new concept in the history of warfare, the cult of the 'Unknown Warrior'. Britain's 'Unknown' was buried in London's Westminster Abbey in November 1920, at the same time that France's *Soldat Inconnu* was being honoured at the Arc de Triomphe in Paris. Elsewhere other nations' 'Unknowns' are still being interred: the Australian in 1993, the Canadian as recently as the year 2000. Other concepts which have become enduring reminders of the war include the cult of the Flanders poppy (though in the first years following 1918 the memorial flower chosen was the chrysanthemum), and the two minutes' silence, both powerfully focused on Armistice Day, the 11th day of the 11th month on which the fighting stopped, at 11am, in 1918. Armistice Day has been undergoing a remarkable renaissance in recent years, after being subsumed during the Second World War, and for several decades after, into Remembrance Sunday. Although in this context we inevitably think of the ceremony at the Cenotaph in Whitehall, London, where the Queen, the nation's leaders and a whole cohort of high representatives lay their wreaths on behalf of the country and the Commonwealth, the occasion is commemorated at thousands of smaller memorials throughout the land – and elsewhere. Wherever British service personnel are based or engaged around the world – and now service women are included among those fighting as armed soldiers in the nation's cause – the rituals of remembrance are scrupulously observed.

The above examples relate largely to the mass. But the white headstones in the cemeteries or the incised carvings of names on memorials relate to the individual: to the family member who went to war, whether as eager volunteer or reluctant conscript, and lost his life in one or other of a range of foreign fields, or, in the case of the sailor, somewhere at sea. I myself remember from my childhood in the 1930s a not uncommon experience of that time: seeing on the walls of houses I visited especially-honoured framed photographs, sometimes coloured, not always expertly, for greater effect, of the relative, the father, brother or son, who had gone to war and never come home. Countless people have their own source of memory, their own personal link to that war, the photograph of a grandfather, or now a great-grandfather, in uniform, a medal in a drawer, an ambition, sometimes realised, sometimes still awaiting its moment, to visit a grave in a cemetery in France or Belgium, or nowadays, with the growing popularity of battlefield tours, further afield, say, in Salonika or Gallipoli.

So this book, as well as the exhibition which was its starting point, carry a strong, clear message: that the conflict which took place far back in the last century is not to be shrugged off and dismissed as a matter of ancient quarrels and battles long ago. It must be remembered.

Hence the title of both book and exhibition: *In Memoriam.* How can we interpret that resonant phrase? There could surely be no better answer than the formula devised in the second month of the war, September 1914, by the poet Laurence Binyon and which, through its use on countless state, and private, occasions, is printed indelibly on our common memory – though in this present context it pointedly applies to those who served and survived as well as to those who served and fell:

At the going down of the sun and in the morning
We will remember them

Malcolm Brown,
March 2008

CHRONOLOGY

1914

28 June	Archduke Franz Ferdinand assassinated
1 August	Germany declares war against Russia
3 August	Germany declares war against France
4 August	Germany invades Belgium; Britain declares war against Germany
14 August	Battle of Frontiers (French offensive into Alsace and Lorraine)
23 August	Battle of Mons
23-29 August	Battle of Tannenberg (Eastern Front: German victory over Russia)
6-10 September	Battle of the Marne
19 October- 22 November	First Battle of Ypres

1915

10-13 March	Battle of Neuve Chapelle
25 April	Allied troops land at Gallipoli
22 April- 25 May	Second Battle of Ypres
7 May	Sinking of the Lusitania
9-25 May	Battle of Aubers Ridge
23 May	Italy declares war against Austria-Hungary
31 May	First Zeppelin raid on London
25 September- 13 October	Battle of Loos
28 November	Austria, Germany and Bulgaria defeat Serbia
13 December	British and French troops occupy Salonika, Greece.
19 December	Haig replaces Sir John French as British commander-in-chief

1916

8 January	Gallipoli evacuation completed
21 February	Battle of Verdun begins
31 May	Battle of Jutland
4 June	Start of Brusilov's Russian offensive in Galicia
1 July- 18 November	Battle of the Somme
29 August	Von Hindenburg and Ludendorff become chiefs of German General Staff

15 September	First use of the tank, during the Somme
7 December	Lloyd George replaces Asquith as British prime minister

1917

1 February	Germany begins unrestricted submarine warfare
6 April	United States declares war against Germany
9-14 April	Battle of Arras
10 April	Canadians take Vimy Ridge
15 May	Pétain replaces Nivelle as French commander-in-chief, following mutiny in the French army
7 June	British take Messines Ridge (following detonation of 19 huge mines)
25 June	First units of the US army arrive in France
31 July	Third Battle of Ypres begins
24 October	Austrians and Germans defeat the Italians at Caporetto
6 November	British capture Passchendaele Ridge
7 November	Bolshevik Revolution in Russia
20 November	Battle of Cambrai (the first battle where a large number of tanks are used – 378)
15 December	Russo-German armistice

1918

3 March	Germany and Russia sign the Treaty of Brest-Litovsk
21 March	Germans launch a massive offensive against the British and French
26 March	Foch appointed to supreme control of Allied Armies in France
14 April	Foch appointed titular commander-in-chief of Allied armies in France (minus Belgians)
15 July	Germans begin their last offensive against the French
8 August	British attack at Amiens (Ludendorff described this as 'the Black Day for the German army)
26 September	Widespread Allied offensives on the Western Front, including US assault in the Meuse-Argonne sector
20 October	Germany accepts US President Wilson's Fourteen Points for peace
9 November	Kaiser Wilhelm II abdicates and flees to Holland
11 November	Armistice signed by the Germans

1 THE ORIGINS AND COURSE OF THE GREAT WAR

"For days we marched, first westwards towards St Quentin, then Ham. Then northwards uncertain where to. Day and night, often ten and fifteen hours. Not we alone. On all roads bodies of troops of all arms rolled on."

F L KASSELL, GERMAN RESERVIST

On 28 June 1914, the Archduke Franz Ferdinand of Austria-Hungary, heir to the ancient throne of the Habsburg Empire, and his wife the Czech Countess Sophie, made an official visit to the city of Sarajevo, the capital of Bosnia, to open a museum. Bosnia, and its sister province Herzegovina, were former Turkish possessions which had been administered by Austria-Hungary since 1879 and annexed by the Habsburg dual monarchy in 1908. Many of Sarajevo's Serb inhabitants were bitterly resentful at not being allowed to become citizens of Serbia, their homeland, which had achieved formal independence in 1878. Some of them were going to give the archduke a less than friendly welcome in Sarajevo, with the help of fellow Serbs infiltrated from the Serbian capital Belgrade. These were members of 'Young Bosnia', a secret society backed by Serbian military intelligence, which was pledged to liberating Slav lands from Habsburg rule. They had drawn up plans to assassinate the archduke.

It was a red-letter day for the visiting couple. It marked the fourteenth wedding anniversary of the archduke and his morganatic wife, who was treated as a commoner at the Austrian court and could never sit with her husband on public occasions. However, Sophie was able to bask in the recognition of the archduke's rank when he was engaged on military business (they had attended Army manoeuvres on 27 June). Thus in Sarajevo she could travel with her husand under the warm summer sky in a handsome open-top Gräf & Stift Double Phaeton as they motored through the streets of the city to their first stop, an inspection of the city's barracks.

It was also a day of fierce and melancholy commemoration for Serbs, as 28 June was the anniversary of the Battle of Kosovo (1389), a crushing defeat for the Serbs at the hands of the Ottoman Army under Sultan Murad I. Murad had been assassinated at the height of the fighting by a Serbian nobleman, Milo Obili, but only a handful of those commemorating his death knew that another assassination was about to unfold.

It very nearly did not happen. The assassins' plans were bungled. Two of them, armed with bombs and pistols, froze as the motorcade glided past. Further along the route, near the River Miljacka, a bomb was thrown at the archduke's open car by a third assassin, Nedeljko Cabrinovic, but it bounced off the back of the Double Phaeton and exploded under the following car, injuring two policemen and some bystanders. Chaotic scenes ensued as Cabrinovic swallowed a cyanide pill and threw himself into the Miljacka.

Previous page Manoeuvring into war. The German Army on peacetime exercises. Below Gavrilo Princip, the man who fired the shots which plunged Europe into war. He was spared the death penalty for the murder of the Archduke and his wife because he was only 19.

Neither the suicide pill nor the death leap achieved their aim. The pill failed to work and the water was only a few inches deep. Cabrinovic was dragged from the shallows and assaulted by an angry crowd before he was taken into custody. The motorcade swept on. Another of the Young Bosnians, the 19-year-old consumptive Gavrilo Princip, a terrorist and nihilist straight from the pages of Joseph Conrad, ducked into a sidestreet café – Schiller's delicatessen – to munch a sandwich and pull himself together.

The archduke proceeded to the town hall for a scheduled reception. Rattled by the attack, he interrupted a speech of welcome delivered by the Mayor of Sarajevo, protesting, "Mr Mayor, I came here on a visit and I get bombs thrown at me. It is outrageous!" His wife leaned forward and with a few whispered words calmed Franz Ferdinand before he delivered his speech, the notes for which had been retrieved from the damaged car and were spattered with blood.

Scant attention was paid to the security of the archduke and his wife as they made their way from the town hall to a hospital to visit the victims of Cabrinovic's bomb. A suggestion that troops should be

The Archduke and the Countess Sophie in the Double Phaeton open limousine with Count Harrach on the running board.

brought into the city to line the streets had been overruled because they were on manoeuvres and did not have their dress uniforms. The overstretched Sarajevo police force assumed responsibility for the distinguished visitors, and one of the archduke's party, Count Harrach, took up station on the left-hand running board of the Double Phaeton.

The original route had now been changed and the archduke's driver became confused, taking the Double Phaeton right past the café where Princip was lurking. He watched in disbelief as the car stopped and reversed, then he surged forward towards the unoccupied right-hand running board of the car, firing two shots from the Belgian semi-automatic pistol provided by Serbian military intelligence. The archduke was hit in the neck and his wife in the stomach. Princip later claimed that his intention had not been to kill Sophie but Oskar Potiorek, the governor-general of Bosnia, who was also riding in the car.

The archduke and his wife, sitting bolt upright and dying in the Double Phaeton, were driven away to Potiorek's residence. They both expired within 15 minutes. Franz Ferdinand's last words, as reported by Count Harrach, were "Sophie, don't die, live for our children.".

His mission completed, Princip swallowed his cyanide pill but vomited it up, and had his pistol wrenched from his hand by onlookers before he had a chance to put it to his head. All of the assassins were eventually caught. Princip was tried and condemned to death but because of his age received a prison sentence of 20 years. Before he died in 1918, a prison psychiatrist asked him if he had any regrets over the assassination of Franz Ferdinand and his wife. His shots had been the first of the Great War. The blood-blotched notes for the archduke's speech were soon to be borne away on a crimson tide. Princip remained philosophical, replying that war was inevitable. If he had not killed the archduke, Germany would have found another excuse to precipitate the conflict.

Firepower

Seventy-two years after Princip's shots rang out, in October 1986, the British historian and politician Alan Clark visited Sarajevo on a trade mission and was taken to the spot where the archduke and his wife had been assassinated. In his diary he wrote: "I could still smell it, just as one can in a haunted room. A colossal seismic charge of diabolic energy had been blown, released on that spot … and drawn its awful price."

At first the incident in Sarajevo was barely noted in Britain, whose population was more concerned with the immediate threat of civil war in Ireland, the suffragettes' struggle to win 'Votes for Women' and the tax increase which was the main feature in the May budget announced by the Chancellor of the Exchequer, David Lloyd George. The German Kaiser, Wilhelm II, did not allow the crisis precipitated by the events in Sarajevo to interfere with his planned holiday cruise. The chief of the German General Staff, Helmuth von Moltke, was at a health spa. The chancellor, Theobald von Bethmann Hollweg, was on holiday on his estate.

But the peaceful summers which most of the peoples of Europe had enjoyed since the death of Queen Victoria in 1901 were about to come to an end. The fault lines in Europe's political landscape had been growing since Germany was united in 1871 and its chancellor, Otto von Bismarck, had set out to reassure the

European powers about the ambitions of this vigorous new political power at the strategic heart of the continent. However, in the years that followed, the tangle of great power rivalry, with its shifting alliances and brutal jockeying for imperial advantage, ensured that the prospect was anything but peaceful. Successive crises in the Russian Far East, Africa, the Middle East and the Balkans had flared up but had not exploded into a worldwide conflagration. Each had many important lessons to impart, had they been heeded. But they all seemed too distant to disturb the sense of wellbeing and optimism engendered in Europe by the new century. There was, however, a huge and growing black cloud which threatened to blot out the summer sun.

In the late nineteenth century, the continental powers maintained vast conscript armies. France and Germany operated a system of universal military service; similar military service in Austria-Hungary, Russia and Italy existed more in theory than in practice. Britain, with its volunteer army, was an exception; its national security depended on the dominant British navy.

The armchair admiral. Kaiser Wilhelm II took a keen interest in military strategy and tactics and the latest developments in weaponry. Distrust of his motives was one factor in the militarisation of Europe in the years before the outbreak of the Great War.

In Europe, industrial muscle and healthier, expanding populations had produced deep pools of manpower which could be mobilised as an act of political policy to achieve national ends. Much of the modern state's increasing revenue was spent on military equipment. Artillery and warships – particularly the Dreadnought types which from 1906 dominated the Royal Navy and the German High Seas Fleet – represented the largest outlay, but uniforms, preserved food and modern barracks were equally significant in conferring a new status on the armed forces of a modern state.

The rapid deployment by rail of ever larger numbers of troops to the front had been a feature of warfare since 1859, when France went to war with Austria in northern Italy. In 1866 and 1870 it underlay Prussia's victories over Austria and France, and would play a significant role in the German war plans of 1914. Six principal railway lines stretched across Germany, enabling the rapid transfer of forces between its eastern and western borders. Between 1909 and 1914, Germany undertook a major rail-building programme along the borders with Belgium and Luxembourg. The purpose was clearly military, as many of the stations on the borders were provided with platforms far longer than were needed by the rural communities they ostensibly served.

The technology which built the railways also provided the weapons which enabled the troops of the new mass armies to inflict mass casualties on each other. A torrent of scientific advances produced a firepower revolution which between 1850 and 1900 increased the range of infantry weapons tenfold from a hundred to a thousand yards. The starting gun had been fired on an arms race. Further refinements produced the machine gun and the quick-firing artillery piece, the arbiters of the battlefield in 1914.

These technological and logistic leaps forward did not happen at a uniform pace across Europe. By 1913, Germany had overtaken Britain as Europe's leading industrial power. In contrast, ramshackle Russia, with a population three times greater than Germany's, could field an army of only roughly equivalent size. Its weak industrial base condemned it to inferiority in equipment, particularly artillery. Its rail network lagged far behind in scale and efficiency – in the Russo-Japanese war of 1904–1905, the Trans-Siberian railway could not cope with the problems of supply and this was a significant factor in Russia's defeat.

During the 1880s, Russia realised that its freedom of action in the Balkans depended in large measure on France's ability to maintain its status as a rival power to Germany. France and Russia had reached a preliminary agreement in 1891. This was followed by secret military conventions in 1892 and 1894 which were in turn confirmed and consolidated in 1899 and 1912. This did not prevent France, Russia and Germany from acting in concert outside Europe as imperial powers. In April 1895, for example, they co-operated to relieve Japan of territory it had wrested from China. Nor was the Franco-Russian alliance a material factor in France's claims on Alsace-Lorraine, lost to the Germans in 1871, or in Russia's ambitions in the Balkans. But the fact that the alliance existed nevertheless played an important role in the events leading up to the Great War.

By 1913, Russia was determined to punch its weight. The transformation was to be completed by 1917, when Russia would possess enough railway track, locomotives and rolling stock to transport a re-armed and re-equipped army to defend its borders within three days of any German mobilisation. In 1909 the Tsar's chief minister, Pyotr Stolypin, had boasted to a French journalist, "Give the state 20 years of internal and external peace and you will not recognise Russia."

In Germany, an autocracy in which the military was nevertheless paramount in forcing the strategic pace, there was mounting alarm. German planners were now faced with a continental alliance between France and Russia. For many years the German aim had been to achieve a swift victory against France, as they had in 1870, before turning east to deal with the slowly mobilising Russians. The German military planners urged that now was the time to strike. To wait was to run the risk that Russia might achieve strategic parity.

The Russians, too, were worried. Germany had made successful overtures to the enfeebled Ottoman Empire, the "sick man of Europe". The Berlin-to-Baghdad railway, built by a German consortium, was completed in 1914, shortly after the arrival in Constantinople (now Istanbul) of a German military mission. This was seen as a direct threat by the Russians, for whom the Bosporus (the straits between the Black Sea and the Sea of Marmara) and the Dardanelles (the straits between the Marmara and the Aegean) were the arteries supplying the lifeblood of the southern Russian economy. They guaranteed Russian access to the Mediterranean and carried a huge volume of exports and imports. When Turkey went to war with Italy in North Africa in 1911–1912, the Turks had closed the Dardanelles and had brought the economy of southern Russia to a grinding halt. Now there could be a German foot firmly planted on Russia's economic neck.

War by timetable

Marching as to war. A throng of French reservists stream out of the Gare du Nord on the way to the troop depots.

The imperatives dictated by war industries, imperial ambition and an army of stridently nationalistic newspapers created the conditions for a "perfect storm" to engulf the European powers. The mood of "business as usual" was, moreover, deceptive. In Germany the Kaiser might be on his yacht but Bethmann Hollweg, supposedly holidaying, was in fact hurrying back and forth between his estate and Berlin, busily tying up the government's (and possibly his own) financial loose ends before Germany went to war. We know of this because his expenses claim has survived.

In the years before 1914, no one questioned that great powers were fully entitled to bully smaller ones. Austria-Hungary was prepared to issue threats against Serbia, even to declare war, but was notably reluctant to tangle with Serbia's fellow Slavs in Russia. It took a month from the archduke's death for Austria-Hungary to declare war on Serbia, and this was a diplomatic rather than a military move, as it would take several weeks for the Austrians to mobilise. Then the Russians stepped in. They were not prepared to countenance the humiliation of Serbia, nor permit the Austrians and their German allies to dominate the Balkans and, by extension, threaten Russia's access to the Mediterranean through the Dardanelles straits. Russian mobilisation began on 29 July 1914.

On 1 August Germany declared war on Russia and mobilised, with the aim of having 3,500,000 men ready for action within a week. Russia's ally France also mobilised on the same day. On 3 August, at 6.45pm, Germany declared war on France. The next day Germany invaded Belgium, a neutral country. Now the British were drawn in. They despatched an ultimatum to Germany demanding an immediate withdrawal from Belgium. There was no reply, and by midnight (Berlin time) on 4 August Britain and Germany were at war. As the British foreign secretary, Sir Edward Grey, waited for the deadline, he observed, "The lamps are going out all over Europe. We shall not see them lit again in our time."

In the years before 1914, Europe's politicians had calculated on the deterrent effect of mobilisation to avoid war. They had not anticipated that these great armies, accumulated to keep the peace, would, once mobilised, propel the great powers into war by their own fearful weight. Army staffs had drawn up detailed war plans in advance. Those of Germany and France involved the use of precise railway timetables for the mass movement of men and *matériel*. The technological gears that enabled these movements could not be thrown into reverse by the politicians, who by this time had irrevocably surrendered control to their generals. In the first fortnight of August 1914, some 20 million men – nearly 10 per cent of the populations of the combatant states – donned uniforms and took the trains to war. They were fit, well clothed and equipped, bearing arms of a lethality never seen before, and all were imbued with the conviction that they would achieve swift and decisive victory. In the words of the Austrian writer Stefan Zweig, "As never before, thousands and hundreds of thousands felt what they should have felt in peacetime, that they belonged together."

Boy Recruits

Patriotism and obliging recruiting sergeants meant that many adolescent British men found themselves bound for the front line

In the summer and autumn of 1914, thousands of teenage British boys below the minimum age of 18 joined up, with the help of less-than-scrupulous recruiting sergeants who collected a bonus for every recruit they signed. When the sergeant asked 16-year-old Jim Norton his age, he answered truthfully and was told, "You had better go out, come in again, and tell me different". Norton returned, having aged two years in as many minutes, and joined the 8th Battalion of the Norfolk Regiment. For some, persistence paid off. A E Hollingshead (2nd Middlesex) recalled, "I was only fifteen and every time I tried to join up in London it was no good and they wouldn't have me. So I went by rail to Birmingham, on a penny platform ticket. I went into a recruiting office there and told them I was seventeen. The sergeant said, 'Why don't you go and have something to eat? When you come back you might be a little older'. I told him that I had no money and he gave me two bob. When I came back he spoke to me as though he had never seen me before. I said I was eighteen and, this time, I got in all right". During the First World War some 250,000 underage teenage boys enlisted in the British Army, of whom an estimated 50 per cent were killed or wounded. Youth was also no bar to execution for desertion. In February 1916, the teenage Private James Crozier of the Royal Irish Rifles was shot for desertion. He was taken to the firing squad dead drunk and his executioners deliberately fired over his head. He was then despatched with a pistol by an officer. In November 2006, Crozier was one of 306 executed First World War servicemen who were pardoned by the British government.

Above *Apprehensive first steps on the way to the front. An official takes down the particulars of youthful applicants.*
Below *A young man is eased into his greatcoat as recruits are fitted out.*

The armies of 1914

In August 1914 the intelligence section of the German General Staff had devised a rule of thumb by which every million of Germany's population could support two divisions of soldiers, or approximately 30,000 men. Drawing on a reserve of 4,300,000 trained men, the German army was organised in 25 army corps comprising 87 infantry and 11 cavalry divisions. Technically, in 1914 Germany possessed no Army; it had four armies, those of the kingdoms of Prussia, Bavaria, Saxony and Württemberg. There was no German Army until after the armistice of 1918.

The front-line fighting force was supported by 32 highly capable reserve divisions. The Germans set great store by their heavy guns for use in the field, particularly the 5.9in howitzer. In addition, Germany was the only combatant nation which had fully integrated the machine gun into its order of battle. Each regiment fielded between six and 12 guns, a total of some 12,000. In August 1914, Germany was able to put 1,750,000 men into the field.

The polyglot army of Germany's Austro-Hungarian ally, with its 32 infantry divisions and nine of cavalry (some 1,300,000 men), was more of a liability than an asset. The real peacetime establishment was 450,000 men and the reserve of about one million men was of dubious quality; at least a quarter were illiterate. More than half of Austria-Hungary's troops were Slavs, Czechs and Italians – men whose natural sympathies lay with Austria's enemies rather than the dual monarchy and who, moreover, spoke neither German nor Hungarian. These were factors behind some of the more spectacular Austrian collapses of the war. Although it had a weak industrial base and railway network, the most reliable element in the Austro-Hungarian Army was its heavy artillery, the massive Skoda howitzers, which were to play a significant part in German plans. It also fielded, in the Schwarzlose machine gun, a robust water-cooled weapon with just ten principal working parts.

When mobilised, the Russians could field 114 infantry and 36 cavalry divisions, the legendary "steamroller" comprising some 1,300,000 men, with a reserve of about four million. Although much had been done to revive it following the humiliating defeat by Japan in 1904–1905, the Russian Army remained poorly equipped, with reserves of ammunition and rifles in short supply, desperately short of competent officers at the lower levels and riddled with corruption at the top. In 1914 it was to lose the equivalent of its first-line strength, a dismaying performance which it was to repeat in 1915.

The French Army had made a remarkable recovery from the utter ruin of 1871 to field 70 infantry and ten cavalry divisions. With reservists, this represented a force of some 1,100,000 men. Because of its relatively small population and low birth rate, the mobilisation was achieved by the conscription of just under 85 per cent of eligible French manpower for a period (after 1912) of three years. The Army was infused with the doctrine of all-out attack developed after the disaster of the Franco-Prussian War. Symbolic of this spirit was the infantry's retention of conspicuous red trousers and heavy, dark blue coats. These were not to be replaced by "horizon blue" uniforms until 1915, and on the outbreak of war the only concession to camouflage was the provision of covers for the cavalry helmets and the kepi. The backbone of the French artillery was the quick-firing 75mm guns introduced in 1897. By 1918 some 17,000 '75s' had been produced. The '75's' hydro-pneumatic recoil system made it very stable when fired and its quick-acting breech mechanism gave it a firing rate of up to 20 rounds a minute. It could throw a 12-pound high-explosive or 16-pound shrapnel shell up to 10,000 yards. However, French offensive doctrine meant that the '75' was not ideally suited to trench warfare, and the shells it fired were too light to pose a threat to a heavily defended position.

From their small Regular Army, the British supplied six infantry divisions and one and a half cavalry divisions for the British Expeditionary Force to France (BEF). They went to war in the khaki uniforms that had been standard issue since the Boer War (1899–1902). Both infantry and cavalry were equipped with the Short Magazine Lee-Enfield (SMLE) rifle which had been introduced in 1903, making Britain the first major power to abandon the idea of issuing carbines for cavalry and rifles for infantry. The SMLE was an extremely powerful weapon, its bullets being capable of penetrating

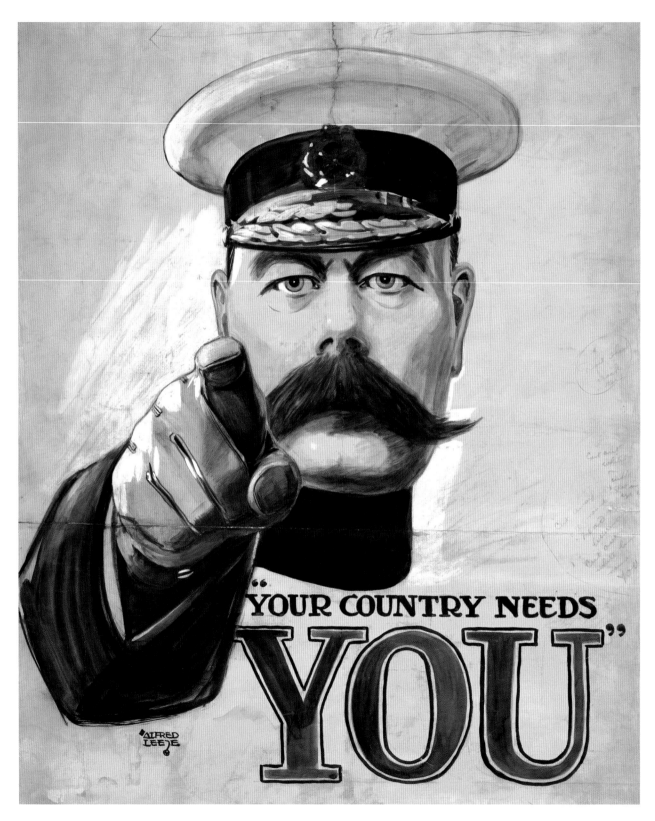

18in (46cm) of oak and 36in (91cm) of earth-packed sandbags. In the hands of a marksman it was lethal at 1,000 yards (915m). In the summer of 1914, each infantry battalion fielded two heavy Maxim machine guns. Compared with its European counterparts, the BEF was lavishly motorised, and its 150,000 men were supported by 1,485 motor vehicles of all kinds. The artillery's lack of heavy guns was balanced by the excellent 18-pounder field gun.

The course of the war

In the 1890s, the Chief of the German General Staff, Field Marshal Alfred von Schlieffen, turned his attention to Germany's fundamental strategic problem – how to cope with a war on two fronts: against Russia in the east and France in the west.

Schlieffen chose to seek a swift decision against France with the bulk of his forces while holding the Russians in check as they slowly mobilised. He intended to draw the bulk of the French Army towards the Rhine by leaving this sector weakly defended. The weight of the German blow was to be delivered in a swinging right hook through Belgium and northern France. Its extreme right would pass south of Paris, crossing the Seine near Rouen to take the French armies in the rear, pinning them against the Lorraine fortresses and the Swiss frontier.

After Schlieffen's retirement in 1906, his plan was steadily watered down by his successor Helmuth von Moltke. The German left wing was strengthened at the expense of the all-important right. In August 1914 the Schlieffen Plan's ratio of forces between north and south had fallen from 7:1 to 3:1, depriving the right wing of the strength to execute a complete encircling movement. It was to exert an inexorable influence on the opening phase of the war.

In August 1914, in scorching summer heat, the Germans drove through Belgium and at first it seemed that a fluid war of movement beckoned. Simultaneously, the French launched their own attack – Plan XVII – a headlong offensive into Alsace-Lorraine where German machine guns mowed down thousands of men advancing in open order. To the north, as the German armies began to swing round into France, the Schlieffen Plan began to unravel. The destruction by the Belgians of much of their railway system had meant that the critical distance between the marching German columns and railheads stretched to about 80 miles. Marching at a pace of 30 miles a day, the German Army was rapidly becoming exhausted before the serious fighting had begun. There was little or no motor transport to help them.

Opposite Britain's Secretary of State for War Lord Kitchener issues his famous appeal in one of the most famous of all recruiting posters, parodied countless times since it first appeared. The artist was Alfred Leete. His design was later copied by James Montgomery Flagg for a similar government poster campaign in the United States in which Uncle Sam replaced Kitchener.

General Alexander von Kluck's First Army, on the extreme right of the German advance, turned south-eastwards, exposing its flank as it marched obliquely across the faces of the defences of Paris. Kluck was now passing east, rather than west of the French capital, and this movement was reported by British aviators on 3 September.

Initially this information made little impact on the massively imperturbable French commander-in-chief, General Joseph Joffre, who was shuffling his forces to the left to protect Paris and to meet the Germans head on. But its significance was not lost on General Joseph-Simon Galliéni, the military governor of Paris. On the morning of 4 September, Galliéni ordered the French Sixth Army to prepare to strike the German flank and rear. Many of the French troops were famously carried to the front by Paris taxis whose drivers nevertheless still kept their meters running.

A German cavalry bugle captured in September 1914 during the Battle of the Marne.

Engaged by the Sixth Army two days later, Kluck turned west to meet the threat, simultaneously opening up a dangerous 30-mile gap between the First Army and General Karl von Bülow's Second Army, which was now taking the brunt of Joffre's counter-offensive. The British Expeditionary Force now advanced cautiously into the gap with the French Fifth Army on its right. The nerve of the Chief of the German General Staff von Moltke, far away in his headquarters in Koblenz, cracked as he cast an anxious eye towards the Channel ports and the threat to his rear posed by the (unrealised) intervention of fresh British armies. On 9 September he ordered Bülow and Kluck to retreat to the Noyon-Verdun line. The Allies tracked the German armies for five days before being halted on the Aisne by a line of hastily improvised German trenches.

Both sides now extended their operations northwards, each trying to work round the other's flank. As this series of leapfrogging manoeuvres reached its conclusion, the BEF sought to deny the Channel ports to the Germans, crashing head on into elements of the German Fourth Army on 20 October. Such was the initial confusion in the British high command that the Commander-in-Chief, Sir John French, believed for at least 48 hours that he was attacking while his heavily outnumbered forces were barely holding their ground. His optimism gave way to something close to panic when he finally grasped the true nature of the BEF's position.

The British line, supported by the French on their right, held. On the British left, the Belgians opened sluice gates to slow the German advance. Bitter fighting on a narrow front continued until 22 November when torrential rain and snow halted the final German offensive. The First Battle of Ypres was the final chapter in the history

of the old British Regular Army. Many of the battalions which had left for France in August some 1,000 strong had been reduced to an average establishment of one officer and 30 men. A tiny corner of Belgium had been kept out of German hands, and the salient around Ypres would see many more battles before the end of the war. From the English Channel to the Swiss frontier, both sides now began to dig in. Trench warfare had arrived, but the losses suffered in the opening months of the war by the BEF would be more than made good by a New Army of volunteers who answered the call made in August by Lord Kitchener, the Secretary of State for War.

In the war of the trenches on the Western Front the role of cavalry had become an anachronism. It remained ever ready but seldom used. When it went into action it was immensely vulnerable to artillery and machine-gun fire. Ironically, the tonnage of fodder required to maintain the BEF's cavalry and transport animals exceeded that for ammunition. Between 1914 and 1918 the horses ate their way through

Roll call of the 2nd Scots Guards on the Ypres-Menin Road, 27 October 1914. The Scots Guards had been involved in heavy fighting in the opening battles of the Great War. On this day, 12 officers and 460 men answered the roll call.

Christmas Truce, 1914

One of the most haunting episodes of the opening months of the Great War was the spontaneous truce of Christmas 1914

The winter of 1914 was particularly hard. The men in the front line were lashed by freezing rain and waded along flooded trenches. The stench of rotting corpses hung heavy on the air. On Christmas Eve, there was a sharp frost as the 1st Battalion The Royal Warwickshire Regiment moved up into the front-line trenches at St Yvon in Belgium. The ground hardened and the smell of putrefying flesh abated. An officer with the Warwicks, Captain Robert Hamilton, heard the Germans shouting across no man's land that they would meet the British halfway and share some cigars. One of his men, a

Private Gregory, volunteered to take up the German offer and ventured unarmed into no man's land, where he met two unarmed Germans covered by a third soldier who aimed a rifle straight at him. Gregory returned unharmed and in the crisp dawn of Christmas Day, Hamilton crossed into no man's land to find an officer of the 134th Saxon Corps with whom he arranged a local truce for 48 hours. Hamilton wrote in his diary, "As far as I can make out, this effort of ours extended itself on either side for some considerable distance. The soldiers on both sides met in their

Above *A snapshot taken by a British officer showing German and British troops fraternising, Christmas 1914.*
Left *Bierstein commemorating the Christmas Truce.*
Below *A meeting in no man's land, Christmas 1914. The British troops are Northumberland Hussars. Fraternisation was subsequently forbidden.*

hundreds and exchanged greetings and gifts. We buried many Germans and they did the same to ours". Among the Saxons was "the chef of the Trocadero who seemed delighted to meet some of his former clients." Along the line both sides agreed not to go into each other's trenches and there was no firing. One participant in the Christmas truce was the artist Bruce Bairnsfather, then a lieutenant with the Royal Warwickshire Regiment. He recalled, "It all felt most curious; here were those sausage-eating wretches who had elected to start this infernal European fracas, and in so doing had brought us into the same muddy pickle as themselves … There was not an atom of hate on either side that day; and yet, on our side, not for a moment was the will to war and the will to beat them relaxed." On New Year's Day the unofficial "live and let live" truce came to an end. Allied commanders subsequently issued strict orders that the Christmas truce was not to be repeated and that anyone attempting to fraternise with the enemy was to be shot.

5.9 million tons of fodder compared with the 5.2 million tons of shells and bullets which crossed the Channel.

In a military convention with France before the outbreak of war, the Russian General Staff pledged to put 800,000 men into the field by the fifteenth day of mobilisation. On the outbreak of war, two Russian armies advanced into East Prussia, a tongue of land projecting across the River Niemen to the heart of Russia, flanked on the north by the Baltic Sea and the south by Russian Poland.

The First Army, commanded by General Paul Rennenkampf, moved against the eastern tip of East Prussia while to the south the Second Army, commanded by General Alexander Samsonov, took the Germans in the rear, cutting off their line of retreat to the River Vistula. The general commanding the German Eighth Army, Max von Prittwitz, panicked. He was immediately replaced by General Erich Ludendorff who, lacking the rank to hold supreme command, acted as chief of staff to a nominal superior, General Paul von Hindenburg, brought out of retirement and squeezed into a uniform now too tight for him.

Even before Hindenburg and Ludendorff had arrived in East Prussia, the situation had been stabilised by one of Prittwitz's staff, Colonel Max Hoffmann. He had exploited the gap between the two Russian armies, separated by the Masurian Lakes, to mount a delaying action in the north while concentrating in the south against Samsonov, whose sluggish advance was spread over a front of 60 miles. Ludendorff finished the job by enveloping the Second Army and taking 125,000 prisoners. The dead included Samsonov, who committed suicide on 28 August. The Germans then turned on the First Army, which fell back in disorder after suffering a crushing defeat at the Battle of the Masurian Lakes. German casualties in both battles were fewer than 25,000 men. These victories ensured that German territory remained clear of Russian troops for the duration of the war.

In the opening campaign of the war in the west, the Germans had occupied much of Belgium and great tracts of industrial north-east France. This enabled them to assume a defensive posture in the west while pursuing territorial ambitions in the east. The French and the British enjoyed no such luxury. For them, regaining the territory lost in 1914 was a strategic necessity. In March 1915, at Neuve Chapelle, the British launched their first attempt to break the German line, attacking on a narrow front. They achieved an initial breakthrough but communications broke down, ammunition ran out and the advance stuttered and failed, setting a pattern for future battles on the Western Front.

The British suffered 13,000 casualties at Neuve Chapelle. In

September, amid the shattered mining communities around Loos, they lost another 65,000 supporting a major French offensive in Champagne. In Britain, a shell shortage caused an outcry which led to the establishment of a Ministry of Munitions under David Lloyd George. The shortage had in part been caused by the raising of Kitchener's New Army, which left industry desperately short of skilled workers.

In April 1915 a sinister new weapon – gas – was introduced in the Ypres sector by the Germans. The grand strategy urged by Lloyd George and First Lord of the Admiralty Winston Churchill – that of defeating Germany by attacking her allies, the so-called "indirect approach" – came to grief in the Dardanelles. Turkey had entered the war on the side of the Central Powers in October 1914. In Britain, operations against the Turks were considered necessary both to safeguard the Suez Canal and to relieve the pressure on the Russians by opening up a supply and communications route through the Dardanelles straits. A lodgement on the Gallipoli peninsula, on the northern side of the straits, would also provide a springboard for an advance on Constantinople, forcing the Germans to withdraw troops from the Western Front.

A Franco-British naval attempt to force the Dardanelles came to grief on Turkish minefields in March 1915. Allied landings on the Gallipoli peninsula followed in April and achieved initial surprise but the chance to break out from the beachheads was frittered away. By the end of the first week in January 1916, the last Allied forces had been withdrawn.

In October 1915, in an attempt to help the Serbs, an Anglo-French force landed at Salonika in north-east Greece, to open up a separate Balkan front against Bulgaria. This too proved a strategic dead-end. The Serbs were overwhelmed by Austro-German forces and their army was driven into Albania. Nearly 600,000 British and French troops were subsequently tied down on the Salonika front which the Germans dubbed "the greatest internment camp of the war".

In May 1915, the Russians suffered a debilitating defeat at Gorlice and were bundled out of Poland with the loss of nearly a million prisoners. Italy declared war on Austria-Hungary in May and was drawn into a slogging match on the River Isonzo, west of Trieste, where strong Austrian forces were deployed in excellent mountain defences.

Meanwhile, the war in the air was gathering pace. At the beginning of 1915 the French developed the forward-firing machine gun. The Dutch aero-engineer Anthony Fokker, who was working for the Germans, introduced a refinement, the interruptor gear. The day of

Kitchener doll.

NETHERLANDS

North Sea

0 — 50 mls
0 — 80 km

Ostend

Antwerp

Dunkirk

FLANDERS

Calais

Ypres ● Passchendaele

GERMANY

Boulogne

● Brussels

Armentières

BELGIUM

● Liege

Lille

Vimy

Mons

Arras ●

● Cambrai

Rhine

Moselle

Amiens

St Quentin

Oise

LUX

F R A N C E

Aisne

● Luxembourg

Oise

Soissons

Reims ●

Chantilly

Marne

Verdun

Saar

● Metz

Epernay

Seine

Meaux ●

Meus

Paris

Nancy

Strasbourg

Seine

Moselle

Western Front

Furthest German advance 1914
Trench warfare 1914–17
Armistice Line 11 Nov 1918

the fighter ace was about to dawn. The strategic bomber also appeared on the scene in the form of the colossal rigid Zeppelin airships which began raiding London on 31 May 1915.

Another new weapon, the U-boat, was also beginning to make its presence felt. At the beginning of February 1915, the German Navy began a blockade of the British Isles. On 7 May a U-boat sank the British liner *Lusitania*, killing some 1,200 passengers, including 124 Americans. Fear of drawing the United States into the war prompted the Germans to bring a halt to "unrestricted" submarine warfare in September 1915.

In the winter of 1915 German attention had fixed on the French fortress system at Verdun on the River Meuse. The Chief of the German General Staff, General Erich von Falkenhayn, planned to force the French to defend this historic bastion for emotional and nationalistic reasons which transcended those dictated by purely military necessity, and in the process to "bleed France white".

Falkenhayn intended to achieve this objective with guns rather than men. On an eight-mile front, he committed nearly 1,400 artillery pieces supplied with 2.5 million shells. In fact the French, anticipating a crushing bombardment, had stripped the fortress system of most of its armaments and moved its garrisons to field works. On 25 February the virtually undefended Fort Douaumont fell to a patrol of Brandenburgers.

This lucky *coup de main* drew 78 French divisions into the fight for Verdun. The French stabilised their defences and the Germans began to substitute men for munitions. Now they were being bled white. The German effort was halted at the end of June when the British bombardment began on the Somme and the Russians attacked on the Eastern Front.

The burden of fighting on the Western Front was now transferred to the British forces on the Somme, where the French and British lines met. Previously, this had been a 'quiet' sector where battalions had, on occasion, drilled undisturbed in open fields in full view of the enemy. In December 1915, the British and French began to plan a joint offensive.

After the terrible struggle at Verdun, the main burden of the fighting on the Somme was to be shouldered by the British Third and Fourth Armies. Their all-too-visible preparations were noted by the Germans, who strengthened their front-line defences to meet the attack, announced by a massive bombardment which began on 24 June 1916.

The British high command confidently anticipated that the bombardment – which expended over 1.5 million shells, many of which turned out to be duds – would smash the German barbed-wire entanglements, bludgeon their batteries into silence and entomb the defenders in their dugouts. They were wrong on all three counts. At 7.30 on the sweltering morning of 1 July, the bombardment moved on to the German second line. The German machine-gunners emerged from their dugouts to pour a withering fire into the men of 13 British divisions advancing at a walking pace across no man's land.

By nightfall, they had suffered 60,000 casualties, 19,000 of them dead, the greatest loss suffered in a single day by the British Army. The gains the British made were minor. On 15 September the British introduced a new weapon to pierce the German line: the tank. There was no breakthrough, only torrential autumn rain and seas of mud. The Battle of the Somme ended on 18 November, by which time the British had sustained some 420,000 casualties.

German Atrocities

A credulous British public and a jingoistic national press
ensured that there was no shortage of stories about the "frightfulness"
of the German military to helpless civilians

The earliest allegations of atrocities in the Great War concerned the conduct of German troops as they advanced through Belgium in the execution of the Schlieffen Plan. In August and September 1914, rumours began to circulate in British government and military circles about the German Army's brutal treatment of civilians. In January 1915, the French government published their findings on these stories, and in the following May the British issued the Bryce Report, which reached the conclusion that the Germans had committed numerous atrocities as part of a strategy of terror. Among the charges were the raping of women and girls, the amputation of children's hands, the chopping off of women's breasts and the use of civilians as "human shields". However, the report was deeply flawed and little or no attempt was made to verify the hundreds of depositions made to the Bryce committee. Moreover, the report was published days after the sinking of the *Lusitania* by a German submarine, U-20, and a month after the first use by the Germans of gas on the Western Front. Anti-German feeling was running at fever pitch. It is true, however, that some 5,500 Belgian civilians died at the hands of the German Army in the opening months of the war and much property was looted and destroyed. Moreover, the German military was greatly preoccupied with the supposed threat of *francs-tireurs* (irregular troops, or guerrillas in modern parlance) whom it had encountered in the Franco-Prussian War of 1870–1871. Nevertheless, in 1915 the atrocity stories were grist to the mills of the Allied popular press. The Germans incurred further Allied wrath in August 1915 when they arrested Edith Cavell, the English matron of a Belgian nursing school, who had been helping Allied soldiers separated from their units. Cavell was shot after a trial *in camera*.

REMEMBER
·BELGIUM·
Buy Bonds
Fourth
Liberty
Loan
ELLSWORTH
YOUNG
6-8

At the Battle of Jutland, on 31 May 1916, the British Grand Fleet and the German High Seas Fleet clashed in a unique naval passage of arms. Screened and supported by dozens of smaller warships, 37 British capital ships sailed against 27 of their German equivalents. It was the only occasion on which two modern battle fleets have engaged each other in European waters, but the encounter was inconclusive. The Germans claimed a tactical success but the Grand Fleet remained intact. For the rest of the war, the Germans did not risk the High Seas Fleet in a major battle in the North Sea.

Deadlock on the Western Front led to renewed demands in Germany for the reinstatement of unrestricted submarine warfare. On 31 January 1917, the Germans announced that all shipping, including neutral vessels, would be sunk on sight in the war zone of the eastern Atlantic. This was the measure that finally brought the United States into the war in April 1917. The German high command did not lose much sleep over this. They had calculated that Britain could be starved into submission in five months, before the US intervention could become effective.

In the spring of 1917, plans for a joint Anglo-French offensive were dislocated by the German withdrawal to the heavily fortified Hindenburg Line. The French, having mopped up the battlefield at Verdun with a series of lightning counterstrokes, nevertheless pressed on and in April launched an attack on a 40-mile front east of Soissons. In the first four days they suffered 120,000 casualties. Morale plummeted and in May discontent flared into open mutiny. Order was restored by General Philippe Pétain, the hero of Verdun, with a mixture of concessions and brute force.

At the end of July, the British Commander-in-Chief, Sir Douglas Haig, opened a fresh offensive in the Ypres salient, with the aim of reaching Ostend to capture the German submarine bases there and also to sever the Belgian railways on which the German communications depended. The enemy had ample warning and when the attack went in there were some two million combatants packed into the Ypres salient. The offensive foundered in a sea of mud and was called off at the beginning of November, only five miles from the original start line. Each mile had cost 50,000 casualties. Three weeks later, at Cambrai, the British achieved initial surprise and a limited amount of psychological success when they used tanks en masse for the first time. The Italians, however, had been driven back to the River Piave after the twelfth battle on the Isonzo (also known as Caporetto). The Austro-German advance was halted by lack of supplies and the timely arrival of 11 British and French divisions.

Opposite HMS Iron Duke, Admiral Jellicoe's flagship, in the North Sea, with a superb view of the battleship's forward 13.5-inch guns.

In June and July London came under attack by German Gotha IV bombers flying from Belgium. On 1 September the capture by the Germans of Riga, the capital of Latvia, brought Russia to its knees. Thousands of troops threw down their arms and walked home. They had "voted with their feet", as the Bolshevik leader Vladimir Ilyich Lenin observed.

In April Lenin had returned to Russia, with German connivance, in a sealed train. In November the Red Guards seized the Winter Palace in Petrograd and the following month the Bolsheviks opened peace talks with the Germans. German forces were within 100 miles of Petrograd when, on 3 March 1918, the Russian delegates signed a peace treaty, giving up Poland, Lithuania, the Ukraine, the Baltic provinces and Transcaucasia. Germany then moved 40 divisions to the Western Front. In the Middle East, General Allenby had successfully carried out his instructions to take Jerusalem by Christmas when he entered the Holy City on 9 December.

On 21 March 1918 the Germans launched a new offensive on the Western Front. They hoped to drive a wedge between the French and the British, the former focusing on the defence of Paris and the latter anxiously eyeing their communications with the Channel ports. On 12 April, Haig issued his famous "backs to the wall" order, forbidding withdrawal.

The Germans were initially checked, but by 3 June a renewed drive had brought them back to the Marne, near Château-Thierry, less than 60 miles from Paris. In their first offensive action of the war, the Americans made a decisive intervention, checked the German advance and then counter-attacked with the French. The Germans were fought to a halt.

On 8 August the British and French attacked on the Somme. Learning the lessons of Cambrai, they concealed their preparations, dispensed with a preliminary bombardment and supported the attack with 462 tanks. Fog masked the initial thrust which within 24 hours had driven ten miles into the German lines. It was the "black day" of the German Army. The Kaiser concluded that the war must be ended.

The final assault on the Hindenburg Line began at the end of September after a preliminary operation by the Americans against the St Mihiel salient, the first independent action they had undertaken in the war. By mid-October, after sharp fighting in which the Americans suffered heavy losses in the Argonne Forest, the German Army was stretched to breaking point and was fast running out of allies. On 30 September Bulgaria sued for peace. In Palestine, Turkish forces were in full retreat after a comprehensive defeat at Megiddo in September.

Damascus was occupied on 1 October 1918 and Turkey capitulated three weeks later. In Italy the Austro-Hungarian Army was on its last legs and signed an armistice on 3 November.

Ludendorff, who in April 1918 had come within an ace of snatching victory on the Western Front, resigned his command on 27 October. Inside Germany, hunger and an influenza epidemic were taking a savage toll. In the port of Kiel 40,000 sailors mutinied. On 9 November a socialist government seized power in Germany and the Kaiser abdicated. Since 7 November a German delegation had been closeted with the French Marshal Ferdinand Foch, the Allied Commander-in-Chief, in his headquarters in a railway carriage at Compiègne. The Germans had been given instructions to sign whatever terms the Allies offered. When they asked Foch about the precise nature of his peace terms, he replied "None". The Germans confessed that they could not fight on. Foch helpfully replied, "Then you have come to surrender." At dawn on 11 November a message was circulated to all the Allied armies. Its opening words were, "Hostilities will cease at 11 hours today, 11 November." One German commander who remained unaware of this development was General Paul von Lettow-Vorbeck, whose 4,000 German and askari troops had tied down a British force of 140,000 in a four-year guerrilla war in German East Africa. He surrendered on 25 November and, as a gallant foe, was afforded the honours of war.

In the summer of 1918, Germany occupied a vast chunk of western Russia, containing more than half of Russia's industry and one-third of its agricultural land. Through its Bulgarian and Austrian allies, Germany also held the upper hand in the Balkans. At the high point of the Ludendorff offensive in the spring of 1918, German armies were only 50 miles from Paris, the point they had reached in August 1914. But it was the Allies, and not Germany, who had emerged victorious from the Great War.

In November 1918 Germany remained in the field and its army's order of battle contained more than 200 divisions. But it effectively demobilised itself and marched home. Many Germans felt that they had been "stabbed in the back". The overwhelming feeling of betrayal was exacerbated when the victorious Allies met in Paris in January 1919 to redraw the map of Europe.

Their task was made all the more urgent by the collapse of four empires – Russian, Ottoman, Austro-Hungarian and German – all of which had gone to war but had failed to survive the bloodletting. The Allies themselves were in an ambiguous position, as they were now eager to disarm and the certainties of the war years had given way to

Opposite The last act at sea as the German High Seas Fleet steams to surrender on 21 November 1918 with the Kaiser class battleship Friedrich der Grosse *leading the way followed by the* Koenig Albert.

grave anxieties about the future. Germany was now prostrate, and seemingly in the grip of socialist revolution, but many felt that her potential to rise again remained intact. To the French, above all, the establishment of a lasting peace could only be won by the neutralisation of Germany by political and economic means. While the Germans considered the final terms with which they were presented on 16 June 1919, the Allies remained ready, however reluctantly, to resume the war and the naval blockade on Germany remained in place.

2 THE WESTERN FRONT

"My Dear Mother,

I am writing this in the trenches. I came up last night after travelling and messing about in Belgium for 12 hours. I am surprised to find how quiet it is here. Except sniping there is nothing doing. We are in good trenches and hold good positions. It was a fine sight coming up last night to see all along the line as far as you could star shells going up. It was like a fireworks display. I was surprised that far from being in a funk as I expected I did not mind coming up at all. It is not all bad here because there are plenty of funk holes if the Bosche gets really nasty."

SECOND LIEUTENANT GEOFFREY LILLYWHITE, MAY 1916

Previous page
"It is impossible to consolidate porridge." The sergeant pulls a cheerful face for the camera. However, too long in a flooded trench could bring on an very painful condition known as "trench foot", which in extreme cases led to amputation.

The dominant image of the Great War is that of "the trenches", the long, seemingly static strip of murdered nature on the Western Front, stretching 475 miles from the North Sea to the Swiss border. Even today the two words have a horrible ring to them, and in the years following 1918, set the men who had seen or served in that unique environment apart from those who had not. Such service left its mark. Something of the same shadow passes over the faces of German veterans of the Second World War when they talk of the Eastern Front. They need not tell you of the horror they witnessed there. You can see it in their eyes.

Among the regulars who crossed the Channel in the summer of 1914 and the men who rushed to answer Lord Kitchener's call to arms, there was little doubt that the war would be over by Christmas. But the Secretary of State for War and hero of Omdurman was not so optimistic. He estimated that the war would last three years. His determination to create a mass force of civilian volunteers – the "Kitchener Armies" – ensured the survival of the British Expeditionary

Force after the destruction of the better part of Britain's small regular army in the first few months of fighting on the Western Front. By December 1914, one million British and Irish men had joined up. The first trained units of "Kitchener men" sailed for France in 1915 and formed the greater part of the armies which went over the top on 1 July in the Battle of the Somme. By then the rhythms of trench warfare had been long established, both in myth and frightful reality.

The eagerly anticipated war of movement lasted just a few weeks. Trenches had already made their appearance by then, but had provided only improvised and temporary cover in the fashion of the foxholes and slit trenches of the Second World War. On 12 September, the German First Army pulled back across the Aisne and took up strong defensive positions along a ridge on the north side of the river. This sector of the Western Front came to be known as the Chemin des Dames after the road which had been built along the ridge in the eighteenth century for the daughters of Louis XV to enjoy their carriage drives. In the late summer of 1914, gun carriages rather than royal coaches were rattling into action.

British and French forces were only 24 hours behind the First Army and lost no time in attacking across the river on 13 September. However, the Germans had established a rudimentary trench system and the Allies could not break through. On 14 September they began to dig their own trenches. Within a few weeks the entire battle line to the north and south had congealed. The position of neither side could be outflanked, the trenches had taken over, and the pattern was set for the next three and a half years.

Digging in

By the spring of 1916, the line occupied by the British Expeditionary Force ran south for approximately 70 miles, from north of Ypres to the River Somme, and east, from Albert to the English Channel, for some 60 miles. From 30 March 1916, the British general headquarters was at Montreuil, 45 miles east of the centre of the line. On the coast, five miles north-east of Montreuil and 15 miles south of Boulogne, was the Base Area at Etaples ("Eat Apples" or "Heel Taps"), which received fresh units from England and those recuperating after a spell in the line.

Dubbed the "Bull Ring", Etaples had a grim reputation for spartan conditions and harsh discipline. The poet Edmund Blunden, who arrived there with the Royal Sussex Regiment in 1916, described Etaples as a "thirsty, savage and interminable training ground",

Left Although the British Army eventually fielded some 650 buses in France, most men made their way up to the front line by foot, marching over unforgiving and immensely slippery cobbles. Fifteen miles a day, with a heavy pack, placed an immense strain on the men's endurance.

Men of the Royal Scots Fusiliers muffled against the winter chill at La Boutillière in 1914. The white goatskin worn by the man in the foreground was an especially prized item.

presenting "endless vistas of dismal tents, huge wooden warehouses, glum roadways, imprisoning wire". On the training ground, Blunden soon had an introduction to the randomness of death in France:

"The machine guns there thudded at their targets, for the benefit of those who had advanced through wire entanglements equally with beginners like myself. And then the sunny morning was darkly interrupted. Rifle grenade instruction began. A Highland sergeant-major stood magnificently before us, with the brass brutality called a Hales rifle-grenade in his hands. He explained the piece, fingering the wind vane with easy assurance; then stooping to the fixed rifle, he prepared to shoot the grenade by way of demonstration. I … was listlessly standing on the skirts of the meeting, thinking of something else, when the sergeant-major having just said, 'I've been down here since 1914 and never had an accident', there was a strange hideous clang. Several voices cried out. I found myself stretched on the floor, looking upwards in the delusion that the grenade had been fired straight above and was about to fall amongst us. It had indeed been fired, but by some error had burst at the muzzle of the rifle: the instructor was lying with mangled head, dead, and others lay near him, also blood-masked, dead and alive. So ended the morning's work on the Bull Ring."

Shortly afterwards Blunden left Etaples to move up the line to the rest sector behind the trenches. At the beginning of 1915 the British established a three-line trench system: front, support and reserve. In the low-lying, frequently flooded plain of the Yser, the waterline was only three feet below the surface, which meant that in addition to the Germans, the ever-present enemies of the men at the sharp end were water and mud.

The British answer was the parapet or command trench which was about three feet deep. The rest of the trench was built up to a height of eight feet with stout walls of earth-filled sandbags – sometimes ten feet thick at the top and 20 feet at the base – to absorb bullets or shell fragments. In some sectors even this proved all but impossible. Near Loos, in the Artois sector, the front line was below sea level, obliging the British to build a system of ferroconcrete emplacements. On one 2,000-yard front the construction of the reserve trench line involved the men of the 42nd East Lancashire Division not holding the front line in manhandling up to 900 tons of material – 5,000 bags of cement, 19,400 bags of shingle and 9,700 bags of sand.

The front line comprised connected fire and command trenches. On the side facing east – the parapet – was a three-foot-high ledge, known as the firestep, which was used by sentries or by an entire unit when repelling an enemy attack. The fire trenches were continuous but not straight. They consisted of sections known as firebays up to 10 yards long, separated from each other by traverses. When seen and photographed from above by reconnaissance aircraft, they formed a crenellated pattern. Their purpose was to break up the line of the trench and protect the soldiers holding it from enfilading fire. The Germans adopted the same system but the French made do with a simple zigzag solution.

The back wall of the fire trench was known as the parados and was also built up with sandbags. To prevent subsidence caused by rainfall and shellfire, the British, Germans and French revetted both the parapet and parados, the British and Germans using sandbags and timber, the French hurdles. The command trenches contained dugouts for rest, latrines and officer command posts. Leading back to the support line, 100 yards to the rear, were communications trenches, down which ran telephone cables to battery and battalion headquarters and up which fresh supplies and reserves were moved

Mud

Although the 475 miles of the Western Front featured several contrasting terrains, the dominant image of the war in the sector occupied by the BEF is that of a mud-clogged wasteland pockmarked with shell craters and barbed wire

The sector occupied by the British Expeditionary Force on the Western Front was low-lying and with a very high water table. It was only possible to dig down for a foot or two before hitting water. Constant shelling destroyed the intricate pre-war drainage system, and a succession of extremely wet winters ensured that one of the abiding images of the Great War is that of a sea of mud and shattered tree trunks stretching as far as the eye can see. Prolonged occupation of flooded trenches could cause "trench foot", a condition in which the feet swelled horribly and then went numb. One soldier claimed that, "You can stick a bayonet into them and not feel a thing. If you are fortunate to lose your feet and the swelling begins to go down, it is then that the agony begins. I have heard men cry and even scream with the pain and many had to have their feet and legs amputated". During the First World War some 75,000 British troops were admitted to hospitals in France suffering from trench foot and frostbite. In March 1916 a battalion of the Royal Scots lost 100 men from exhaustion and trench foot, 25 per cent of their strength. The simple business of moving along waterlogged trenches often condemned troops to exhausting hours spent in traversing a few hundred yards, their progress hampered by sodden, mud-caked greatcoats whose weight had increased by anything up to 34 pounds. Shell holes filled with water were often death traps for the unfortunates who fell into them. It was estimated that in the Ypres salient these claimed nearly 1,000 wounded men a month as they made their way painfully back to the dressing station along the Menin Road.

Men of the Border Regiment shelter in so-called "funk holes" scraped out of the trench wall on the Somme in 1916. Sleep in this situation came fitfully. Harry Patch, a private in the Duke of Cornwall's Light Infantry, recalled sleeping for up to two hours "head in your hands, but the least noise you would be awake and wonder for a moment where the hell you were and what you were doing there".

at night. The communications trenches were built in zigzags, to minimise blast effect and, in common with all the other trench lines, were provided with dugouts which afforded some protection from German artillery. Communications trenches then zigzagged their way back some 500 yards to the reserve line of trenches, where more reinforcements were held. Further back, and well beyond the range of small-arms fire, were the artillery positions.

The fire trench was not the most forward defensive position. Narrow passageways, known as saps, extended towards the enemy line. They led to isolated listening posts, often established in shell craters and held by only two or three men. Men from the front line would take it in fretful turns to mount a three-hour watch in these saps, straining to hear the smallest sound from the enemy line. Beyond the trenches, at a grenade's throw distance, lay barbed wire entanglements, and beyond that the narrow strip which divided the opposing trenches – no man's land – punctuated by points of entry for patrols. Its width varied from sector to sector, from as much as 500 yards to as little as 50. Near Zonnebeke in the Ypres salient in 1915, the British and Germans were only ten yards apart.

The world of the trenches

The French trenches soon acquired a reputation for slovenliness. The writer Robert Graves, who joined up in 1914, observed that bodies were buried in the floor of their trenches, making them shallower as the casualties rose. In part the problem stemmed from the French reluctance to accept a permanent German presence on the soil of France and their understandable desire to expel them at the earliest opportunity.

In this the British and French were joined at the hip. To win the war, they had to adopt an offensive strategy. The Germans always had the option of remaining on the defensive, in positions which were on higher ground and easier to fortify than those occupied by the Allies. In the early part of the war, the Germans tended to pack troops into the front line with little immediate support beyond some machine-gun positions. However, their approach to trench engineering rapidly became more flexible. Single lines of trenches manned by the entire available garrison turned into more complex defensive geometry several miles in depth, criss-crossed with belts of barbed wire and incorporating deep dugouts protecting reinforcements from heavy Allied artillery fire. The lightly held first line could be easily evacuated in the event of an enemy attack. Then the exhausted attackers could be dislodged from their hard-won gains by a concerted counter-attack launched from the second and third trench systems.

In 1916 a German officer, Friedrich Steinbrecher, lamented this development:

Troops fix scaling ladders on 8 April 1917, on the day before the Arras offensive, This was a series of limited attacks on a narrow front which, in spite of being hampered by appalling weather, achieved the objective of drawing in German reserves from the River Aisne.

"The poetry of the trenches is a thing of the past. The spirit of adventure is dead … We have become wise, serious and professional. Stern duty has taken the place of keenness … a frigid mechanical doing of one's duty … formerly the dugouts were adorned with pictures – now they are covered with maps, orders and reports. Formerly the men christened their dugouts … now they are numbered."

FRIEDRICH STEINBRECHER, GERMAN OFFICER

In the autumn of 1916, the Germans prepared an even more formidable defensive line running from Neuville-Vitasse, near Arras, to Cerny, east of Soissons. The Hindenburg Line consisted of three lines of double trenches to a depth of two miles, the first of which was protected by six belts of barbed wire, the densest of them 100 yards thick. Dozens of communications trenches linked the lines and to the rear were sited hundreds of guns zeroed in to plaster no man's land with shrapnel and high-explosive or gas shells. Further forward, machine guns with interlocking fields of fire were positioned to strafe no man's land the moment the enemy mounted an attack. Railways were built up to the rear areas to speed reinforcement and supply.

Wallpaper from a captured German dugout. Occupying higher and less waterlogged ground than the BEF, the German dugouts behind the front line were luxurious by British standards, well ventilated, lit by electric light and often panelled with timber.

The British responded to these German innovations with modifications of their own, dividing their trench system into three zones – forward, battle and rear. The forward zone was to contain the machine guns and one-third of the available manpower; two miles back, in the battle zone, were to be found the artillery and two-thirds of the men; the rear held a mobile reserve.

The tactical pack was often shuffled but the men on the ground in the British trenches did not notice any changes to their daily lives, which seemed an endless mixture of toil and confusion. In 1916 a soldier of the 1/4th Battalion, The Loyal North Lancashire Regiment, described "Beek trench", near Ypres:

"A mass of slime and rotten sandbags which it was part of our job to drain, duckboard and rivet [sic] with corrugated iron. As nearly every trench in the salient was in like state, and repairs were soon spotted and strafed by the Hun … it will be seen that 'Old Bill's'[1] opinion, that the war would end only when the whole of Belgium had been put into sandbags, had much to justify it. Going up Beek trench on a dark night was no picnic. You started along a long narrow alley winding uphill, your hands feeling the slimy sandbag walls, your feet wary for broken duckboards; now and again a hot stuffy smell, a void space in the wall, and the swish of pumped up water under foot proclaimed the entrance to a mine. Gradually the sandbag walls got higher and the alley narrower, and in places you stumbled where the trench had been blown in and got covered in blue slime … round corners you dived under narrow tunnels two or three feet high, finally emerging into the comparative open of the front line trench."

What struck Edmund Blunden on his arrival in the front line was the "sense of the endlessness of the war". To his poet's mind, the

An Anzac officer, probably the official historian C E W Bean, contending with the glutinous mud in the Somme sector in the winter of 1916. Such trying conditions could reduce experienced men to tears.

skulls which poked through the mud "like mushrooms" in the Festubert trenches seemed like relics of ancient battles. Gazing at the weatherbeaten sandbag walls around him, Blunden sensed that he and his comrades shared the past with the men who had stood on the walls of Troy. An old trench captured from the Germans in 1915 "lay silent and formidable, a broad gulley, like a rough sunk lane rather than a firing trench. It was strewn with remains and pitiful evidences. The whole region of Festubert, being marshy and undrainable, smelt ill enough, but this trench was peculiar in that way. I cared little to stop in the soft drying mud in the bottom of it; I saw old uniforms, and a great many bones, like broken bird cages. One uniform identified a dead German officer; the skeleton seemed less coherent than most, and an unexploded shell lay on the edge of the fragments. What an age since 1914! Meanwhile, so many bullets cracked with whip-like loudness just above our heads that it seemed we were actually being aimed at, though it was night and the enemy at half a mile's distance."

Out of the Line

A straw bed, a shave and a square meal were the highly prized rewards for troops
who came out of the trenches to snatch a short time out of war

Every front-line soldier longed for the moment when his battalion moved from the reserve trenches, which were within German artillery range, to rest billets well clear of the battle zone. Here it was possible to enjoy simple pleasures: a pile of clean straw in which to sleep; a clean shirt and a bath; a hot meal – usually egg and chips – and a drink in an *estaminet* (tavern). The *estaminet,* invariably run by a formidable woman, was the nearest thing to a soldier's club on the Western Front. However, not every *estaminet* was a haven of benevolent good cheer. "No 4" in St Omer had a notorious reputation. According to the gunner Aubrey Wade it was "where licence was raised to the fourth power". "No 4", bizarrely, was next to the cathedral and at night attracted crowds of troops queuing to get in. Wade and a companion saw "Canadians, Australians, English troops, British West Indian blacks with rolling eyes and all-embracing smiles, non-combatant corps conscripts, Chinks [Chinese][2] out for the evening in clean overalls – taken all round, it was well representative of the allied forces with the sole exception of Frenchmen, of whom there was none". Inside, Wade came face to face with the owner, "a middle-aged, shapelessly fat woman with black hair greased down over her forehead. From her dirty ears dangled long, sparkling earrings which brushed her shoulders as she turned her head to shriek obscenities at the jeering crowd of soldiers who mocked her attempts

at English. Her skirt terminated halfway to her knees and was raised still higher as she slipped small bundles of notes into a bulging stocking." Behind this harridan waited some of the women and girls who could be purchased for the price of "five francs in one hand". Wade noticed that "one of them did not seem to be much more than fourteen, but others were a good deal older. All were practically naked, except for a single corset-like garment which left nothing to the imagination." They found plenty of customers. "The pudgy hands of the 'madame' were continually busy transferring notes to her stockings as men went upstairs, selected a partner and disappeared behind closed doors." Sickened, Wade and his companion beat a hasty retreat.

Opposite *Canadian troops find a comfortable billet behind the lines in a ruined barn at Villers-au-Bois, in June 1917. The troops' delight in a brief time out of war was caught by Private Archie Surfleet of the East Yorkshire Regiment: "We don't need much, now, to make us happy: a pile of clean straw, a clean shirt, ten francs, an estaminet out of Jerry's range and we are as happy as sandboys."*
Below *Coffee for the troops near Armentières, May 1916.*

At the front

In the British Army, as a rule of thumb, an infantryman would spend about a week in the fire and support trenches and one week in the reserve lines each month. The rest of his time he spent behind the line. Inevitably, some drew the short straw, particularly when a big offensive was launched. In 1916, during the Battle of the Somme, the 13th Battalion The York and Lancaster Regiment, part of the 94th Brigade, spent 41 consecutive days in the front line.

Examining his diary, Lieutenant Charles Carrington of the Royal Warwickshire Regiment calculated that in 1916 he had spent 65 days in the front line and another 36 in supporting positions. He was in reserve for another 120 days "near enough to the line to march up for the day when work or fighting demanded". Carrington also spent ten days in hospital, 73 in rest camps clear of the fighting zone, 17 days on leave and the remaining days travelling. The 101 days under fire in the front line and supporting positions comprised 12 tours in the trenches, the longest for 13 days and the shortest for a single day. He concluded with the observation that he had been in action four times:

"Douglas", a ventriloqist's dummy used by gunner Arthur Langley Handen to entertain his comrades in France.

"Once I took part in a direct attack, twice in bombing actions, and once we held the front line from which other troops advanced. I also took part in an unsuccessful trench raid."

One of the striking features of life in the trenches was the infrequency with which the troops saw the enemy. Nevertheless, they were always aware of his presence. Earth over-enthusiastically tossed over the parapet by a digging party might attract the attention of German artillery or machine guns and, on occasion, messages would be exchanged. Edmund Blunden recalled that he first became aware of the death of Lord Kitchener when the Germans opposite hoisted a large placard above their trench bearing the news. (Lord Kitchener was drowned on 5 June 1916 when en route to Russia. The warship on which he was travelling, the cruiser HMS *Hampshire*, struck a mine laid by the German submarine U-75 and sank with heavy loss of life. On the same day the last division of Kitchener's New Armies arrived in France.)

In quiet sectors, where boredom was a deadly enemy, artillery, sniper and mortar fire could cause a steady stream of casualties. During two months in the Neuve Chapelle sector in late 1916, the 13th York and Lancasters lost 255 men although they had been standing on the defensive the whole time. German snipers took a heavy toll on the unwary. Edmund Blunden recalled, "my excellent sentry in the longest sap, looking too faithfully through his loophole, was shot clean through the head".

Snipers

During the course of the war, sniping became a deadly art. In 1914 the snipers on the Western Front were principally pre-war gamekeepers or sportsmen. The Germans were quick to systematise this aspect of trench warfare, and by 1916 Bavarian regiments were being supplied with three sniper rifles per infantry company. In addition they received binoculars, periscopes and sniper's protective steel plates (loops) which were incorporated into the trench fortifications. By the end of the war, there were 24 snipers in each German battalion.

The optimum target for the sniper was always the head, where a hit meant either death or a disabling wound. The American Herbert McBride, who served with the Canadians, was a keen observer of the impact of a sniper's bullet:

"At short ranges, due to the high velocity, it does have an explosive effect and not only that effect but, when it strikes, it sounds like an explosion … all of a sudden, you hear a 'whop' and the man alongside goes down. If it is daylight and you are looking that way, you may see a little tuft sticking out from his clothes. Wherever the bullet comes out it carries a little of the clothing … the sound of a bullet hitting a man can never be mistaken for anything else … the effect of the bullet, at short range, also suggests the idea of an explosion, especially if a large bone be struck. I remember one instance when one of our men was struck in the knee and the bullet almost amputated the leg. He died before he could be taken to the dressing station."

HERBERT MCBRIDE, AMERICAN SOLDIER

At first the British approach to sniping was essentially amateurish. Nevertheless, rigour was injected by the enthusiasm of remarkable individuals like Hesketh Vernon Hesketh-Pritchard, a former big-game hunter, who was the driving force behind the formation, in the spring of 1916, of the BEF's first officially sanctioned sniper training establishments. In his own words, Hesketh-Pritchard saw it as his mission to "irritate the Germans". On the afternoon of 6 October 1915, he was duelling with a sniper in the enemy trenches and watching him through a telescope: "At 4.15 we could see the brim of his cap, and he lighted a pipe – I could see the tobacco smoke … Then he fired a shot resting his rifle on the board … I think he was shooting at a dummy plate … Then at 4.55 he looked over, his chin resting on the parapet. The rifle was well laid, and I had not to move it more than an inch; then the shot. Later a Bosche with a beard looked over, and this man was killed by the sergeant-major.

Hits achieved at ranges over 300 yards were relatively rare. Moving targets and the vagaries of weather (wind, rain, heat haze) saw to that. Snipers often achieved their best results at relatively short range, crawling into no man's land under cover of darkness, taking up a good position for several hours and firing one or two well-aimed shots before moving back to the relative safety of the trenches.

As the war dragged on, dedicated sniping officers strove to refine techniques and equipment. Elaborate methods of concealment were devised, including dummy trees or even simulated dead horses. They were used as hides or as a means to attract the attention of enemy snipers and force them to show their hand. Hesketh-Pritchard devised an elaborate system of dummy heads which could be raised or lowered to goad enemy snipers into revealing their positions.

Both sides fought to gain the upper hand. In January 1917, the British Summary of Recent Information Regarding the German Army and its Methods noted that "snipers have been discovered wearing uniforms made of sandbags, merging themselves with the parapet". In December 1917 the hard, practical experience gained by the British over three years was distilled in the manual *Scouting and Patrolling*, which also noted the importance of using snipers' intimate knowledge of the enemy's positions in the gathering of intelligence. By the end of the war, each British infantry platoon had its own two-man team (sniper and spotter in interchangeable roles) working as intelligence gatherers and marksmen. Humans were not their only targets. They were also used against enemy machine-gun positions to destroy the weapons' breech-block mechanism with a single well-aimed shot. The war of the snipers was fought to the bitter end. The last Allied infantryman to die on the Western Front was killed by a German sniper at 10.55am on 11 November 1918, five minutes before the Armistice took effect.

Patrols and trench raids

Troops quickly adapted to the demands of life in the trenches. There was a routine to staying alive. Harry Patch, a machine-gunner with the Duke of Cornwall's Light Infantry who had been called up in the autumn of 1916, remembered:

"Anyone who tells you that in the trenches they weren't scared, he's a damned liar; you were scared all the time. We constantly reminded each other, 'Keep your head down, don't look up.' If you didn't duck low enough behind the parapet, or if you were fool enough to look to see where the German lines were, then death could be instant. There's a sniper ready every time, see a tin hat, bang. There was an officer in C Company and out of the line he was very fond of seeing that your buttons were polished and shined. Of course this was the worst thing you could do in the front line as any reflection, any unnecessary glint, would attract attention, so

Above Star shells light the night sky over the Western Front. The nights were always busy in the front line; reserves and rations were brought up from the rear and wire obstacles were set up under cover of darkness. Below A rare photograph of the moment of attack as an officer of the 9th Battalion, The Cameronians (Scottish Rifles) leads the way out of a sap in the spring fighting of 1917.

Medical Services

The Great War witnessed a massive expansion of the medical services
supporting the troops in France and back in 'Blighty'

The British Army began the First World War with a small and relatively well-equipped medical service. However, the rapid increase in the size of the BEF, and the steadily rising number of casualties suffered in the battles of 1915, led to a root-and-branch overhaul of medical services stretching from the front line in France back to Britain. In 1914 there were some 20,000 personnel in the Royal Army Medical Corps (RAMC); by 1918 it consisted of nearly 200,000. Dealing with the wounded depended on a chain of treatment centres, beginning with the regimental aid posts behind the reserve trenches, then moving back to the advanced dressing and casualty clearing stations (CCSs) further to the rear, and behind them the base hospitals. The chain continued all the way to hospitals, nursing homes and converted country houses in the United Kingdom. The locomotive links in this chain were provided by stretcher-bearers carrying men away from the front line, motor-powered and horse-drawn ambulances, hospital trains, barges and ships, all of which were

Above: *A casualty on his way to the regimental aid post near the front line.*
Opposite: *Seven men battle through gripping mud at Pilckem Ridge, carrying a single casualty, in August 1917.*

run by the RAMC, which was unfairly stigmatised by the troops as "Run Away Mother's Coming" or "Rob All My Comrades". On the Western Front, lightly wounded men were expected to make their own way to aid posts, while the more serious cases waited to be collected by stretcher-bearers. With the exception of amputations, little or no surgery was carried out at the aid posts and advanced dressing stations – the aim was to get the wounded to the CCS as quickly as possible. A CCS – the closest point to the front at which nurses could serve – was designed to handle up to 2,000 patients, and the strain of working in these places, filled with dying and mutilated men, was unremitting. It was often equally grim at the big hospitals in the rear areas. Private John Martin was an orderly at No. 9 General Hospital in Rouen: "There was an incinerator in the hospital and I remember an old sweat who operated it recounting the incredible number of arms and legs he had disposed of in one day. I should estimate that during three days three hundred men went through our ward. There were nineteen other wards and a dozen further hospitals. Was it a nightmare? No, because we had no time to stop and think. We were too hard worked to feel at all. The only appropriate adjective was bloody and after it we were lousy as well from carrying discarded clothing to the incinerator."

whenever we were going up the line we used to smear them with mud … To calm nerves almost all men smoked, and if they could get enough cigarettes they would chain smoke. To hide any glow from the pipe I smoked I turned it upside down, placing my thumb over the tobacco so it didn't fall out. During the day I could always get under a groundsheet with a cigarette or pipe so no telltale smoke rose above the parapet."

A club used on trench raids, one of the many improvised weapons employed on this frequently nerve-racking and savage aspect of the war on the Western Front.

The British high command was not prepared to permit the troops to sit passively in the trenches and soak up the punishment administered by the German snipers and trench mortars (see below). In February 1915 Field Marshal Sir John French, Commander-in-Chief of the BEF, called for "constant activity" even though his army stood on the defensive. The fighting spirit of the British troops was to be fostered by a regime of patrols, intended to deny no man's land to the enemy, and trench raids, aimed at boosting morale and securing vital intelligence.

Many of the men tasked with these potentially hazardous nocturnal duties doubtless had a less sanguine view of them than Sir John French. Patrols were usually undertaken by an officer and six men and were invariably nerve-racking affairs. Alan Thomas, who served with the Royal West Kents, was a bolder soul than most and remembered his nights on patrol with some relish:

"Scrambling over the parapet always gives one a kick. Taking your bearings you made for the gap in [your own] wire … Once through … the fun – if you can call it that – began. Every object seemed to take on a human shape. If you gazed at it long enough you could swear that it was moving … Nearing the German lines one might (or might not) catch some sound of the enemy – a voice, a footfall, the metallic sound of a rifle being shifted, or maybe only a cough or a clearing of the throat … Even then you might find that what you had been listening to was nothing but the sound of loose wire blowing in the wind."

ALAN THOMAS, ROYAL WEST KENTS

Trench raids, euphemistically called "minor local enterprises", were more ambitious affairs, sometimes involving up to 200 men and elaborate equipment and preparations. A raid of 16 November 1915, mounted by two Canadian battalions, was used as a model for many subsequent operations. Two 70-man groups were divided into different sections, from wire-cutters and bombing and blocking parties to trench rifle groups. On the night of the raid, artillery suppressed the enemy defences in the targeted sector – particularly the wire and machine-gun posts – and covered the withdrawal, which was successfully achieved with the loss of one wounded man and another killed by a "negligent discharge".

Subsequently, trench raids became more frequent, although by no means as successful. On the night of 28 June 1916, 55th Division launched a raid in the Somme sector. The masking clouds of gas and smoke were blown away when the wind changed direction. The raiders came under heavy fire just 50 yards from the German trenches. One of the raiders recalled: "He opened up with machine guns, rifles and trench mortars. It was like Hell let loose, but someone shouted 'on the Kellys', and on we went, but were cut down like corn. The Jerrys were two deep in their trench, and we realised we were done. Sixteen men answered the roll call out of 76. The worst part of a stunt is always after, when they have a roll call. To stand there and listen to the names being called and try to answer 'He's killed' – no one can picture it who hasn't seen one."

The survivors came back with one German cap. A private who covered the withdrawal won a Victoria Cross. Veterans of the trenches would have agreed that "Many a muddle means a medal".

Just as with snipers, experience led to the development of specialised clothing and equipment for trench raids. *Scouting and Patrolling* had some handy hints:

"Men on patrol should be lightly equipped. A cap-comforter is least visible, the face and hands should be darkened and gloves may be worn. Each man should carry two bombs, a bayonet or knobkerrie and a revolver or rifle. A revolver is more convenient, but men so armed should be expert in its use. The rifle is best for purposes of protection. Scouts going out on patrol should have nothing on them which would assist the enemy if they were captured."

The Germans sent their own trench raiding parties to the British lines. Edmund Blunden encountered the aftermath of one of their operations on a winter's morning:

"Our own dead had been carried away, but just ahead were stretched two or three of the raiders. One was an officer of forty, sullen-faced, pig-nosed, scarred and still seemingly hostile. In his coat pocket were thirty or forty whistles which evidently he had meant to issue to his party before the raid. Another corpse was that of a youth, perhaps eighteen years old, fair-haired, rough-chinned. He was lying in the snow on his back, staring at the blue day with eyes as blue and icy; his feet were towards the German lines, and his right hand clutched the wooden handle of a bomb."

The Allied Commanders

Until the arrival of the US Expeditionary Force in 1917, the principal Allied commanders in France were British and French

Commanders laboured under several signal disadvantages during the First World War. The war was unique because the commanders lacked voice control over their armies. On the Western Front, communications broke down almost immediately after the troops left the trenches and went over the top. The trenches themselves proved almost insuperable obstacles, making cavalry obsolete on a battlefield dominated by artillery and the machine gun. The weapon with the potential to break the deadlock – the tank – was, in 1914–1918, an unreliable instrument. Its time would come in 1940. The "big four" Allied commanders were Haig, Joffre, Pétain, Pershing and Foch. General Sir Douglas Haig, who was appointed Commander-in-Chief of the British Expeditionary Force in December 1915, was a cool personality, virtually inarticulate at meetings, but a wily political infighter with the ear of King George V. In recent years a number of attempts have been made to rehabilitate his reputation, but the fact remains that in 1916-1917 his generalship cost the British Empire over 700,000 casualties to no discernible effect. His survival recalls the Tommies' melancholy dirge on the Western Front, "We're 'ere, because we're 'ere, because we're 'ere." Haig was there because he was there and no one better could be found to replace him. For the French, Joffre's massive imperturbability, rather than any great insight as a commander, saw France through the first great crises of the war. However, it was his failure to prepare adequately for the German offensive at Verdun in 1916 that led to his removal in December of that year. As a consolation prize, he was created a Marshal of France. Pétain, the hero of Verdun, was a master of defensive warfare and a firm believer in wearing down the enemy with limited attacks, "striking continually against the arch of the German structure until it collapses". On 8 May 1917, Pétain became Commander-in-Chief of the French Army, which had been undermined by a series of mutinies, and halted the threatening military collapse with firmness and restraint. Foch, who was appointed the Allied Commander-in-Chief in April 1918, embodied the bristling spirit of all-out attack, although he was canny enough to sanction the use of a less expensive strategy in the summer of 1918. Both Haig and Foch believed that Pétain had a defeatist streak. They were proved right, long after their deaths, when after the fall of France in 1940, the aged Marshal became head of France's Vichy puppet government.

Above *Haig's cap.*

Right *The imperturbable Joffre (left), the inarticulate Haig and the dapper Foch (right), bristling advocate of the offensive at all costs.*

73

Days in the trenches

Daily life in the front line assumed a mixture of the mundane and the morbid. For everyone, each day conformed to a basic pattern which was crisply summarised by Major Walter Vignoles, who arrived at the front near Armentières with the 10th Battalion, The Lincolnshire Regiment in February 1916:

"At dawn we 'stand to arms' every one turning out. When it is light, all rifles are cleaned and inspected, and the men have a tot of rum. Then breakfast, after which I let them turn in to sleep till dinner, with the exception of day sentries, just a few men watching the enemy's lines through periscopes. After dinner the men turn out for work in repairing periscopes etc and put in about three hours at that. We 'stand to' again at dusk. After dark we have to get out over the parapet to do any repairs that may be required to the wire entanglements, or repairs to the front of the parapet. In the salient here there is a good deal of work to be done, and there are several places where the trenches are old and broken, from whence one can peep at the enemy; we filled and put in position nearly 4,000 sandbags while we were in the trenches."

The "tot of rum" to which Major Vignoles referred had been introduced in the winter of 1914 to mitigate some of the worst effects of life in the trenches. The rum came up to the front in one-gallon jugs marked with the letters SRD (Service Rations Department) which the troops modified to "Soon Runs Dry". By 1918 each British division was consuming some 300 gallons of rum a week, an average of about one-third of a pint per man. It was Navy rum and its strength caught many a new arrival to the trenches unawares, leaving them coughing and spluttering. After a freezing night, however, it was heartily welcomed.

The French and Germans drank a rough brandy rather than rum and also had a daily wine ration. In summer the British also issued a ration of neat lime juice. There were reports that some units threatened a mutiny when this was substituted in error for the rum ration. Troops might also have been forgiven for feeling mutinous about their food rations. Officially each soldier was to receive, every day and in addition to his rum, one and a half pounds of fresh meat or a pound of salt meat, one pound of biscuits or flour, four ounces of bacon, three ounces of cheese, half a pound of tea, four ounces of jam, three ounces of sugar, two ounces of dried or eight ounces of fresh vegetables, and two ounces of tobacco. In the front line, this rarely arrived. Private Clarrie Jarman of the 17th Battalion, The

Opposite Grub's up! A *regimental cook in the* *Ancre Valley in 1916.*

Queen's Royal West Surrey Regiment observed, "our main food in the line was bully [beef] stew. We shared one loaf between four men. Sometimes a ration of cheese or butter would arrive, usually when we had no bread. Tins of biscuits were always there to eat. They were like dog biscuits."

Hardtack biscuits were as tough to bite into as a chunk of concrete. They were often vigorously broken down with a rifle butt and fried with bully beef or mixed into a duff with currants and other dried fruit. In cold weather the biscuits also provided a handy fuel substitute, and some were made into souvenirs such as photograph frames. Parcels from home were always welcome and often arrived within days of a request being made. The parcels provided a poignant link to friends and family. However, some were more welcome than others. John Dalton, who served with the Tank Corps, received a parcel from a schoolgirl in his home town which contained "three pairs of very small socks, boiled sweets, a crushed fruit cake, a Bible, a tin of vermin powder and a tract exhorting the reader to give up alcohol".

When it came to parcels, officers fared better than the men under their command. On Christmas Day 1916, Captain Harry Yoxall, of the 18th Battalion, The King's Royal Rifle Corps, wrote in his diary:

A poignant contrast to the Yuletide blow-out enjoyed by Captain Yoxall (see opposite). Christmas Day in a shell-hole at Beaumont-Hamel, on the Somme, in 1916. The first-day objective of the 29th Division on 1 July, the village was not taken until 13 November.

"At seven-thirty we had our Christmas dinner; The Menu was as follows:

Tomato Soup
Curried Prawns

Roast Turkey and Sausages
Roast and Mashed Potatoes

Christmas Pudding Minced Pies
Devonshire Cream Rum Butter
Scotch Woodcock on Toast

Cheese Caviare
Apples Oranges Tangerines Almonds and Raisins Nuts
Candied Fruit Chocolate

Coffee

Veuve Cliquot 1906
Whiskey Rum Port
Liqueur Brandy 1891
Rum Punch."

CAPTAIN HARRY YOXALL, THE KING'S ROYAL RIFLE CORPS

Yoxall's Christmas blow-out was , by any standards, exceptional. More typical, perhaps, is an entry from the diary of Corporal James Brown Gingell of the Royal Engineers: "Xmas Day, day off. Not much to do, we only had our ordinary rations with the exception of a bit of Xmas pudding."

Squalor

Human detritus and dead bodies attracted swarms of rats to the trenches. Harry Patch remembered that they were quite fearless: "They would pinch your rations and gnaw at your leather equipment and they would have a go at your leather bootlaces if you stood there long enough. When you went to sleep, you would cover your face with a blanket and feel the damn things run over you. They were quite tame and they certainly weren't afraid of you. Most rats will scamper away from you but not those in the salient."

The rats could be intimidating. Second Lieutenant Geoffrey Lillywhite recalled: "There was one old fellow who was quite well known in our sector. I met him one day in a communication trench. He could walk on top of the mud into which I sunk at every step. He was enormous, with ferocious and venomous eyes, and I freely admit I flattened myself against the trench wall and let him go past which he did without turning his head."

No one who served in the trenches could count on escaping infestations of lice which caused agonising scratching and carried trench fever, leading to shooting pains in the shins and a soaring temperature. In 1917 trench fever accounted for some 17 per cent of all cases of sickness in the BEF. Nits found a home in the men's hair and vast clouds of blue and green flies feasted on corpses. Men could never escape the stench that hung like a miasma over the trenches. One soldier recalled a "combination of mildew, rotting vegetation and the stink which arises from the decomposing bodies of men and animals".

Australian troops wait their turn outside outside a bath house at Ypres in 1917. Often housed in converted breweries, the bath houses struggled to launder the troops' lice-infested shirts. Harry Patch, who served with the Duke of Cornwall's Light Infantry June to September 1917, recalled that during those four months he never had a bath or a change of clothes.

Boredom and terror

Life in the trenches was often characterised as a mixture of boredom and terror – approximately 90 per cent of the former and some 10 per cent of the latter. The main agent of the short spells of terror endured by every man in the front line was the enemy artillery.

With the arrival of fixed trench systems, the war on the Western Front took on many of the aspects of a gigantic siege, requiring colossal quantities of all types of guns and projectiles. In August 1914, the six divisions of the BEF fielded 486 guns, all but one of them light field pieces. By November 1918, the number of British guns in France had risen to 6,432 of all types.

During the war, the British artillery loosed off over 170 million rounds, representing more than five million tons. During the two weeks preceding the Passchendaele offensive in July 1917, British guns fired some 4.3 million rounds. At Messines in June 1917, the British concentrated 2,338 guns (808 of them heavy) and 304 large smooth-bore trench mortars on a nine-mile front, a ratio of one gun every seven yards or 240 to the mile. In the 17-day preliminary bombardment, 5.5 tons of ammunition were delivered to each yard of enemy front. Until 1918 the British remained firm believers, in spite of all evidence to the contrary, in the heavy bombardment of the enemy line for protracted periods before the launching of an offensive. As early as January 1915, the British Commander-in-Chief Sir John French had declared, "Breaking through the enemy's lines is largely a question of expenditure of high-explosive ammunition. If sufficient ammunition is forthcoming, a way can be blasted through the line. If the attempt fails, it shows, provided that the work of the infantry and artillery has been properly coordinated, that insufficient ammunition has been expended, ie either more guns must be brought up or the allowance of ammunition per gun increased."

In 1914, the German Army was particularly well prepared for this new form of warfare on the Western Front. In addition to its large stocks of machine guns and heavy artillery, it possessed 180 trench mortars, or *minenwerfers* (bomb throwers). Trench mortars were not a recent innovation – they had been used in the American Civil and Russo-Japanese War – but only the Germans had grasped their potential.

The principal advantage of the trench mortar was that it provided the infantry with its own portable artillery. It was light, compact, robust and simple to manufacture in quantity. Its high-angle fire made it an ideal weapon with which to bombard enemy positions. The German trench mortars came in a variety of calibres, ranging from

War of the Tunnels

The Western Front recalled a vast medieval siege given a hideous technological twist by modern methods of mining

As trench warfare took hold, digging tunnels towards and under the enemy's lines ("sapping"), and then detonating one or more mines to create a breach in the defences, became an increasingly important feature on the Western Front. The Germans were the innovators, when in December 1914 they tunnelled under the Allied lines in Belgium and detonated ten small mines, the largest of which weighed 300 pounds, to blow up an Indian brigade. The French responded with their own *sapeurs-mineurs* units, working with primitive equipment. Initially, the BEF had no dedicated tunnelling companies but by the beginning of 1915 it had formed brigade mining sections from troops with neither experience of tunnelling nor specialised listening equipment to discover where the Germans were digging. They were quickly joined by tunnelling companies consisting of former coalminers. The men soon found themselves engaged in a grim new war fought under the shell-churned surface of no man's land. Each side would listen intently for the other, ready to blow a small charge, which would entomb the hostile tunnellers while leaving one's own workings undamaged. Sometimes the tunnellers broke into the enemy's sap and vicious hand-to-hand fighting with picks and shovels would ensue. Twelve-hour shifts were normally worked in freezing, waterlogged conditions where gas might ignite or asphyxiate and shortage of oxygen was a constant peril. By 1917 the British and French tunnellers had overtaken the Germans and were deploying a

sophisticated range of equipment, including listening devices, silent air and water pumps and ammonal explosive charges, which had replaced volatile gunpowder and guncotton. In June 1917 the attack on Messines Ridge was preceded by the detonation, at dawn, of nearly a million pounds of explosives under the German positions. The artilleryman Aubrey Wade witnessed the results:

" … at the fall of a handkerchief the earth seemed to stop its ears in terror. The ground under our feet literally rocked. It writhed again as the spreading wave of shock from the annihilated Messines Ridge broke upon us and passed on. A sudden rising wind blew back over the lines into our faces, a fearful wind hot like the breath from the Pit itself, a wind that was the aftermath of the crack of doom …"

Some 6,500 German prisoners, dazed and disorientated by the explosion, were taken in the Allied attack.

The detonation of British mines underneath the German positions on Hawthorn Ridge, near Beaumont Hamel, at 7.20am on 1 July 1916, 10 minutes before Zero Hour. This gave the Germans ample warning of the coming attack.

3in to 9.8in; the larger types were crew-served weapons. The range of the smaller-calibre trench mortars was short, but in a situation where the opposing lines were as little as 100 yards apart, this was no handicap. Edmund Blunden saw at close quarters the sudden and devastating effects of a *minenwerfer* shell plunging into a trench where a group of engineers were tunnelling under the German line:

"The tunnellers who were so busy under the German lines were men of stubborn determination, yet, by force of the unaccustomed, they hurried nervously along the trenches above ground to spend their long hours listening or mining. At one shaft they pumped air down with Brobdingnagian bellows. The squeaking noise may have given them away, or it may have been mere bad luck, when one morning a *minenwerfer* smashed this entrance and the men working there. One was carried out past me, collapsing like a sack of potatoes, spouting blood at twenty places … Not far away from that shafthead, a young and cheerful lance-corporal of ours was making some tea as I passed one warm afternoon. Wishing him a good tea, I went along three firebays; one shell dropped without warning behind me; I saw its smoke faint out, and I thought all was lucky as it should be. Soon a cry from that place recalled me; the shell had burst all wrong. Its butting impression was black and stinking in the parados where three minutes ago the lance-corporal's mess tin was bubbling over a little flame. For him, how could the gobbets of blackening flesh, the earth wall sotted with

British infantry advancing towards Thiepval during the later stages of the Battle of the Somme. Thiepval had been a first-day target on 1 July 1916. In the initial attack the 36th (Ulster) Division took very heavy casualties but nevertheless reached the German second line north of Thiepval. However, the village was not taken until 26 September, by the 18th (Eastern) Division.

blood, with flesh, the eye under the duckboard, the pulpy bone be the only answer?"

By the spring of 1916 the British had caught up, and their standard trench mortar was the 3-inch Stokes, which initially was used to fire only smoke rounds. As the year wore on, the British introduced medium and heavy mortars with respective ranges of 150 and 1,000 yards. By 1918 the British had some 3,000 mortars on the Western Front.

Artillery accounted for up to 70 per cent of the casualties between 1914 and 1918. Troops subjected to heavy bombardment endured physical and mental torture. In December 1917 Aubrey Wade, a gunner with a battery of horse artillery, spent a very uncomfortable night in a sap under heavy fire:

"Before I, the Jonah, arrived at the position the battery had escaped serious shelling. Therefore we were all the more surprised when, in the early hours of the next morning, we were pounded into wakefulness by heavy explosions on the hillside overhead. Literally the ground quaked with the impact of each shell. They came at intervals of about ten or fifteen seconds; inexorable, closer overhead every time; roaring through the night under the stars and embedding themselves yards deep in the ground before exploding with a concussion that struck through and through the hillside and left it shuddering for the climax of the next scream; still closer, instantaneously extinguishing the feeble candle with the terrific shock. Small pieces of earth fell on us from the roof at each burst, making us crouch in expectation of the whole thing falling in on us bodily at the impact of the next one."

AUBREY WADE, GUNNER

Nevertheless, after even the heaviest artillery bombardment, sufficient troops survived to emerge from their dugouts to break up an infantry attack when enemy troops clambered out of the trenches and advanced into no man's land. In a week-long preliminary bombardment on the Somme at the end of June 1916, the British fired 1.7 million shells. On the first day of the Battle of the Somme, 1 July 1916, German machine guns took a terrible toll of the British divisions as they advanced at a slow walk across no man's land. Second Lieutenant Alfred Bundy of the 2nd Battalion The Middlesex Regiment (Duke of Cambridge's Own) remembered:

"An appalling rifle and machine gun fire opened against us and my men commenced to fall. I shouted 'down' but most of those that were not hot had already taken what cover they could find. I dropped in a shellhole and occasionally attempted to move to my right or left but bullets were forming an impenetrable barrier and exposure of

The Front on Film

"War has always been dreadful, but never, I suppose, more dreadful than today."
H Rider Haggard's reaction to *The Battle of the Somme*

The Battle of the Somme began on 1 July 1916 and ended four and a half months later, on 18 November. Long before the outcome of the battle was known, in mid-August 1916, an 80-minute silent documentary film was released in Britain chronicling the opening days of the Allied offensive. It was greeted with warm reviews at home and was even shown to the Royal Family at Windsor and troops in France. The footage had been shot by two film cameramen, Geoffrey Malins and J B McDowell, who had arrived in the Somme sector in late June. They wore officers' uniforms but had no

badges or rank, and their original assignment had been to make a series of short documentary films on a number of aspects of life at the front. However, their brief expanded, largely because of the quality of the footage they were sending home and the scale of events it revealed. Like Topsy, the film just grew. On its release, *The Battle of the Somme* was endorsed by David Lloyd George, then Secretary of State for War, who declared, "I am convinced that when you have seen this wonderful picture, every heart will beat in sympathy with its purpose, which is no other than that every one of us at home and

abroad shall see what our men at the Front are doing and suffering for us, and how their achievements have been made by the sacrifices made at home." In 1916 the technical difficulties of filming a major battle on a 20-mile front were formidable, and these may account for the inclusion of some staged footage of troops "going over the top". These were in all probability filmed at a trench mortar training school, and nowadays would be flagged up as "reconstructions". Nevertheless, on 11 August 1916 *The Times* noted, "In years to come, when historians want to know the conditions under which the great offensive was launched, they will only have to send for these films and a complete idea of the situation will be revealed before their eyes – for we take it as a matter of course that a number of copies of them will be carefully preserved in the national archives.".

Above *An authentic image of war, captioned "British Tommies rescuing a comrade under shell fire (this man died 30 minutes after reaching the trenches)".*
Below *A questionable sequence, in all probability filmed at a trench mortar training school several days before the start of the battle. Wholly authentic or not, some 20 million cinemagoers saw the film after its release.*

An 18-pounder gun crew pose for the camera during the battle of Pozières Ridge, on the Somme, 30 July 1916. The line of horses visible to their front indicates that they would not actually be firing. The ammunition lying ready is high explosive shell. Clearly visible is the pole trail which limited the gun's elevation and thus its range.

the head meant certain death. None of our men was visible but in all directions came pitiful groans and cries of pain. I began to suffer thirst as my water bottle had been pierced with a bullet … I finally decided to wait until dusk and about 9.30 began to crawl … At last the firing ceased and after tearing my clothes and flesh on the wire I reached the parapet and fell into our own trenches now full of dead and wounded."

The two-week-long British bombardment which preceded the Battle of Passchendaele, in which 4.3 million shells were fired, had the disastrous effect of destroying the area's drainage system. The infantry moved forward into a morass which prompted the poet Siegfried Sassoon to write:

> *I died in hell –*
> *(They called it Passchendaele);*
> *My wound was slight*
> *And I was hobbling back, and then a shell*
> *Burst slick upon the duck-boards; so I fell*
> *Into the bottomless mud, and lost the light*

Breaking the deadlock

Both sides sought technological answers to the stalemate on the Western Front. At 5pm on 22 April 1915, two sinister greenish-yellow clouds crept across no man's land towards the Allied lines at Ypres. The clouds were pressurised chlorine gas released from more than 500 cylinders in the German trenches as the preliminary to a major offensive.

German prisoners and a deserter had warned of this new weapon, but no countermeasures had been taken. The two French colonial divisions on the north flank of the salient were engulfed by the cloud and fled in panic, leaving a four-mile gap in the front peopled only by the dead and those who lay suffocating in agony from chlorine

British infantry manning a Vickers machine gun during the Battle of the Somme, July 1916. They are wearing grey flannel anti-gas hoods fitted with mica eyepieces and are exhaling through rubber-tipped metal tubes clenched between their teeth.

Shell Shock

The effects of modern weaponry, particularly artillery, often left physical and mental scars

There were two types of shell shock. The first was a condition which applied to men who had survived a shell burst but had nevertheless suffered physical damage which upset the working of the brain. The second, which was triggered by the cumulative effect of life in the front line, was much more difficult for army doctors to diagnose or quantify. The official figures, which state that during the First World War there were some 80,000 cases of shell shock – a wastage rate of 2 per cent – are clearly an underestimate. Many men who were never classified as suffering from shell shock nevertheless were on occasion overwhelmed by a complete loss of self-control which triggered a nervous collapse. Symptoms of shell shock could be physical or mental, such as losing the ability to walk or talk, nightmares, profuse sweating and amnesia. These were likely to occur during a "big push" when men were repeatedly sent over the top and had to contend with equally frequent enemy counter-attacks, plus lack of food, water and sleep. In the late summer and autumn of 1917, during the Battle of Passchendaele, the ratio of officers and other ranks diagnosed with some form of shell shock ran at 1:38. Significantly, the proportion of officers to other ranks was about 1:30. During the next twelve months, however, the shell shock ratio narrowed to one officer for every 14 men. Officers affected by the condition received better treatment than the men, often being sent to convalesce in the South of France, and were more likely to be sent back to Britain permanently rather than returned to the trenches.

The intolerable strain of the fighting is etched into the faces of these battle-scarred British troops

poisoning. Having achieved total surprise, the Germans failed to exploit the breakthrough. Nevertheless, the gas had caused at least 15,000 casualties, 5,000 of them fatal.

Chlorine gas poisoning led to a slow and agonising death by asphyxiation. On 25 September 1915 the British released chlorine gas on the German lines at Loos, but little of it reached the enemy trenches. Thereafter increasing use was made of gas shells, and by 1918 no fewer than 63 different types of gas had been developed, each with its own smell and grisly effects on the human body. Chlorine smelled of a mixture of pineapple and pepper; phosgene reeked of rotten fish; the most familiar was mustard gas, which was reminiscent of soap and sweets. Its effects were often delayed by up to 12 hours before it began to blister the skin, close the eyes, attack the bronchial tubes by stripping off the mucous membrane and cause violent vomiting. It was also known to destroy the testicles of those who took shelter in shell craters where it lingered.

The first countermeasures taken against gas were primitive, among them pads of cotton waste soaked in urine; chlorine gas was partially neutralised by the ammonia in the urine. The summer of 1916 saw the introduction by the British of grey flannel hoods impregnated with the chemical compound phenol and fitted with mica eye-pieces. The wearer was able to breathe by using a rubber-tipped metal tube clenched between the teeth. From 1917, these stopgap measures were replaced by box respirators which used filters containing chemicals to neutralise the gas. Jim Marshall, a machine-gunner, was caught in a bombardment of gas shells at Arras as his unit moved into position:

"Our sergeant noticed that some shells were not exploding, and called, 'Gas! Gas!'. We dropped everything and pulled our masks on, but not before we had taken a whiff of it. I was coughing something terrible, but didn't dare take the mask off. We had to lug the guns into position, mount them and stand at readiness, all with the masks on. It was a couple of hours later that an officer came up and asked why we still had our masks on, as the all clear had been sounded ages before. Our sergeant felt a right fool, but we reckoned better safe than sorry. We were all frightened of gas."

The long-term effects on those who had been gassed and had survived were often horrifying. In the immediate post-war years, many American cities passed laws against disfigured gas or shell-burst victims being seen in public, in an attempt to protect the sensibilities of women and children. The maimed veteran was required to wear a hood or a mask. If he ignored this injunction in Chicago, the veteran ran the risk of facing criminal prosecution for "Being Ugly on the Public Way".

Opposite A line of British troops blinded by tear gas at an Advanced Dressing Station near Béthune, in the spring of 1918. The image is very similar to that in the famous painting Gassed *by John Singer Sargent.*

The changing battlefield

A new weapon but all-too-familiar conditions. A tank stuck fast in the mud at Passchendaele in the autumn of 1917. In 1916 an aide-de-camp to Field Marshal Haig had observed at a tank demonsrtation, "The idea that cavalry will be replaced by these iron coaches is absurd, It is little short of treasonous."

At a conservative estimate, gas caused about a million casualties during the First World War, but it did not prove to be the breakthrough weapon sought by the Allied and German high commands. The trenches still gripped the front in the Ypres salient. By the time the offensive at Passchendaele (sometimes known as the third Battle of Ypres) slithered to a halt in November 1917, the front itself had been reduced to a morass which swallowed trench lines whole. Machine guns on the Somme and the glutinous mud of Passchendaele had dictated the terms of this seemingly endless slogging match between blind and exhausted boxers. At Passchendaele men and mules had drowned in the mire. A survivor recalled finding: "A khaki-clad leg, three heads in a row, the rest of the bodies submerged, giving one the idea that they had used their last ounce of strength to keep their heads above the rising water. In another miniature pond, a hand still gripping the rifle is all that is visible while its next door neighbour is occupied by a steel helmet and half a head, the eyes staring icily at the green slime which floats on the surface almost at their level."

However, a new breakthrough weapon was already at hand. Two months after the outbreak of war, in October 1914, the official British war correspondent, Colonel Ernest Swinton, approached General Headquarters (GHQ) with a proposal to use the pre-war Holt agricultural tractor as a means of overcoming barbed wire and broken ground.

GHQ was not interested but Swinton's scheme eventually found a backer in Winston Churchill, First Lord of the Admiralty. In the autumn of 1914, the armoured cars operated in northern France by the Royal Naval Air Service (RNAS) had enjoyed some success but had been hampered by trenches which the Germans had dug across the roads. The Admiralty's work on a solution to this problem coincided with Swinton's proposal and led to the establishment, in February 1915, of an Admiralty Landships Committee.

A series of trials led to a prototype armoured vehicle known as "Big Willie" which was successfully tested at Hatfield Park at the beginning of 1916. Kitchener dismissed "Big Willie" as a "pretty mechanical toy" but Sir Douglas Haig, commander of the BEF from 19 December 1915, was keen to use the machines – codenamed "tanks" – in France as soon as possible. They were first employed in significant numbers on 15 September 1916 during the Battle of the Somme, but were thrown forward in uncoordinated fashion. At Passchendaele they stuck fast in the mud. The tank pioneer Colonel J F C Fuller recalled:

"I waded up the road which was swimming a foot or two in slush … The road was a complete shambles and strewn with debris, broken vehicles, dead and dying horses and men; I must have passed hundreds of them as well as bits of men and animals littered everywhere. As I neared Poelcapelle our guns started to fire … the nearest approach to a picture I can give is that it was like standing in the middle of a gigantic Primus stove. As I neared the derelict tanks the scene became truly appalling; wounded men lay drowned in the mud … The nearest tank was a female[3] . Her left sponson doors were open. Out of those protruded four pairs of legs; exhausted and wounded men had sought refuge in this machine, and the dead and dying lay in a jumbled heap inside."

COLONEL J F C FULLER, TANK PIONEER

In November 1917, tanks were first used successfully at Cambrai. One of them was commanded by Second Lieutenant Gordon Hassell, whose memoirs contain an evocative description of the perils of riding in one of the monsters:

"Terribly noisy, oily, hot, airless and bumpy! Without any sort of cushions, as we had no springs and had thirty tons' weight, any slight bump and crash was magnified and many a burn was caused by a jerk throwing the crew about. Instinctively one caught a handhold, and got a burn on the hot engine. The crew had very little knowledge of where they were going, only by peeping through slits and weapons apertures could they see anything. In action if the tank was hit slivers of hot steel began to fly – bullets hitting the armoured plates caused melting and the splash, as in steel factories, was dangerous to the eyes. For protection we used to wear a small face mask."

At Cambrai on 20 November 1917, without a preliminary bombardment, 324 fighting tanks, using specially devised tactics, tore a six-mile gap in the Hindenburg Line. The next day church bells rang out in London for the first time to mark a land victory. But once again the breakthrough was not exploited and most of the ground gained was lost to a German counter-attack. The tank had not proved to be the perfect weapon, and to the end of the war it remained prone to mechanical failure, vulnerable to artillery fire and too slow fully to exploit a breakthrough. But when movement returned to the battlefield in the spring and high summer of 1918, the tank offered an indication of the kind of warfare which would underpin German triumphs in 1940 and Allied victories in 1944.

Above Protective face mask worn by Second Lieutenant Gordon Hassell in the Battle of Cambrai, 1917. *Opposite* Many questions, few answers. A British soldier pauses in front of a streetside crucifix near Armentières.

However, it is worth noting that in the final campaigns of the war, during which the movement which had flickered so briefly in 1914 was restored to the battlefield, the casualties on both sides rose at an alarming rate. In August 1917, at the height of the Battle of Passchendaele, British casualties ran at 81,000. Exactly a year later, at the Battle of Amiens, the British achieved an initial breakthrough on a narrow front but were checked by the Germans who rushed up reinforcements. When the offensive was called off by Haig a few days later, the British had suffered 122,270 casualties. Mere occupation of the trenches could not bring victory, and was a hellish ordeal, but in the long run it did save lives.

Thirty years before D-Day, as Germany and France fought the first key battle of the war on the Marne, their armies and their generals looked back to an earlier conflict, the Franco-Prussian War of 1870–1871. In 1918 the armies locked in the final struggles on the Western Front anticipated a conflict which lay in the not-too-distant future. It came in 1939 and was a war of aircraft, armour and mass mobilisation. The era of Total War had dawned.

3 THE WAR
IN THE AIR

"When I got over the harbour I could see no signs of any submarine. I therefore determined to bomb the batteries just to the south of the town, where there would be little risk of killing civilians."

W R SAMSON ON BOMBING OSTEND, 25 DECEMBER 1914

Previous page A pilot of
No. 1 Squadron of the
recently formed Royal Air
Force at Clairmarais on
3 July 1918 demonstrates
the use of the Foster
mounting on the upper
wing of his SE5a as he fixes
a drum of ammunition on
the Lewis gun.
Below An aerial view of the
so-called "Concentration
Camp" at Netheravon in
June 1914, at which the
squadrons of the Royal
Flying Corps (RFC) came
together for trials and
tactical exercises.

In the high summer of 1914, less than 11 years after the Wright Brothers had made the first heavier-than-air powered flight, the moment arrived for the European powers to put their infant air services to the test.

The German Army's air service was the largest, some 260 aircraft in all, of which half were the Rumpler Taube (Dove) type. The French could put 138 aeroplanes into the field. Their pilots had gained valuable operational experience in the previous two years while serving in Morocco. The British deployed the smallest air service. Sixty-three fragile but inherently stable aircraft of the Royal Flying Corps (RFC) accompanied the British Expeditionary Force to France.

At this stage in the war, all three nations' air services anticipated that the principal role of their aircraft would be reconnaissance. In the land war they would act as scouting auxiliaries for the cavalry, flying over the theatre to discover, and report on, enemy troop movements and concentrations which lay beyond the range of cavalry patrols.

Reconnaissance was to remain the principal operational activity of the combatant air forces throughout the war. Air fighting began when bolder souls went aloft armed with carbines, darts, grenades stuffed into their pockets, and even bricks, to ensure that their duties continued uninterrupted.

The RFC nevertheless remained an engagingly untried force

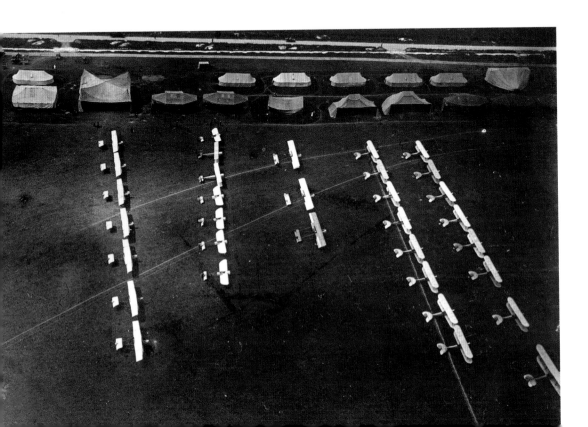

which boasted an intriguing mixture of hastily commandeered transport vehicles, one of which – No. 5 Squadron's ammunition and bomb lorry – still bore the scarlet livery of a famous sauce manufacturer and the legend "The World's Appetiser".

One aggressive RFC pilot was Lieutenant L A Strange of No. 5 Squadron. On 28 August he was aloft in his Farman biplane, No. 341, with Captain Penn Gaskell as his observer:

"I spent the morning … fixing up a new type of petrol bomb to my Henri Farman and in the morning Penn Gaskell and I went to try it out. We dropped two bombs on either side of the road north of St Quentin, where we found a lot of German transport; returning ten minutes later to have another go at the same lot, we found them moving south, so we dropped down to a low height and flew along the road, where we managed to plant our bombs right on to a lorry which took fire and ran into a ditch. The lorry behind it caught fire as well, and both were well ablaze when we left. It was not a serious loss to the German army, but it sent us home very well pleased with ourselves. That same evening a German machine dropped three bombs in our aerodrome and one fell fairly close to our transport, but luckily it did not burst. We all made a rush to the spot to grab bits of the bombs as souvenirs and found that they were full of shrapnel bullets."

Before the storm. Lieutenant (later Major) H D Harvey-Kelly sprawls nonchalantly by a Yorkshire haystack. He became the first RFC pilot to land in France on the outbreak of war and later commanded No.19 Squadron. On 29 April 1917, he was shot down by the German fighter ace Kurt Wolff of Jasta 11 and died of his wounds three days later.

The wings of a dove

In August 1914 the German air service was completely subordinated to the tactical requirements of the German Army. Its machines were initially unarmed and dedicated to reconnaissance, a task which they performed with spectacular success in East Prussia during the campaign which preceded the crushing German victory at Tannenberg.

The most numerous German type was the elegant, bird-winged and inherently stable Rumpler Taube. In the west, the Taube added bombing to its reconnaissance duties when on 30 August a German pilot flew over Paris, dropping four bombs on the Gare de L'Est, killing one civilian and injuring four others. In a nearby street a message fell to earth written on a streamer attached to a sand-weighted rubber pouch: "The German army is at the gates of Paris. There is nothing for you to do but surrender. Leutnant von Hiddessen."

The citizens of Paris were not cowed and, over the coming days, Taube missions became the source of enormous popular interest. When on 3 September three Taubes chugged over the rooftops of the French capital, its citizenry was well prepared for the visit, arming themselves with binoculars and opera glasses and newspaper diagrams of the Taube's distinctive silhouette. The profit-minded did brisk business selling seats in the best vantage points, particularly Montmartre. The German pilots entered into the carnival spirit, flying circuits round the Eiffel Tower while French riflemen blazed away at them from the upper storeys.

The Taubes paid another visit on 8 September as the Schlieffen Plan was coming apart at the seams and the German armies were falling back from Paris. This time their arrival was received with less good humour, although they dropped no bombs. One of the Taubes was brought down by ground fire north of Paris. The pilot crashed near a unit of troops on trench-digging duty. When he pulled out a pistol and attempted to resist capture, he was beaten to death with shovels and picks. The stakes in the air war were now considerably higher.

The RNAS and strategic bombing

In Britain, the naval air arm, the Royal Naval Air Service (RNAS), was more innovative and experimental than the cautious, bureaucratic RFC. The Navy had traditionally played a wide-ranging strategic role, with the emphasis on mobility and flexibility of response, and the air enthusiasts in the RNAS grasped the opportunity offered by the aircraft as an offensive weapon.

The RNAS already envisaged its aircraft flying long distances to bomb enemy warships, dockyards and shore installations. While army pilots had groped their way across the country using the maps in Bradshaw's railway guide, the RNAS was developing navigational aids and bombsights, taking machine guns aloft and conducting bomb-dropping and torpedo-launching trials.

On 3 September 1914, the hard-pressed British War Office had ceded the air defence of the British Isles to the Royal Navy. In keeping with its own offensive philosophy, the Admiralty believed that, in the event of war, German army and navy airships (Zeppelins) would be despatched across the North Sea to bomb Britain's cities. The Royal Navy was unwilling to wait passively for their arrival overhead and concluded that the best form of defence was attack and that the German airships should be destroyed in their hangars. Already in Belgium was the Eastchurch Squadron of the RNAS, led by Flight Commander C R Samson. On 27 August Samson had flown to Ostend at the head of a mixed unit which included a semi-rigid airship, which at the time was the only RNAS aircraft armed with a machine gun.

Reinforced with an improvised squadron of armoured cars, Samson threw his tiny command into the confused spasm of land fighting – the so-called Race to the Sea – which followed the breakdown of the Schlieffen Plan and preceded the arrival of trench warfare. While his armoured cars raced back and forth across the Belgian countryside, Samson drew up plans to bomb the Zeppelin sheds at Cologne and Düsseldorf. He had 12 aircraft at his disposal, a motley collection of Sopwiths, Blériots, BE2as, a Deperdussin monoplane and two Bristol TB8s. These aircraft were hardly more sophisticated as fighting machines than Samson's collection of primitive armoured cars. The principal available weapon for bombing was the pear-shaped, impact-detonating 20-pound Hale bomb armed by a fusing mechanism activated by a small propeller which started to revolve when the bomb was dropped.

It was not until 22 September that the RNAS launched its first raid on Germany, attacking the Zeppelin sheds at Düsseldorf and Cologne. Two weeks later it scored its first clear-cut success. On 8 October Flight Lieutenant R L G Marix bombed the shed at Düsseldorf. Arriving over his target, Marix dived to 600ft before releasing his bombs. Thirty seconds later, the roof of the shed collapsed as the fully inflated army Zeppelin Z9 inside exploded, sending sheets of flame to a height of

500ft. Marix's Sopwith Tabloid had been badly damaged by ground fire and, with his fuel exhausted, he force-landed some 20 miles from Antwerp. He borrowed a bicycle from a friendly Belgian peasant and rode most of the way back to base, completing the journey by car.

The RNAS eventually established itself at Dunkirk, which remained its largest single operational base for most of the war. Its location, strategically placed on the left flank of the Allied line and at the end of one of the vital cross-Channel arteries, encouraged the RNAS to diversify its operations into virtually every aspect of aerial activity from sea patrolling to strategic bombing. This was encouraged by the relative freedom which the Admiralty allowed successive RNAS commanders and the elasticity of the RNAS's organisation compared with the RFC's strict dependence on the requirements of the Army in the field.

On 21 November 1914 the target was the Zeppelin factory at Friedrichshafen, on Lake Constance (the move to Dunkirk had placed the Zeppelin sheds on the Rhine out of range). Taking off from the airfield at Belfort on the French-Swiss border, three Avro 504s headed for Lake Constance. One was piloted by Flight Lieutenant S V Sippé, who later wrote in his log:

"11.30am: arrived at extreme end of lake and came down within 10ft of the water. Continued at this height over lake, passing Constance at a very low altitude, as considered less likelihood of being seen. Crossed lake and hugged north shore until five minutes from objective. Started climb and reached 1200ft. Observed 12 or 14 shrapnels bursting slightly north of Friedrichshafen. Presumed these were directed against No. 873 [the Avro flown by Squadron Commander Briggs].

11.55am: When half a mile from the sheds put machine into dive and came down to 700ft. Observed men lined up to right of shed, number estimated at 300–500. Dropped one bomb in enclosure to put gunners off aim, and, when in correct position, two into works and shed. The fourth bomb failed to release. During this time very heavy fire, mitrailleuse and rifle, was being kept up, and shells were being very rapidly fired. Dived and flew north until out of range of guns, then turned back to waterside shed to try to release fourth bomb. Bomb would not release; was fired on by machine guns, probably mitrailleuse, dived down to surface of lake and made good my escape."

Of the 11 bombs released over the target, two had fallen on the airship sheds, damaging one of the Zeppelins under construction and blowing up a gasworks in a spectacular explosion.

Heartened by this success, Samson flew a raid on Bruges with 16-pound bombs on 14 December and on 21 December made the first

Opposite Two outstanding aircraft of the war. Dwarfed by a Handley Page 0/100 bomber, which features experimental rear engines, is the reliable SE5a fighter, which was operationally armed with a nose-mounted Vickers and a wing-mounted Lewis gun.

night flight of the war, in a Maurice Farman, when he raided the U-boat base at Ostend. In his autobiography, Samson recalled:

"When I got over the harbour I could see no signs of any submarine. I therefore determined to bomb the batteries just to the south of the town, where there would be little risk of killing civilians. The lights of the town were all lit and the view was splendid. The flash of the guns and the glare of the bursting shells was a wonderful sight all along our line from Dixmude to Ypres. By the time I reached 1,000ft I opened out my engine and turned south, passing along the seafront of Ostend. As soon as the noise of my engine was heard, pandemonium started. Star shell rockets and searchlights played into the sky, and the lights of the town went out in about two minutes, but they stayed long enough for me to pick out my objective. I let go my 18 bombs in salvos of threes, and the flash of their explosions was a most satisfying sight. Having unloaded my cargo, I set out directly to seaward. By this time the air was alive with shrapnel, but all well away from me; the searchlights were sweeping the sky, but all the beams were well above me. Getting out to about four miles to seaward, I headed for home, turning round every now and then to look at the view. The air behind me was a mass of bursting shells. Rockets and star shells, and it was certain that the Hun was badly shaken."

FLIGHT COMMANDER C R SAMSON

The birth of the bomber

On 6 February 1915 Samson submitted a memorandum to the Admiralty: "Practical experience has shown me that bomb dropping is only successful at the present moment when carried out by aeroplanes carrying a number of bombs. 100-pound bombs are wanted against submarines. I am quite confident of being able to use 200hp Short seaplanes adapted as aeroplanes for this work. They should carry four 100-pound bombs and would be used at night."

The vigorous bombing campaign mounted by the RNAS in the opening months of the war played an important part in the development of the first series of large British bombing aircraft, dubbed "bloody paralysers" by the Director of the Admiralty Air Department, Commodore Murray F Sueter. In contrast to the general-purpose types which had been pressed into service at the beginning of the war, the Handley Page 0/100, powered by two 250hp Rolls-Royce Eagle engines, was the first true British bomber. It entered service with the RNAS in September 1916. The observer lay prone, just behind the pilot, to aim and release the bombs, tugging on the pilot's left or right boot to alter direction on the bombing run. Sub-Lieutenant Paul Bewsher, who flew 0/100s with 3 Wing, described the crucial moments in a raid:

"I lifted my seat and crawled to the little room behind, which vibrated fiercely with the mighty revolution of the engines. I stood on a floor of little strips of wood, in an enclosure whose walls … were of tightly stretched canvas which chattered and flapped a little with the rush of the wind from the two propellers whirling scarcely a foot outside. Behind was fitted a petrol tank, underneath which hung 12 yellow bombs. I lay on my chest under the pilot's seat and pushed to the right a little wooden door, which slid away from a rectangular hole in the floor through which came a swift updraught of wind. Over this space was set the bombsight with its ranging slide bars painted with phosphorescent paint. On my right, fixed to the side of the machine, was a wooden handle operating a metal drum from which ran a cluster of release wires to the bombs further back. It was the bomb dropping lever, by means of which I could drop all my bombs at once, or one by one, as I wished."

SUB-LIEUTENANT PAUL BEWSHER

Tactical bombing

During the opening months of the war, the RFC had focused its attention almost entirely on reconnaissance. But the arrival of trench warfare forced a reappraisal of the value of bombing operations. By its very nature, this new form of warfare resulted in the more or less static concentration of large numbers of troops and quantities of equipment in or immediately behind the front line. The increasingly familiar features of the trench system – troops moving up to the front or back to the rear areas, ammunition dumps, billets and headquarters buildings – presented a range of inviting targets to bomb-carrying aircraft.

Of greater significance than these harassing operations was the role allotted to the RFC in the big offensives planned for the spring of 1915. When the first big push was made against the German line, the

RFC would be called upon to prevent or delay the arrival of enemy reinforcements, with particular attention being paid to the rail systems which brought them up to the front line.

The RFC's first attempt to coordinate tactical bombing operations with a major offensive came on 10 March 1915 when 2 and 3 Wings supported the attack made by the First Army at Neuve Chapelle. On the first day of the Neuve Chapelle offensive, Captain L A Strange of No. 6 Squadron was flying a BE2c loaded with three 25-pound bombs. His target was the railway station at Courtrai. When Strange took off,

Reconnaissance

Static trench warfare on the Western Front ensured that
aerial reconnaissance became a vital weapon in the intelligence armouries
of both the Allies and the Germans

In the opening weeks of the Great War, aircraft successfully conducted strategic reconnaissance on the Eastern Front, at the Battle of Tannenberg, and on the Western Front, in the build-up to the Battle of the Marne. The arrival of trench systems, whose rear areas were accessible only from the air, underlined the importance of aerial reconnaissance. At a strategic level, effective reconnaissance could only be conducted by aircraft equipped with cameras. In addition wireless was needed, for the rapid transmission of reports. Although the British had tested an airborne wireless before the outbreak of hostilities, it did not enter general service until 1915. In May 1915, during the Artois offensive, the Royal Flying Corps sent aircraft aloft to spot targets and communicate with the British artillery by using Morse code. However, it was difficult to use Morse keys while in the air, and at the beginning of 1916 airborne wireless telephony – the transmission of voice messages – was tested for the first time. The first sets had a trailing wire, which could be reeled in when necessary and which acted as an aerial. By early 1917, reliable transmitters became available, but the aircraft equipped this way were mostly retained for home defence around London. Only two squadrons so equipped were deployed on the Western Front. By the end of the war, their sets had a range of about 200 miles. Observation at a tactical level, and the direction of artillery fire, could be conducted from tethered balloons linked by telephone cable to command posts on the ground. By 1918 the British Army fielded a balloon company for each of their five armies on the Western Front. The balloons' two-man crews were often exposed to "balloon-busting" enemy fighters, the gunner Aubrey Wade recalled:

"The favourite time for a raid was late afternoon on a day when the sky was hung with cumulus clouds. Out of one of these a racing German fighter would drop straight for the nearest balloon; then he would circle around it pouring a stream of bullets into the fabric. After two or three bursts of fire the 'tracer' bullets did their work and sent the balloon up in flames like a gigantic torch hanging in the sky, with the observers dropping slowly to earth on their parachutes. Never once did we see a 'plane firing at the parachutes as they floated down, but occasionally a terrible thing happened; on a windless day the balloon, heavier than the men, would drop faster and engulf them in the blazing debris."

Above *A British Caquot-type observation balloon being hauled down near Fricourt, 1916. Balloon observers were issued with parachutes.*
Left *Aerial photographs taken over the German lines are assembled into a mosaic at an RFC office near Arras.*

the weather was breaking up, with clouds at 2,000ft and poor visibility. Strange crossed the lines below the clouds but a shell bursting nearby sent him up into them to emerge north of Courtrai. Diving through a low bank of cloud east of the town, he came down to within 200ft of the railway, following the track towards the station. A sentry on the platform opened fire as he approached, but Strange silenced him with a grenade thrown over the side of his BE2c. His aircraft flashed over the station roof and Strange dropped his bombs on a train standing on the other side.

The RFC's first ventures into tactical bombing provided a catalogue of exceptional gallantry and heavy loss. On 26 April, during fighting in the Ypres salient, Lieutenant W B Rhodes-Moorhouse of No. 2 Squadron, flying a BE2b loaded with a 100-pound bomb, also attacked Courtrai railway station. Met with heavy rifle and machine-gun fire, he descended to 300ft before releasing his bomb. Mortally wounded, he flew 35 miles back to his airfield and on his return insisted on delivering his report before receiving any attention. He died the following day and a month later was awarded a posthumous Victoria Cross, the first VC given for valour in the air.

At the beginning of August 1915, representatives of the RFC, RNAS and the French Groupes de Bombardement met to review air policy. One of the gloomier documents they studied was an RFC memorandum containing a detailed analysis of the results of bombing operations undertaken by the three services on the Western Front between 1 April and 18 June. In 483 operations a total of 4,062 bombs had been dropped with little apparent material result. Urgency was added to their deliberations by the appearance in the skies over the Western Front of the Fokker prototype M5K single-seater monoplane – the Eindecker – fitted with a machine gun synchronised to fire directly through the propeller arc. The first true fighter aircraft had burst on the scene.

A Morane Saulnier Type N "Bullet", piloted by Lieutenant T H Bayetto. Note the steel deflector plates fitted to the propeller blades in line with the fixed forward-firing machine gun.

The Fokker scourge

In February 1915, two Frenchmen, Roland Garros and Raymond Saulnier, had experimented with a forward-firing machine gun, fixing steel plates to the propeller of their aircraft to deflect the small percentage they calculated would strike it. In April, Garros came down behind German lines and his captured aircraft enabled the Dutch-born aero-engineer Anthony Fokker to produce a mechanical interrupter gear which allowed the gun to fire only when no propeller blade was in the way. It was fitted to the Eindecker monoplane, which gained its first victory when Leutnant Kurt Wintgens shot down a French two-seater.

In the hands of fighter aces[1] like Max Immelmann and Oswald Boelcke, the Eindeckers took a heavy toll of relatively defenceless Allied aircraft. Boelcke, who claimed 40 victories, codified the basic techniques of air combat in a pithy set of rules for pilots, the *Dicta Boelcke*, which were still being issued in booklet form to Luftwaffe pilots in the Second World War. Boelcke also drew on his experience in the fierce aerial fighting over Verdun between February and June 1916 to form specialised fighting squadrons, the *Jagdstaffeln* (hunting flights), known as Jastas. An early recruit to Jasta 2, commanded by Boelcke, was Manfred Freiherr von Richthofen, the "Red Baron".

A Fokker EI monoplane, the Eindecker, which was powered by an 80hp Oberursel rotary engine and armed with a single 7.92mm LMG 08 machine gun. The Eindecker was a pre-war machine which used wing-warping, governed by wires, to control aircraft roll.

Unlike Immelmann and Boelcke, Richthofen was not from the outset a natural flier. Anthony Fokker recalled, "he was slow to learn to fly, crashing on his first solo flight and only mastering the plane at last by sheer force of superior will. Time and again he escaped death by a miracle before he managed to conquer the unruly plane which later became his willing slave."

Flying an Albatros DII, Richthofen gained many of his early kills over sitting-duck two-seater reconnaissance aircraft which he nailed after long, stalking pursuits. On 23 November 1916, at the close of the Battle of the Somme, he achieved his eleventh victory in a tense, circling 31-minute dogfight with the RFC ace Major L G Hawker of No. 6 Squadron, who was flying a DH2.

There is a saying that there are old pilots and bold pilots but never old and bold pilots. Fokker was of the opinion that "one of the reasons Richthofen survived so long was his ability to keep guarding himself while he attacked. Many other aces were shot down during a fight unexpectedly, as they were training their guns on an enemy pilot. Richthofen would fight very close to his wing men, and not until it was a real dogfight, with the whole air in confusion, would he release his formation to permit every pilot to shift for himself. He was an excellent teacher, and young pilots who showed exceptional skill and courage were sent to his *Staffel* to get experience. At first they were taken along to observe the fighting from a distance, and forbidden to engage in combat at all during the first three flights, for it had been found that many of the new pilots were killed in their first fight, before, as Fokker acknowledged, they had learned to be "all eyes in every direction".

On 16 January 1917, Richthofen was awarded the Pour Le Mérite (popularly called the Blue Max, after Max Immelmann) and given his first command, Jasta 11, packed with some of the finest fighter aces on the Western Front. The RFC tended to spread their talented and experienced

Above *Anthony Fokker with aces Hauptmann Bruno Loerzer (44 victories) and Oberleutnant Hermann Goering (22 victories) on his left.*
Below *Pilots of Jasta 11 at Roucort aerodrome in April 1917 after the unit had scored its 100th victory. Richthofen is seated in the cockpit of his Albatros DIII and his brother Lothar is sitting cross-legged at the front.*

Allied Fighter Aces

Air warfare came of age in the skies over the Western Front and with it came the burgeoning cult of the "fighter ace", an individual who fought high above the trenches where mud, machine guns and artillery barrages dominated the lives of millions of men

In August 1914 war was seen as a glamorous occupation. This illusion was swiftly shattered in the terrible slogging match on the Western Front, where death became wholly industrialised. There was no glory here. What shreds of glory remained were celebrated in a new dimension, in the air, where the fighter ace, in popular imagination at least, inherited the mantle of the medieval knight. The first Royal Flying Corps pilot to win a Victoria Cross in aerial combat was Captain (later Major) Lanoe Hawker, who shot down three enemy aircraft – all of them armed – on 25 July 1915. Hawker himself was shot down by Manfred von Richthofen on 23 November 1916, becoming the 'Red Baron's' eleventh victim. Richthofen's younger brother Lothar is sometimes wrongly credited with shooting down another highly decorated British ace, Captain Albert Ball, on 7 May 1917. Ball was found dead at the controls of his SE5, his body badly mutilated and only isolated bullet holes in his aircraft. Two weeks later King George V presented Ball's parents with a posthumous VC. Another pilot who was awarded a posthumous VC was Major Edward "Mick" Mannock, an outstanding patrol leader and tactician whose 73 victories made him the top-scoring British fighter pilot of the war. Mannock was a firm believer in the advantage in air fighting conferred by height and his motto was "Always above; seldom on the same level; never underneath". Mannock was killed by ground fire on 26 July 1918. One of the great French heroes of the war in the air was the frail Capitaine Georges Guynemer, who was credited with 54 victories after 660 hours' flying and more than 600 combats. He failed to return from a patrol on 11 September 1917 and no trace of him or his machine was ever found. In all probability Guynemer and his crashed aircraft were pulverised by a British artillery bombardment. The leading American fighter ace of the Great War was the former racing driver Captain Edward V Rickenbacker, who between 29 April and 11 November 1918 scored 28 victories. Rickenbacker was older than most of his fellow pilots and flew with a cool and calculating flair. He survived the war to combine a distinguished business and public life with a native American genius for machines.

Left *Captain Albert Ball in a new SE5 at a snowbound airfield outside London during No. 56 Squadron's working up period in March 1917. Ball modified the fighter, removing the original windscreen and fuselage Vickers machine gun.*
Below *The smashed windscreen from the fighter piloted by RFC ace James McCudden, VC, who downed 57 enemy aircraft. He died in 1918.*

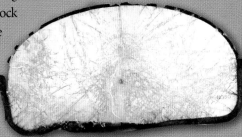

Above *Major (later Air Marshal) W A "Billy" Bishop, VC, DSO, MC, DFC, with his Nieuport 17 Scout in August 1917.* Opposite *Aircraft of Jasta 11 at Douai, early in 1917. Richthofen's all-red Albatros DIII is the second from the front. In the spring of 1917, Jasta 11 combined with Jastas 6,10 and 4 to form an independent fighter wing, the so-called "Richthofen Circus", which from 26 June was known as Jagdgeschwader 1 or JG1.*

pilots thin along the front line. In contrast, Richthofen had in his hands a superb fighting unit equipped with the best machines. He wanted his enemies to know it – hence the all-scarlet machine of the *Staffelführer* and the scarlet and second colour of the pilots he commanded. The Canadian ace Billy Bishop recalled the remarkable impact made by these garish machines:

"Every day our pilots were bringing home fresh stories of the fantastic German creations they had encountered in the skies. Some of them were real harlequins of the air, outrivalling the gayest feathered birds that had winged their way north with the spring. The scarlet machines of Baron von Richthofen's crack squadron, sometimes called the 'circus', heralded the new order of things. Then it was noticed that some of the enemy craft were painted with great rings about their bodies. Later, nothing was too gaudy for the Hun. There were machines with green planes and yellow noses; silver planes with gold noses; khaki-coloured bodies with greenish-grey planes; red bodies with green wings; light blue bodies and red wings. Every combination the Teutonic brain could dream up. One of the most fantastic we had met had a scarlet body, a brown tail, reddish-brown planes, the enemy markings being white crosses on a bright green background."

Bishop claimed the last of his 72 victories, a German two-seater, in June 1918. By then the day of the "lone wolf" fighter ace was long gone and the sentimental code of chivalry in the air – if it had ever existed – had been replaced by the grim pragmatism of attrition.

Above *Oberleutnant Ernst Udet, who scored 62 victories to become the second highest-scoring German fighter pilot of the war. His Fokker D VII bears the name "Lo" after his fiancee Lo Zink whom he married in 1920. In the 1930s Udet became head of the technical branch in the new German air ministry and later served as the Luftwaffe's Director-General of Equipment. He committed suicide in 1941.*
Below *Captain H W von Poellnitz, a flight commander of No. 32 Squadron RFC, takes off in a DH2 from Vert Galand aerodrome in July 1916.*

Bishop, who survived the war to follow a distinguished career in business and public life, had a notably unsentimental attitude towards the business of air warfare:

"In ordinary fight or duel we had tactics, of course, to suit the occasion. The great thing is never to let the enemy's machine get behind you, or 'on your tail'. Once he gets there it is very hard to get him off, as every turn and every move you make, he makes with you. By the same token it's exactly the position into which you wish to get, and once there you must constantly strive for a shot as well as look out for attacks from other machines that may be near. It is as well if you are against odds never to stay long after one machine. If you concentrate on him for more than a fraction of a second, some other Hun has a chance to get a steady shot at you without taking any risks himself."

BILLY BISHOP

The Red Baron was shot down and killed, probably by ground fire from Anzac troops, on 21 April 1918. His body lay in a hangar of No.3 Squadron, Australian Flying Corps before being laid to rest in a grave at Bertangles. A wreath from his enemies bore the inscription, "To our gallant and worthy foe". In 1925, Richthofen's remains were borne by train to Berlin. Bells tolled and flags flew at half mast across Germany. Richthofen was reburied at the Invalidenstrasse Cemetery, with President Hindenburg throwing the first handful of earth into the grave. Twelve years later Hermann Goering, who had himself flown with the Richthofen 'circus' on the Western Front and was now commander of the Luftwaffe, unveiled a much larger memorial on the spot. Once again the Richthofen legend had become the property of the German propaganda machine.

Zeppelins

In *The World Crisis,* Winston Churchill wrote that from the beginning of the war there was a widespread fear that "at any moment half a dozen Zeppelins might arrive to bomb London, or what was more serious, Chatham, Woolwich or Portsmouth".

In August 1914, the German armed forces had 30 rigid airships, all of them of the Zeppelin type named after their designer Count Ferdinand von Zeppelin. In 1914 these massive machines of war sent shivers down the spines of Britain's military establishment. The First Sea Lord, Admiral Jackie Fisher, was so alarmed that he predicted a horrible massacre and suggested that the only counter would be to announce that, if bombs were to fall on London, German prisoners of war would be shot as a reprisal. The Kaiser was also queasy about attacking the British capital. At first he sanctioned the bombing of docks, shipyards and other military installations on the Lower Thames but forbade any attacks on private property and historic buildings in the capital itself.

It was not until the end of April 1915 that the first effective raid on England was launched by the German Army airship LZ38, a four-engined Zeppelin commanded by Hauptmann Erich Linnartz. Crossing the coast north of Felixstowe in the small hours, LZ38 bombed Ipswich and Bury St Edmunds. The ban on attacking the capital was lifted at the end of May when the Kaiser gave permission for the bombing of targets in East London. On the night of 31 May/1 June LZ38 scattered 30 small high-explosive bombs in an arc stretching from Stoke Newington to Leytonstone. Rioting broke out in London's East End as the population vented its fury on premises owned by people of German descent.

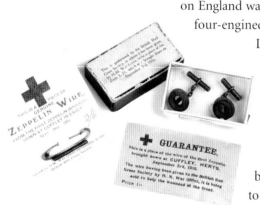

Brooches made from Zeppelin wire.

At this stage in the war Britain's air defences were wholly inadequate to deal with the airship threat. The motley collection of aircraft tasked with intercepting the enemy raiders not only had the utmost difficulty in locating their targets at night but they also struggled to return safely to their airfields. To defend London there were only some 20 obsolescent types. One of the more optimistic weapons fitted to some of them was the 'Fiery Grapnel', a grappling iron on a cable which was meant to engage the outer envelope of a Zeppelin and detonate an explosive charge.

There was an extraordinary contrast between the porous front line of London's air defences and their colossal prey. The early wartime

Zeppelins were some 520ft long. The men who flew them worked in a strange world of throbbing engines, dimly glowing dials and gauges and the ceaseless squeaking of wires and struts under strain. The commander of the Army airship LZ12, Oberleutnant Ernst Lehmann, described what it was like to fly against England:

"Under us, on the shimmering sea, cruised enemy patrol boats. I prudently ordered the lights out. In the control car the only light was on the dial of the machine telegraph … On the narrow catwalk between the rigging and the tanks we balanced ourselves as skilfully as if we were walking in the broad daylight down a wide street. I was wearing fur-lined shoes; and this thick footwear was not solely a protection against the cold. The hobnailed army boot might have damaged the ship's metal frame [or struck fatal sparks], and shoes with rubber or straw soles were therefore regulation … I continued the inspection and descended to the aft engine car, which swayed under the ship like a celestial satellite. The car was enclosed and so crowded by the two 210hp Maybach motors that the two mechanics could scarcely turn around. The noise of the motors drowned out every word, and the Chief Machinist simply raised his hand which meant that everything was OK. The air in this nutshell was so saturated with gasoline fumes and exhaust gases I almost choked until I opened the outlet and let the icy stream in …"

COMMANDER OF AIRSHIP LZ12

On the night of 16–17 May 1915, RNAS pilots based on the Channel coast of northern France engaged Zeppelins for the first time when Flight Sub-Lieutenant R A J Warneford and Flight Commander Spenser Grey intercepted and attacked LZ39 as it returned from a raid on Calais. Grey's machine gun and a rifle firing incendiary bullets handled by Warneford's observer had little effect. Ten minutes later Lieutenant A W Bigsworth joined the fight in an Avro 504B. Over Ostend he climbed above the Zeppelin at a height of about 10,000ft and dropped four 20-pound bombs on the huge target below him. Five gas cells were ruptured on board LZ39 and the rear engine was badly damaged, but the Zeppelin was able to limp home.

On the night of 6–7 June, LZ37 was returning from a raid on London when it had the misfortune to encounter the determined Flight Sub-Lieutenant Warneford, who was flying to bomb the Zeppelin sheds at Berchem St Agathe with six 20-pound bombs hanging from the racks of his Morane-Saulnier monoplane. Warneford spotted LZ37 over Ostend and after a patient hour-long pursuit, during which he came under heavy defensive fire from the Zeppelin, he managed to coax his Morane to 11,000ft, some 4,000ft

Skat *was a popular card game played in the trenches of the Western Front by the German and Austrian armies. This pack, manufactured in Germany in 1917 and sold to raise money for the widows of airmen, depicts heroes of the new war in the air. From top left to right* Army observer's breast badge; Naval airship crew's motto, "Don't forget the murder of L19 by the *King Stephen* (an incident in 1916 when a British steamer allowed the crew of a ditched airship to drown in the North Sea; Naval pilot's breast badge; Hauptmann Oswald Boelcke; Crown Prince Rupprecht of Bavaria; Oberleutnant Freiherr von Pechmann, the first observer to win the Pour le Mérite; Otto Lilienthal, the German glider pioneer; a Gotha seaplane; a Rumpler reconnaissance aircraft; aero-engine maintenance; the Prussian Eisernes Kreuz; Dr Parsifal, inventor of the Drachen reconnaissance balloon and airship pioneer; "I will be like Boelcke", the motto of German pilots; greeting of airship crews; Drachen balloon with a Paulus parachute for the observer; a Schutte-Lanz airship coned by searchlights.*

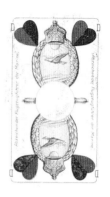

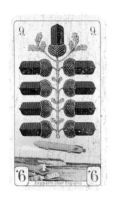
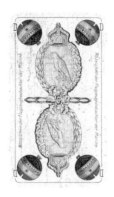

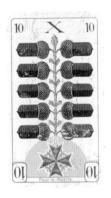

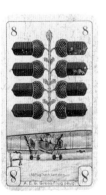

From top left to right *A truck-mounted anti-aircraft gun; a Zeppelin crossing the English coast; a Marine Naval Observer's breast badge; Fegattenkapitan Peter Strasser, the naval airship commander; aerial photo-reconnaissance; the Pour Le Mérite, or "Blue Max"; Prince Albrecht; Anthony Fokker; a rear gunner; Manfred von Richthofen; Graf Zeppelin; a red Albatros; a bomber taking off to raid London; an Army pilot's breast badge; Prince Leopold of Bavaria; Crown Prince Wilhelm.*

above his target. He put his aircraft into a steep glide, levelling out some 150ft above LZ37 and releasing his six bombs. The last bomb was still in the air when LZ37 exploded in a mass of flame, tossing the tiny Morane around the sky in the blast.

Remarkably, one of LZ37's crew survived the fiery descent. He was trapped in the forward gondola, which fell one and a half miles before crashing through the roof of a convent and depositing him on a bed. Warneford was awarded the Victoria Cross for downing LZ37, but only ten days after the duel over Ghent he was killed in a flying accident.

In spite of Warneford's success over Ghent, the 1915 balance sheet for Britain's air defences made depressing reading. In 19 raids, Zeppelins had dropped 37 tons of bombs, causing nearly a million pounds of damage, much of it on the night of 8 September when the German naval airship L13 raided London to drop a line of bombs running from Euston to Liverpool Street and killed 26 people.

In 1916 the German Naval Airship Division introduced a new class of airship, the 640ft-long R-types which were dubbed "super-Zeppelins". On the icy, windswept reaches of the R-type's streamlined upper hull were two gun platforms. The main platform was located at the bow 60ft above the control gondola, and housed three 8mm Maxim-Nordenfelt machine guns firing a mixture of armour-piercing and explosive shell. When not in use, the guns were swathed in cloth jackets to prevent the cooling water freezing solid. More machine guns were installed in the control and rear engine gondolas.

The Zeppelins' crews learned to live with the intense cold they experienced when flying at altitude. The temperature in the control gondola rarely rose above freezing point, and layers of fur-lined clothing were supplemented by wads of newspaper stuffed inside the crewmen's overalls. Food provided some comfort. A crew member recalled, "We got sausages, good butter, Thermos flasks containing an extra brew of coffee, plenty of bread, chocolate and 50 grams of rum or brandy per man … We had several peculiar and very practical kinds of tinned food, which might be described as chemical and gastronomical miracles. There were tins containing hashes and stew which were heated up by a certain chemical process as soon as you opened them. We were not allowed to cook anything on account of the danger from inflammable gas."

Impressive though they were, the "super-Zeppelins" did not represent a great technological leap forward. Neither their speed nor their ceiling were significantly greater than those of previous types. Moreover, the British aircraft were now armed with incendiary ammunition designed specifically to deal with Zeppelins.

Opposite The destruction of LZ37 by Flight Sub-Lieutenant Warneford of No.1 Squadron, RNAS, flying a Morane Saulnier L3253. LZ37 was 518 feet long and powered by three 630hp engines. Both its gondolas were of the open type, with the propellers mounted on outriggers. The keel was externally mounted and widened at the centre to accommodate a small cabin wireless and bomb racks.

On the night of 2–3 September 1916, the German Army and Navy combined for the first and last time to attack London. Sixteen airships set off but only one, the Army's SL11, found the target. In the small hours it was intercepted over North London by Lieutenant William Leefe Robinson of No. 39 Squadron flying a BE2c armed with a Lewis gun firing explosive and incendiary bullets. Robinson recalled:

"I sacrificed height (I was still at 12,900ft) for speed and made nose down in the direction of the Zeppelin. I saw shells bursting and night tracer shells flying around it. When I drew closer I noticed that the anti-aircraft aim was too high or too low; also a good many some 800ft behind. A few tracers went right over. I could hear the bursts when about 3,000ft from the Zeppelin. I flew along about 800ft below it from bow to stern and distributed one drum along it. It seemed to have no effect; I therefore moved to one side and gave it another drum distributed along its side – without apparent effect. I then got up behind it (by this time I was very close – 500ft or less below) and concentrated one drum at one point (underneath rear). I was then at a height of 11,500ft when attacking the Zeppelin. I had hardly finished the drum before I saw the point fired at glow. When the third drum was fired there were no searchlights on the Zeppelin and no anti-aircraft was firing. I quickly got out of the way of the falling, blazing Zeppelin and being very excited fired off a few red Very lights and dropped a parachute flare."

LIEUTENANT WILLIAM LEEFE ROBINSON

Leefe Robinson's destruction of SL11 stirred the commander of the Naval Airship Division, Fregatenkapitan Peter Strasser, to redouble his efforts. On the night of 23–24 September he despatched eight Zeppelins to raid the Midlands and the "super-Zeppelins" L30, L31, L32 and L33 to attack London. Struck by anti-aircraft fire and harried by home defence fighters, L33 came down near the Blackwater estuary as it struggled home. L32 was intercepted over London by Lieutenant F Sowrey in a BE2c. Sowrey got so close underneath L32's hull he could see the great wooden propellers churning the air. It took three drums of ammunition to bring L32 down in a ball of fire. Near the wreckage, embedded up to the waist in the ground was found the body of L32's executive officer, who had jumped rather than burn to death. The charred remains of the other 21 members of the crew were found trapped in the shattered gondolas and crushed under the Zeppelin's twisted girders. A third Zeppelin, L31, was coned by searchlights near London and shot down by Lieutenant Wulstan Tempest of No. 39 Squadron RFC.

Strasser strove to wrest the initiative back by introducing a new class of Zeppelin, dubbed "height climbers" and designed to operate at 20,000ft, well beyond the range of home defence fighters and anti-aircraft guns. Crew comfort – never any Zeppelin's strong point – was slashed to a minimum. To freezing temperatures was added the agony of altitude sickness, which could only be partially eliminated by bottles of compressed oxygen. Without these, crews suffered a disabling fatigue at heights over 16,000ft; a 50-yard trip to one of the Zeppelin's flush toilets was so exhausting that it made a man useless for the rest of the night.

On the clear summer night of 6–7 June 1917 two of Strasser's "height climbers", L42 and L48, raided England. L48 was intercepted and shot down by three home defence fighters and crashed into a Suffolk field. There were three survivors. One of the crew, executive officer Otto Mieth, recalled his ordeal. A bright light had flooded the gondola and for a moment Mieth thought that L48 had been coned by a ship's searchlight:

"When I glanced up from my position, six or eight feet below the body of the ship, I saw that she was on fire. Almost instantly our

The "height climber" L48 was the first of its class to carry a streamlined control gondola. The underside of the hull and the gondolas were doped black to counter British searchlights.

600ft of hydrogen was ablaze. The quickest death would be the best; to be burned alive would be horrible. So I sprang to one of the side windows of the gondola to jump out. Just at that moment a frightful shudder shot through the burning skeleton and the ship gave a convulsion like the bound of a horse when shot. The gondola struts burst with a snap, and the skeleton collapsed with a series of crashes like the smashing of a huge window. The gondola was now grinding against the skeleton, which had assumed a vertical position and was now falling like a projectile … I wrapped my arms around my head to protect it from the scorching flames … That was the last thing I remember … There was a tremendous concussion when we hit the earth. It must have shocked me back to consciousness for a moment, for I remember a thrill of horror as I opened my eyes and saw myself surrounded by a sea of flames."

Shortly afterwards Mieth was dragged from the wreckage by civilians and police who had arrived on the scene. Strasser's optimism, however, remained unquenchable and on 5 August 1918 he flew against England in L70, just under 700ft long and, with a top speed of 81mph and a bomb load of 8,000 pounds, the last word in height climbers. L70 was one of five Zeppelins flying their last big raid of the war. The massive height climber was shot down off the English coast by Major Egbert Cadbury, flying a rugged DH4, the outstanding day bomber of the war. In a head-on attack, Cadbury's gunner blew a gaping hole in L70's outer fabric, starting a fire which rapidly spread from stem to stern. For a moment L70's bow reared up, as if in a final struggle to escape, and then it plunged seaward, a blazing mass which broke in two as it disappeared into a thick layer of cloud at 11,000ft.

The first Battle of Britain

The Zeppelins of the German Navy continued to fly against England until the late summer of 1918. However, the German Army had lost faith in Zeppelins a year before this and abandoned airship operations in mid-1917. The airships were immensely hard to navigate with any degree of accuracy, particularly in bad weather, and were now threatened by the improved British air defences. Moreover, Germany had developed a heavier-than-air bomber capable of raiding targets in Britain, and the Kaiser was urging that Germany's dwindling rubber and aluminium reserves should be devoted to the bomber programme.

The Gotha GIV was flown by a three-man crew, commanded by

the observer, who was also the navigator and bombardier, occupying the "pulpit" position in the Gotha's bulbous, box-like nose. The GIV had a maximum bomb load of 1,100 pounds which could be carried either externally or internally.

The twin-engined GIV was flown by men of the Englandgeschwader (England Wing), based in Belgium. On the morning of 13 June 1917, 14 Gothas flying in a diamond formation at a height of 16,500ft attacked London. Conditions were perfect as each Gotha broke formation to select a target almost at leisure. One bomb hit a school in Poplar, killing 16 children. Home defence fighters failed to make a single interception on the Gothas' inward journey and only a handful struggled to within combat range as the German aircraft droned back to their base in occupied Belgium unscathed.

The Gotha GIV bomber, whose three-man crew were provided with oxygen equipment for operating at altitude. They were, however, reluctant to use it not only because of the unpleasant side effects but also because it was thought "unmanly". Studied bravado was the norm in GIV units.

Daylight raids by the Gothas caused a public furore about the state of Britain's air defences, and their rapid overhaul soon forced the Gothas to bomb by night. By the end of the war some 60 Gothas had been lost in operations against the British mainland, 24 of them being shot down or disappearing over the sea. None of the GIVs' successors, the four-engined Staaken RVI, was lost to defensive action over England.

The R-types' robustness was demonstrated on the night of 16–17 February 1918 when R12 blundered into the balloon apron at Woolwich. The balloon apron was London's defensive system of tethered balloons flying at 9,000ft and linked with cables from which 1,000ft steel wires hung vertically at 25yd intervals. After striking it with its starboard wing, R12's commander, Oberleutnant Hans-Joachim von Seydlitz-Gerstenberg, later wrote:

"The aircraft was first pulled to starboard, then port and finally slipped out of control to the port side. The first pilot, Leutnant Gotte, immediately throttled down all engines, then opened up the throttles on only one side, whereby the aircraft gained equilibrium once again after having fallen 300m. The impact of the balloon apron was so severe that the starboard mechanic fell against the glowing exhaust stacks, which severely burnt his hands, and the port aileron control cables sprang from their roller guides. The aircraft itself remained intact with the exception of minor damage to the leading edge of the starboard wing, propeller and mid-fuselage section."

OBERLEUTNANT HANS-JOACHIM VON SEYDLITZ-GERSTENBERG

The Independent Force

The German raids on London had prompted the British to establish their own strategic bombing force, which emerged in the spring of 1918 as the Independent Force of the fledgling Royal Air Force, based in France and tasked with attacking German war industry.

The Independent Force's main weapon was the Handley Page 0/400, which could carry a maximum bomb load of 2,000 pounds. Bad weather and demands for their use in a tactical role meant that the 0/400s flew only a fraction of their missions against German war factories. On the night of 25 August two 0/400s attacked the Badische chemical works near Mannheim, one of the most difficult targets in Germany.

The movements of the two aircraft were coordinated in advance. The 0/400 piloted by Captain W B Lawson was to approach Mannheim at 5,000ft, drawing enemy fire. When he was joined by the

Opposite The shape of things to come. The damage caused to homes in Baytree Road in Brixton after a German Zeppelin raid on the night of 23–24 September 1916.

RE8s (Nicknamed "Harry Tates", after the comedian) of No. 15 Squadron, RFC, lined up by the roadside near Albert on 25 March 1918, during the German offensive in Picardy. The RE8 was a reconnaissance and artillery-spotting aircraft which by 1918 had become obsolete

0/400 flown by Lieutenant M C Purvis, Lawson was to "veer off four miles, shut off our engines, turn and glide silently towards the target". The four-mile glide was calculated to bring him over the target at an altitude of 1,000ft at which the 0/400 would be safe from blast.

The two bombers made a successful rendezvous over Mannheim, but Lawson began his glide too soon. Lieutenant H N Monaghan (a pilot who had volunteered to fly with Lawson as a gunner) remembered, "The silence was startling, with only the whistle of the flying wires and the soft sound of the wind to break the quiet … I stood on a wooden lattice support with my arms resting on the fuselage, gazing at the countryside below."

Lawson's mistimed glide brought him over the Badische factory at 200ft, the 0/400 bucking wildly as its bombs exploded below. A searchlight probed for the bomber, obligingly illuminating a church steeple directly in its path, while Monaghan tossed 20-pound Cooper bombs over the side, "looking down a long street and seeing, with astonishment, a house topple in the roadway".

Lawson remained over the target for several minutes, strafing the works and its searchlights with machine-gun fire. As he flew away Purvis glided in to bomb from 400ft and sweep the town with 1,100 rounds of machine-gun fire. A division of the works was put out of action for two weeks, but the damage was limited by the failure of many of the bombs to explode.

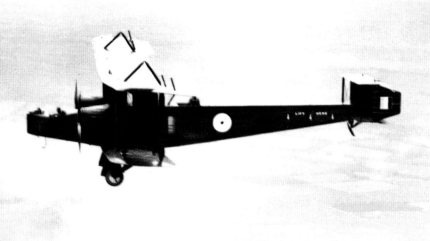

As the war drew to a close, frantic efforts were made to bring the massive Handley Page V/1500 into service to launch "terror raids" on Berlin, but the huge biplane never flew in anger against Germany. In the final analysis, bombing – whether strategic or tactical – did not alter the course of the Great War, but in four years had nevertheless achieved a degree of technical sophistication undreamt of in 1914, when pilots had gaily lobbed grenades from their cockpits on to enemy cavalry below. As with the German Zeppelins, the most tangible achievement of the Independent Force was to divert enemy equipment and personnel from front-line service.

Reacting to the Gotha raids, the British Prime Minister Lloyd George had appointed a member of the Imperial War Cabinet, General Jan Smuts, to head a committee of enquiry into the air defence of Britain. By the time he had submitted his conclusions, Smuts had been captivated by a vision of air power:

The Handley Page 0/400, which had a maximum speed of 95mph, an operational ceiling of 8,500ft and a maximum, bomb load of 2,000lb. By the end of the war the 0/400 had the Course-Setting Bombsight which remained standard RAF equipment for the next 20 years. A modified version was still in service at the start of the Second World War.

"As far as can at present be foreseen there is absolutely no limit to the scale of its future independent war use. And the day may not be far off when aerial operations, with their devastation of enemy lands and destruction of industrial and populous centres on a vast scale, may soon become the principal operations of war, to which the older forms of military and naval operations may become secondary and subordinate."

GENERAL JAN SMUTS

4 THE WAR AT SEA

"For 30 years I have been waiting for this day!"

ADMIRAL SIR DAVID BEATTY, COMMANDER OF THE
ROYAL NAVY'S BATTLECRUISER SQUADRON, AUGUST 1914

In the summer of 1914, Britain was the world's pre-eminent naval power, its capital ships the guardians of the largest empire the world had ever seen. In contrast, Germany could only dream of such imperial pre-eminence but it did field the most powerful army on the continent of Europe. However, since 1906, the year in which the Royal Navy's revolutionary all-big-gun battleship HMS *Dreadnought* entered service, at a stroke making all other capital ships obsolete, the naval gap between the two nations had been steadily closing.

It had not closed completely by July 1914. On the eve of the Great War, the Royal Navy's order of battle included 20 Dreadnought class battleships and nine Dreadnought-type battlecruisers, the latter a warship of the same weight as the original *Dreadnought* but faster and less heavily armoured. The German High Seas Fleet, by comparison, had 13 Dreadnought class ships and five battlecruisers. Moreover, their Dreadnoughts were smaller and more lightly armed than their British opposite numbers.

Crucially, however, they possessed a number of significant advantages over the British warships. They were more strongly armoured. The belts along their waterlines, which protected machinery and magazines against shells, were markedly thicker. They were broader in the beam, making them more stable gun platforms. They were also internally subdivided into numerous watertight compartments, the *sine qua non* of survival in action. The Royal Navy's ships adopted the same "honeycomb" system but, with fewer cells, were less battleworthy. If they were badly hit, they would have to slacken speed or pull out of the line to repair the damage.

The weakness of the British battlecruisers' thin armour was compounded by inferior magazine protection, carelessness in the handling of ammunition and insufficient awareness of the dangers of flash being transmitted from the turrets to the magazines below. These vulnerabilities would become apparent long before the Grand and High Seas Fleets clashed at Jutland in 1916, but the lessons were not heeded.

Yet these magnificent ships, when cleaving through a seaway, spray cascading in torrents down their superstructures, were among the most beautiful engines of war ever built, pure fighting machines utterly useless for any other purpose than that which dictated their design. However, their vulnerability to other threats in the shallow coastal waters of the North Sea – "contact" mines and torpedo-firing submarines – was well appreciated by the Royal Navy's high command. On 30 October 1914, the commander of the British Grand Fleet, Admiral Sir John Jellicoe informed the Admiralty, "It is quite within the bounds of possibility that half our battle fleet

might be disabled by underwater attack before the guns opened fire at all, if a false move is made."

This apprehension played a part in the Royal Navy's decision, at the beginning of the war, to mount a "distant" rather than a "close" blockade of the High Seas Fleet from its deep-water Scottish bases at Cromarty in the Moray Firth, Rosyth in the Firth of Forth, and Scapa Flow in the Orkney Islands, some 30 hours' steaming distance from the German naval bases on the Ems, Jade, Weser and Elbe estuaries. These dispositions effectively blocked the High Seas Fleet's access to great waters via the Scotland-Norway gap. The Royal Navy calculated that the High Seas Fleet would not risk a breakout through the bottleneck of the English Channel.

No place for big ships

The Royal Navy was given a sharp reminder of the danger posed by the submarine when on 22 September 1914 the obsolescent cruisers *Aboukir*, *Cressy* and *Hogue*, which were patrolling off the Dutch coast, were coolly sunk, one by one, by the U-boat U-9. Each of the cruisers was hit by a single torpedo. Some 2,300 sailors went into the water, of whom 300 were rescued by the Dutch trawler *Titan*. One of the survivors was a 15-year-old midshipman, W H "Kit" Wykeham-Musgrave, who had joined *Aboukir* on the outbreak of war. When *Aboukir* was fatally hit, he swam to *Hogue*. When *Hogue* was holed, he took to the water again and swam to *Cressy*. As the stricken *Cressy* disappeared beneath the waves, he was in the North Sea for a third time and was rescued by *Titan*. He wrote to his grandmother, "I don't remember being picked up as I was unconscious. But I woke up in the trawler *Titan* which was Dutch. They were awfully kind to us and did every possible thing for us. We were taken off on a destroyer called the *Lucifer* which took us to Harwich. I had no clothes on when picked up [he had been taken to the sick bay on *Cressy*] but was provided with most funny clothes on the destroyer."

Wykeham-Musgrave, who was back at sea again within a few

The victors of Coronel steaming to a fatal encounter off the Falkland Islands. Admiral Graf von Spee's squadron in line ahead off the Chilean coast in November 1914.

weeks, went on to live to the ripe old age of 90. Others were not so lucky. Twenty young midshipmen lost their lives in the disaster off the Dutch coast. The press dubbed them "Winston's babies", an implied criticism of the First Lord of the Admiralty Winston Churchill, though the real villains of the piece were the naval staff at the Admiralty who had countenanced such foolhardy use of the cruisers. As one submarine officer commented, "The North Sea is no place for big ships. I only hope the person responsible for putting them there gets hung."

The Germans remained equally cagey about risking their battle fleet in the North Sea. Nevertheless, on 28 August Commodore Roger Keyes, commander of the Harwich cruiser force on the east coast, successfully lured a force of German cruisers from their estuaries when he attacked a destroyer patrol in the Heligoland Bight. Keyes was covered by three of Admiral Sir David Beatty's battlecruisers, which stood off and sank three light cruisers and a destroyer.

Four months later British battlecruisers overwhelmed another inferior German force. On 1 November 1914, at the Battle of Coronel, Germany's detached East Asiatic Squadron of commerce raiders, commanded by Admiral Graf von Spee, had surprised and destroyed some obsolete British cruisers off the Pacific coast of Chile. In the engagement, Vice-Admiral Sir Christopher Cradock went down with his flagship *Good Hope*.

The British responded by sending a powerful force, including the battlecruisers *Inflexible* and *Invincible*, to exact revenge. On 8 December, they encountered the East Asiatic Squadron off the Falkland Islands in the South Atlantic; the British were in Port Stanley harbour taking on coal as two of von Spee's ships imprudently appeared on the horizon.

On seeing the tripod masts of the battlecruisers, the East Asiatic Squadron beat a hasty retreat, but were run down by the pursuing British. The Germans' two most powerful ships, the armoured cruisers *Scharnhorst* and *Gneisenau*, then turned to fight in an attempt to enable the weaker elements of the squadron to escape. While the *Inflexible* and *Invincible* engaged *Scharnhorst* and *Gneisenau*, the remainder of the East Asiatic Squadron, the light cruisers *Nürnberg*, *Leipzig* and *Dresden*, came under the guns of the British cruisers *Glasgow*, *Carnarvon*, *Cornwall* and *Kent*.

Petty Officer H S Welch later described in his diary the height of the duel between *Kent* and *Nürnberg*:

"The crash and din was simply terrific – first our broadsides were going off and shaking our bodies to pieces, deafening, choking and nearly blinding us, then the shells from the enemy hitting and bursting, throwing death-dealing pieces of shell and splinters of steel in all directions and nearly poisoning us with the fumes. Shells were scorching all round us and as they whizzed by the bridge and the deck I could feel the rush of air. One hit the corner of the fore turret casing, glanced off and tore through the deck into the sick bay crumpling and tearing steel plating as thought it were paper."

PETTY OFFICER H S WELCH

Kent eventually gained the upper hand. Welch recalled that "… several of *Nürnberg*'s guns were smashed clean up and one of her 5.9-inch guns on the forecastle was blown overboard and the other was falling about the deck. Her upper works were a picture – funnels all splintered and torn and jagged pieces sticking out."

Ninety minutes later, *Nürnberg* foundered. The German cruiser "gave a sudden lurch to starboard and sank smoothly down into the deep amid a mass of wreckage and dense clouds of smoke. The sight was one of fearful awe, and yet she turned over and sank with a graceful gliding motion as would a cup of tea or tumbler pressed over into a bowl of water. Those who went down in her were game to the end for we saw a party of her men standing on the quarter-deck waving the German ensign (tied to a pole) as she sank and so they went down to their watery grave. One can only feel that they were brave men and died as their beloved Fatherland would have them. They fought well and to a finish."

All but two of von Spee's force – the auxiliary *Seydlitz* and the light cruiser *Dresden* – escaped destruction. *Dresden* was scuttled off the Juan Fernandez Islands in March 1915. Admiral von Spee and his two sons were among the 1,871 German sailors who died in the battle. Richard Steele, a clerk in *Invincible*, watched as the battlecruisers picked up survivors from *Gneisenau*:

"As they're hauled on deck, they're taken below into the Wardroom ante room, or the Admiral's spare cabin. Here with knives we tear off their dripping clothes, then with towels try to start a little warmth in their ice-cold bodies. They are trembling, violently trembling, from the iciness of their immersion. Most of them need resuscitation. Some on coming to consciousness give the most terrible groans as if there was represented to their minds some very awful picture. What frightful sights they must have witnessed, some of them! Our shells did terrible damage, sometimes wiping out an entire gun's crew. One or two are horribly burned and some of their bodies are red where they have been peppered with lyddite. We get what spare warm clothing we can, such as blankets and sweaters. We have three surgeons on board and these do what best they can, relieving suffering frequently with morphia. I will draw a veil over the rest of this. I myself don't like to think of it. The human body is not beautiful in all circumstances! That's all I will say."

Tip and run

The High Seas Fleet continued to play tip and run in the North Sea, hoping to bait a trap for the Grand Fleet, but it was a dangerous game. At the beginning of the war the Royal Navy had come into possession of the German naval codes. Three cypher books had been captured by the Royal Australian Navy in the Pacific; another had been recovered from a wreck on the bed of the North Sea; and yet more cyphers, for the High Seas Fleet itself, had been handed to the British by the Russians, who had retrieved them from a cruiser wrecked in the Baltic.

A week after the destruction of the East Asiatic Squadron, on 16 December 1914, German battlecruisers bombarded the coastal towns of Scarborough, Hartlepool and Whitby. Five weeks later, on 24 January 1915, on another sweep into the North Sea, a German force of three battlecruisers, five cruisers and 18 destroyers, commanded by Rear-Admiral Franz Hipper, was intercepted by Beatty's battlecruiser squadron, which consisted of *Lion, Tiger, Princesss Royal, New Zealand* and *Indomitable*, supported by three light cruisers and 35 destroyers. The interception was no accident. Thanks to the Royal Navy's possession of the German code books, Beatty had advance warning of the German sorties.

However, he was unable to achieve a comprehensive victory in the subsequent Battle of Dogger Bank. On being found and fixed, Hipper immediately turned for home but was overhauled by the British battlecruisers, which opened fire at a range of 20,000 yards. A series of muddled and misunderstood orders then allowed the German battlecruiser *Derfflinger* to engage *Lion*, Beatty's flagship, unopposed. *Lion* was badly mauled and was forced to

Vice-Admiral Sir David (later 1st Earl) Beatty, commander of the Royal Navy's battlecruiser fleet at Jutland, strikes a characteristically jaunty pose. A flamboyant commander and natural showman, Beatty was ill-served by a streak of impetuosity. He died in 1936, after catching a chill at Jellicoe's funeral.

The stricken Blücher *at Dogger Bank, with sailors clinging to the hull. Some 260 survivors were picked up by British ships.*

drop out of the line. Thereafter the British battlecruisers concentrated their fire on the heavy cruiser *Blücher*, which was slow and undergunned, while the remainder of the German force raced for home.

Blücher was pulverised by four battlecruisers while a German reconnaissance Zeppelin, L-5, circled overhead. One of her officers noted the final moments of the stricken ship: "*Blücher* was left behind as our forces steamed off and she was unable to follow. The four English battlecruisers fired at her together. She replied for as long as she could, until she was completely shrouded in smoke and apparently on fire. At 1207 she heeled over and capsized."

On board *Blücher* there were terrible scenes. A survivor recalled:

"The shells … bore their way even to the stoke-hold. The coal in the bunkers was set on fire. Since the bunkers were half empty the fire burned merrily. In the engine room a shell licked up the oil and sprayed it around in flames of blue and green … The terrific air pressure resulting from explosions in a confined space …roars through every opening and tears its way through every weak spot … As one poor wretch was passing through a trap-door a shell burst near him. He was exactly halfway through. The trap-door closed with a terrific snap … Men were picked up by that terrific air pressure and tossed to a horrible death among the machinery."

A SURVIVOR, *BLÜCHER*

Hipper had been let off the hook but one of his battlecruisers had taken a near-fatal battering. *Seydlitz* had been struck by a 13.5in shell which penetrated the roof of an after turret and caused a raging fire which rose as "high as a house" above the turret. The flames then licked down into the munition chamber and through a connecting door, which should have remained closed, into a second munition chamber and from there to a second turret, where the crew were also engulfed by flame.

The detonation of 14,000 pounds of propellent in *Seydlitz*'s munition chambers did not set off the battlecruiser's magazine, thanks to the bravery of an officer and two ratings who opened flooding valves to allow 600 tons of water into the ship. *Seydlitz*, mauled and down by the stern, limped away. The High Seas Fleet noted *Seydlitz*'s lucky escape and immediately introduced measures to counter the danger of turret fire: the number of anti-flash shutters was increased, and the amount of combustible material stored in or near the turrets cut back.

The British failed to draw similar lessons from the damage inflicted on *Lion*. The hits she had sustained allowed 300 tons of water into the battlecruiser, slowed her to a crawl, robbed her of electrical power and threatened fire in her magazine. However, the fire started in her forward turret had been relatively small, unlike that in the *Seydlitz*, and had been quickly extinguished. It had not spread to the ammunition-handling rooms and the magazines because, by chance, there had only been a relatively small amount of ammunition stored in the turret lobby. Unlike the Germans, the British took no measures to limit the amount of ammunition, particularly propellent, in the turret lobby or to strengthen the anti-flash devices in the turret trunk, which led to the heart of the ship.

Thus the British battlecruisers' magazines remained vulnerable to "flashback". The habit of feeding charges end to end, from the magazine to the gun – the result of the Royal Navy's obsession with the rate of fire rather than its accuracy – ran the risk of a chain reaction being set off in the event of flame from a hit, producing a fatal explosion. The safety of Beatty's battlecruisers had been sacrificed to the imperative of rapid firing, but an examination of the Royal Navy's accuracy, or rather the lack of it, at the Falklands and Dogger Bank makes sobering reading. In the South Atlantic, it took *Inflexible* and *Invincible* five hours and nearly 1,200 shells to send two inferior ships to the bottom. At Dogger Bank, only six of the 1,150 heavy shells fired had found their targets.

After Dogger Bank, Kaiser Wilhelm II ordered the High Seas

Fleet to remain in its north German bases. From time to time it sailed into the Baltic against the Russians but it did not venture into the North Sea again in strength until the beginning of the spring of 1916. At the end of April 1916, the High Seas Fleet bombarded the port of Lowestoft but broke off the action when a light Royal Navy force threatened to intervene.

Jutland

The new commander of the High Seas Fleet, Admiral Reinhard Scheer, remained a proponent of the "risk" theory which had animated German strategy in the North Sea in 1914. He hoped to entice elements of the Grand Fleet into a series of isolated actions in unfavourable circumstances in which the latter's strength would be worn down. The Lowestoft raid was part of this strategy but Scheer had decided that it had been launched too far south to draw the Royal Navy's capital ships into a trap. He now focused on laying minefields which would play havoc with the major elements of the Grand Fleet and expose the Fleet's crippled casualties to his battleships, battlecruisers and submarines.

Reviewing his building plans, Scheer also concluded that the balance of naval forces would not improve in his favour. It was now or never. At the end of May 1916, he ordered his squadrons to sea, ostensibly to bombard Hartlepool but in reality in a bid to provoke a fleet action which would inflict unacceptable losses on the Royal Navy.

Thanks to their codebreakers, the British were once again able to anticipate some of Scheer's opening moves, which had begun two weeks earlier when his U-boats had set out for their patrol lines. Scheer had successfully concealed this development from the British by anchoring a ship in the River Jade to transmit signals purporting to come from his flagship. He was not so fortunate on 30 May when Jellicoe learned, via intercepted and decoded wireless messages, that the High Seas Fleet was about to leave Wilhelmshaven.

Armed with this information, Jellicoe was able to set his own trap. The Grand Fleet's 24 battleships left Scapa Flow on an interception course, while Beatty's nine battlecruisers, reinforced by four fast new battleships of the Queen Elizabeth class, sailed from Rosyth, passing undetected through the German U-boat line. In so doing, they gained two hours' steaming time on the High Seas Fleet and were thus within striking distance long before their enemy expected to encounter them.

Admiral Reinhard Scheer, who was appointed commander-in-chief of the German High Seas Fleet in January 1916. At Jutland he could claim a tactical victory but in strategic terms the battle represented a defeat. After the Kaiser expressly forbade any further forays by the surface fleet into the North Sea, Scheer urged a return to unrestricted submarine warfare, a move which was eventually to bring the United States into the war.

In the German vanguard was Vice-Admiral Hipper's scouting force of battlecruisers and light cruisers, the bait to lead Beatty's battlecruisers on to the guns of Scheer's battleships before Jellicoe could come to Beatty's aid. Screened and supported by dozens of smaller ships, 37 British capital ships were sailing against 27 of their German equivalents. It was the only occasion on which two modern battle fleets have clashed in European waters.

In the mid-afternoon of 31 May the two battlecruiser fleets crashed into each other. Beatty had hoisted flags to engage the enemy but his fast battleships missed the order and maintained a northward turn to join forces with Jellicoe. The British battlecruisers, silhouetted against the western sky, came under heavy fire at a range of 18,000 yards. One German gunnery officer described the British ships as " black monsters; six tall, broadbeamed giants steaming in two columns".

A counterpart in HMS *New Zealand*, the fourth ship in the line, described his sensations as battle was joined: "I had great difficulty in convincing myself that the Huns were in sight at last, it was so like Battle Exercise the way in which we and the Germans turned up on to more or less parallel courses and waited for the range to close

The Fourth Battle Squadron of the Grand Fleet Fleet cruising in line abreast columns in the North Sea.

143

sufficiently before letting fly at each other. It all seemed very cold-blooded and mechanical, no chance here of seeing red, merely a case of cool, scientific calculation and deliberate gunfire. Everyone seemed cool enough, too, in the control position, all sitting quietly at their instruments waiting for the fight to commence."

In closing with the enemy, Beatty had allowed his battlecruisers to press on to within the German ships' fire zone. At 4pm *Lion*'s Q turret amidships was struck by a 12in shell from *Lützow*, killing the entire gun crew. One of the dying gunners involuntarily sent a loading cage packed with cordite down into the working chamber, starting a fire which raced through the turret trunk towards the magazine. The turret officer, Major F J W Harvey, who had lost both his legs when the shell struck, managed with his last breath to give orders to close the magazine doors and flood the magazine. This action saved the ship and won Harvey a posthumous VC.

The fire which burned below the turret proved fatal for all the men at work above the magazine. *Lion*'s gunnery officer later noted its effects:

"(It) passed down the main trunk into the shell-room and handling room and up the escape trunk into the switchboard compartment. In this latter compartment were stationed, beside the switch board men and certain of the electrical repair party, the after medical party under the charge of a surgeon. All these men, together with the magazine and shell-room crews, were killed by cordite fire … (their) bodies and clothes were not burnt and, in cases where the hands had been raised involuntarily, palms forward, to protect their eyes, the backs of the hands and that part of the face screened by the hands were not even discoloured. Death to these men must have been instantaneous."

GUNNERY OFFICER, *LION*

On *Lion*'s bridge, Beatty and his officers remained "blissfully ignorant of the fact that two large shells had exploded in the ship; the rush of wind and other noises caused by the high speed at which we were travelling, together with the roar of our own guns as they fired, four at a time, completely drowned the noise of bursting shell. There was no doubt, however, that we were under heavy fire, because all round us huge columns of water, higher than the funnel, were being thrown up as the enemy shells fell into the sea. Some of these gigantic splashes curled over and deluged us with water. Occasionally above the noise of battle, we heard the ominous hum of a shell fragment and caught a glimpse of polished steel as it flashed past the bridge."

It was only when a bloodstained marine arrived to report the damage to *Lion* that the men on the bridge craned forward to see the

remains of Q turret, which had been opened up like a can of sardines. Yellow smoke billowed from the gash in its roof and its guns pointed drunkenly upward. None of those on the bridge had heard or felt the detonation, although they were only a few yards away.

At 4.20pm, a magazine explosion sank *Indefatigable*, with the loss of all but two of her crew. At 4.26pm, *Queen Mary* blew up. The battlecruiser had been hit several times and a cordite fire caused a massive explosion in her forward magazine. There were only 20 survivors of a crew of 58 officers and 1,228 men. One of the crew of the battlecruiser *Tiger*, which was steaming behind her, recalled, "the whole ship seemed to collapse inwards … the roofs of the turrets [solid sheets of armour weighing 70 tons] were blown 100 feet high, then everything

HMS Lion suffering a hit on Q turret from the battlecruiser Lützow *at 4pm on 31 May 1916. Lion was saved by the action of the turret Major F J W Harvey who, although mortally wounded, gave orders to close the magazine doors and flood the magazine.*

Jack Cornwell, VC

Mortally wounded at the Battle of Jutland, with his ship ablaze around him,
16-year-old Jack Cornwell stayed at his post manning a gun on the cruiser
Chester. His courage won him the Victoria Cross

John Travers Cornwell, usually known as Jack Cornwell, was born into a working-class family in Leyton, Essex in January 1902. In October 1915 he gave up his job as a delivery boy and enlisted in the Royal Navy. In the spring of 1916, he was assigned to the Town class cruiser HMS *Chester* as a Boy Seaman First Class. On 31 May 1916, at the Battle of Jutland, *Chester* was part of a screen of cruisers covering a battlecruiser squadron. While turning to investigate gunfire in the distance, Chester came under fire at a range of about 4,000 yards from four German cruisers and was repeatedly hit by 150mm shells. Seventeen of the men servicing *Chester's* 5.5-inch guns were killed and 49 were wounded in the action. Many of the wounded had lost limbs because the open-backed gun shields provided little protection from splinters. Among the wounded was Cornwell; he had a shard of his steel in his chest, but he remained by his gun, the sole survivor of the gun crew, awaiting orders which never came. Incapable of further action, the badly damaged *Chester* was ordered back to the port of Immingham, and Cornwell died in Grimsby hospital on 2 June. *Chester's* captain wrote to Cornwell's mother: "I know you would

wish to know of the splendid fortitude and courage shown by your boy on the action of 31 May. His devotion to duty was an example to us all. The wounds which resulted in his death within a short time were received in the first few minutes of the action. He remained steady at his most exposed post at the gun, waiting for orders…" Several months after the Battle of Jutland, Cornwell was awarded a posthumous Victoria Cross, which was given to his mother by King George V at Buckingham Place on 16 November 1916. His body was exhumed and was reburied with full military honours. Cornwell's epitaph reads, "It is not wealth or ancestry but honourable conduct and a noble disposition that maketh men great". The 5.5-inch gun which Cornwell served is on display at the Imperial War Museum, London.

Opposite Jack Cornwell, of whom the captain of HMS Chester *wrote, " His devotion to duty was an example to us all".*
Above The 5.5-inch gun which he was servicing at Jutland. HMS Chester *was launched in 1915 and had entered service only three weeks before Jutland. In the battle 29 of the crew were killed and 49 wounded.*

was smoke". The loss of *Queen Mary* prompted Beatty's famous complaint that "something's wrong with our bloody ships today".

Beatty's shells were now finding their targets but because they were fitted with over-sensitive fuses, they exploded on impact. In contrast, most of the German shells exploded after penetrating their targets' armour. In the former case, the whole ship quivered horribly as the energy of the exploding shell was transmitted from stem to stern. In the latter, where the energy was absorbed by the compartmentation of the hull, the crew in unaffected parts of the ship would remain quite unaware that it had received a mortal blow.

In line following *Queen Mary* was *Tiger*, whose executive officer, Commander E R Jones, coolly noted the disaster: "The *Tiger* being astern of the *QM* we saw their accident closely and a horrible sight it was. First an enormous height of dull red flame, followed by a great mass of black smoke amongst which was the wreckage thrown in all directions. The blast was tremendous. We passed through the smoke and it was very unpleasant."

The gunnery duel was now shifting in favour of the Grand Fleet

The end of Queen Mary, *torn apart after a colossal explosion caused by a cordite fire in the forward magazine. All but two of* Queen Mary's *crew were lost.*

as Beatty's four fast Queen Elizabeth-class battleships, finally redirected to the heart of the action, moved within range and their 15-inch guns opened up at 19,000 yards. The British began to dictate the exchanges with their heavier weight of metal.

Minutes after *Queen Mary* had blown up, Beatty received a signal from one of his scouting light cruisers, *Southampton*, that the enemy battle fleet had been sighted. If he held his course, certain destruction awaited his battlecruisers at the hands of the German battleships. At 4.40pm, he gave orders to turn away towards Jellicoe's squadrons. Beatty's ships were now running north.

Southampton was also racing north under a deluge of heavy shells. The cruiser escaped destruction but Beatty's battleships were not so fortunate. Another muddle over his flag signals delayed their turnaway by several minutes, during which time *Barham* and *Malaya* were hit. Then, as they withdrew, their heavier armament began to punish the Germans. *Seydlitz* was struck by 22 shells but stayed afloat, a tribute to German shipbuilders and seamen.

At 6pm the battle fleets sighted each other. On board the battleship *Vanguard* one of its cooks, Walter Greenwood, was on the quarterdeck, taking a break from baking bread. He recorded what he saw in a letter home:

"While my dough was proving in the tins I went out on the quarterdeck and witnessed a magnificent spectacle, one never to be forgotten. The whole visible horizon was one long blaze of flame. The hulls of the enemy's ships were not visible to the naked eye, but could be seen dimly through the haze with the telescope. And the only means we had of knowing the enemy was there was by spurts of flame from the enemy's guns. I was so intensely interested that I did not realise the risk until observing a cruiser close by on fire. I went back to the bakehouse and endeavoured to save my batch of bread. The dough requires at least twenty minutes more proof. But being very loathe to waste the material and labour, I put it in and trusted to luck if it would be possible to save it later. Then my superior officer gave me orders to leave everything at any critical time. By the time I got to my station we were in the thick of it. Several minutes later I got out a book to read entitled the *Meditations of Marcus Aurelius*. I had not read much when we received the news that the *Invincible* had gone down and we were passing close to her."

WALTER GREENWOOD, COOK, *VANGUARD*

The victor of the Falklands had been sunk at 6.33pm, the victim of another communications breakdown. Half an hour earlier, just before the British and German battleships engaged each other,

Jellicoe had signalled Beatty, "Where is the enemy's battle fleet?" Beatty's reply was ambiguous but nevertheless prompted Jellicoe to deploy from six columns into line, in the process preparing to "cross the enemy's T", a manoeuvre which would bring all his guns into action while limiting the enemy's firepower to his forward guns only.

This manoeuvre, which produced a moving wall of Dreadnoughts seven miles long, took approximately 15 minutes. Meanwhile, masked by mist and out of sight of Jellicoe's main formation, and the German battleships, *Invincible* was sailing ahead of *Indomitable* and *Inflexible* and was effectively isolated from the cover of Beatty's battleships. The mist parted and exposed the battlecruisers to the fire of the German battleships. *Invincible* was hit repeatedly, and at 6.33pm a shell smashed through the Q turret amidships. Flash raced down the turret trunk and the magazine exploded, blowing the battlecruiser in half.

Invincible sank in about 15 seconds with the loss of 1,025 officers and men out of a total of 1,031. Shortly afterwards the British battleship *Temeraire* passed the spot where she had gone down. In a letter home one of *Temeraire*'s officers, Commander T N James, recalled the moment:

"I had been keeping my eye open for the Zepps [Zeppelins] as I felt sure they must be about, and although I couldn't see one in the air great was my joy when I thought I saw one wounded, lying in the water some distance on the bow; as we got closer I found it wasn't a Zepp but a ship, and felt rather elated at seeing the fruit of our labours. Alas, on getting closer found it was the *Invincible*, with her bow and stern above water, sticking up in the air at an angle of about 45 degrees, her back broken and resting on the bottom."

Scheer was still uncertain whether he was engaging the British battlecruisers and their battleship escorts or was facing an imminent encounter with the Grand Fleet. Hipper had a clearer idea but did little to help Scheer by sending a message as murky as some of Beatty's efforts earlier in the day: "Something lurks in that soup. We would do well not to thrust into it too deeply."

Jellicoe, on the other hand, was better placed. He knew Scheer's positions and headings and could place himself between the High Seas Fleet and its line of retreat to the ports of north Germany. In the remaining hours of daylight, he was poised to deliver a crushing blow to the High Seas Fleet.

As they passed *Invincible*, Jellicoe's battleships, deploying from column to line, could pick out their targets on the western skyline. Scheer's observers could only make out the enemy by the ring of

Top *The end of the battlecruiser* Invincible *shortly after 6.30pm, struck by a heavy shell on the starboard midship 12-inch turrret. Flash from this shell ignited the magazine, which held 50 tons of cordite.* Invincible *was blown in half and sank within 15 seconds with the loss of all but six of her crew.*

Bottom The Last of Invincible *by Robert H Smyth.*

heavy gun flashes on the horizon. They could see no ships. The men with the best, albeit partial, view of the unfolding action were the British sailors in the gun control positions located over the bridge on the battleships' foremasts, 60 feet above the forward turrets. The spotters, who observed the fall of their ships' shot with high-magnification instruments, could also see the approach of enemy shells, "appearing as dots getting larger and larger". The phenomenon of being under heavy long-range fire was noted as a "curious sensation" by a midshipman on board the battleship

HMS Iron Duke, *flagship of the Grand Fleet at the Battle of Jutland, where the battleship served in the Fourth Battle Squadron.* Iron Duke *briefly became Beatty's flagship when he assumed command of the Grand Fleet in late 1916. Launched in 1912,* Iron Duke *served as a base ship at Scapa Flow in the Second World War and was broken up in Glasgow in 1948.*

Neptune: "The time of [shell] flight seems more like 30 minutes than the 30 or so seconds that it actually is. A great ripping gush of flame breaks out from the enemy's guns some [10] miles away and then follows a pause during which one can reflect that somewhere in that great 'no man's land' 2 or 3 tons of metal and explosive are hurtling towards one. The mountainous splashes which announce the arrival of each successive salvo rise simultaneously in bunches of four or five to an immense height."

Jellicoe's battleships opened fire at a range of some 14,000 yards. They scored 22 hits on the High Seas Fleet, which responded by inflicting 33 hits on Beatty's battlecruisers and battleships. Jellicoe's ships remained virtually unscathed. After being hammered by the guns of the Grand Fleet for ten minutes, Scheer ordered a *Gefechtskehrwendung* – a "battle turnaway" – under the cover of a smokescreen and destroyer attacks and, hoping to throw Jellicoe off his scent, turned due west towards the British coast.

Gambling that he might still succeed in passing across the rear of the Grand Fleet to regain harbour, Scheer then ordered a change of course and began to steer due east, aiming to work his way back home through the minefields strung around German coastal waters. But his timing was awry and his ships collided with the British rear, now steering southward as Jellicoe strove to cut off Scheer's line of retreat. At 7.10pm the High Seas Fleet came under heavy fire, its T once again crossed and its battlecruisers under the guns of Jellicoe's battleships for a second time. Scheer's battlecruisers sustained 27 hits while scoring only two hits on *Colossus*, one of Jellicoe's battleships.

Scheer ordered another "battle turnaway" and in desperation

instructed his limping battlecruisers to charge the enemy in a "death ride". His light cruisers and torpedo boats were then ordered to launch torpedo attacks before he withdrew, covered by a smokescreen. Scheer recalled the death riders before they were blown out of the water but the torpedo attacks, launched at extreme range, forced Jellicoe to order his own turnaway. When the chase was resumed, Scheer had put a crucial 11 miles between his ships and the Grand Fleet.

The sun set at 8.24pm. The Grand Fleet still held a potentially decisive tactical and numerical superiority. If Jellicoe could ride out the night and block Scheer's escape route, then the High Seas Fleet would be at his mercy when the sun came up. The fleets converged on southerly courses, each ignorant of the other's whereabouts. During the night, there were nine bruising encounters when elements of the two fleets were briefly locked in some brutal jostling. In one of these incidents, the pre-Dreadnought *Pommern* was sunk when a torpedo from the cruiser *Onslaught* found its magazine. *Pommern* was not elaborately subdivided and had no underwater protection. She broke in two and sank, leaving no survivors. In another, the British armoured cruiser *Black Prince* was set on fire by salvoes from a German Dreadnought and blew up. In a third the British cruiser *Southampton* torpedoed and sank the German cruiser *Frauenlob*. The flavour of the fighting was caught by G N Cracknell, an officer in the light cruiser *Champion*, part of the 13th Destroyer Flotilla:

"The night was very thrilling, the sky was lit up with flame and intermittent actions were going on all around us. Saw two or three ships on fire and one huge Dreadnought [*Pommern*] blown up by a torpedo. We had a narrow squeak, ran into some big German ships who turned their searchlights on us and blazed away, but did not touch us although bits of shell were picked up on the deck next day." The destroyer *Ardent*, pinned by searchlights, had the misfortune to take a pounding from the 5.9in guns of the German battleship *Westfalen*. Her captain described the damage on board:

"All the boats were in pieces. The funnels looked more like nutmeg graters. The rafts were blown to bits, and in the ship's side and decks were holes innumerable. In the very still atmosphere the smoke and steam poured out from the holes … perfectly straight up into the air. Several of my best men came up and tried to console me, and all were delighted that we had at length been in action and done our duty. But many were already killed and lay around their guns and places of duty. Most of the engine-room and stokehold brigade must have been killed outright."

CAPTAIN, *ARDENT*

Ardent was hit by more salvoes before sinking with the loss of all but the captain and one other crew member. In the darkness the technical advantage swung back in favour of the High Seas Fleet. Jellicoe could not risk a night engagement. Although the British main armament gunnery was at least as good as that of the Germans, they had not introduced centralised control of the secondary armament and remotely controlled searchlights. Nor did the Grand Fleet possess satisfactory illuminating star shells. The initiative lay with Scheer, who exploited the vital instruments of darkness as he drove through the rear flotillas of the Grand Fleet.

Jellicoe only possessed a partial picture of the unfolding action, as the flash of guns intermittently illuminated the sky to the north and east. The Admiralty had intercepted German signals which gave a clear indication of Scheer's intention, but little of this reached Jellicoe, who never possessed enough information to enable him to make the correct counter-deployment. By 1am on 1 June, the High Seas Fleet was clear of danger and suffered only one more loss when a battleship was damaged by mines. Two and a half hours later it had reached the coast of Jutland and its protecting minefields.

The High Seas Fleet could begin to lick its wounds. The battlecruiser *Lützow* had sunk and of the four remaining only *Moltke* remained battleworthy. *Seydlitz* had to be hauled into harbour stern first. Ten of

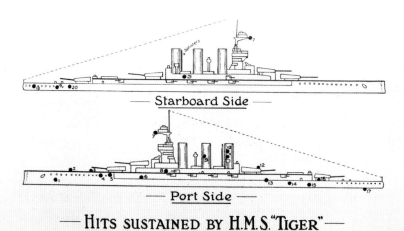

— Starboard Side —

— Port Side —

— HITS SUSTAINED BY H.M.S. "TIGER" —

1	5·9"		9. 10. 11	11"
2	11" Pitched on forecastle · burst in cable locker flat		12	11" Burst on 'Q' turret Blew in Centre sighting hood.
3	Two 11" projectiles burst in Sick Bay just before turn at 4·35 p.m.		13	11" Did more damage than any other projectile.
4	11"		14. 15	11"-Did not penetrate belt.
5	Hit "A" barbette · 12"		16	11"-Burst on 'X' turret.
6	Burst in flour store · 11"		17.18.19.20	5·9"
7	Carried away steaming light · 11"		21	12" Broke back of Steam pinnace & Nº 4 Derrick. Blew away battery door and part of bulkhead
8	11" bounced off without doing much damage.			

Left *Damage to the port side of the battlecruiser* Derfflinger *photographed after Jutland.* Derfflinger *had been hit by ten-15-inch shells, one 13.5-inch shell and two 12-inch shells. When the battlecruiser reached Germany, she was shipping nearly 3,500 tons of water, some of which had been taken in to correct a heavy list.* Opposite *The hits sustained by the British battlecruiser* Tiger.

Scheer's capital ships had been severely damaged; *Seydlitz* and *Derfflinger* had to undergo months of repairs before they were seaworthy. The pre-Dreadnought *Pommern* had also been lost, along with four light cruisers and five destroyers. Casualties amounted to 2,552 sailors killed and approximately 500 wounded.

British losses were heavier. Three battlecruisers had been sunk, along with three armoured cruisers and eight destroyers. The capital ships *Lion*, *Tiger* and *Warspite* had suffered heavy damage. Some 6,100 British sailors had been killed and 700 wounded. The Royal Navy conducted an immediate inquiry into the technical and training faults revealed by the battle. An unexploded German shell was examined to discover why its design was superior. A searching examination was made of the battlecruisers' vulnerability to magazine explosions.

When all was said and done in the aftermath of the Battle of Jutland, one thing remained clear. On 1 June 1916 the Royal Navy had only to replenish coal and ammunition and patch a few holes before it was ready, within a week, to sail back into the North Sea. In contrast, Germany was never able to risk a major encounter again. With the exception of a few abortive forays, the High Seas Fleet did not emerge from harbour until it sailed out to surrender in November 1918. In his report on the battle to the Kaiser, Scheer stated that only U-boat action against British commerce offered an opportunity to win the war.

The U-boat war

In 1914, Germany had a submarine fleet of about 70 U-boats. German admirals, and their British counterparts, initially saw the submarines as auxiliaries to their main fleets, acting as scouts and harrying battleships. Little attention was given to the submarine's potential against Britain's merchant shipping lifeline.

At the beginning of February 1915, the German Navy stepped up its U-boat operations after the declaration of a blockade on the British Isles. Surface hunters forced U-boat commanders to make periscope rather than surface attacks, a tactic which made it hard to identify neutral vessels. On 7 May 1915, U-20 sank the British liner *Lusitania*, bound from New York to Liverpool, off the coast of southern Ireland. The *Lusitania*, one of the most luxurious pre-war liners, sank in 18 minutes. Among the 1,200 passengers who drowned were 124 United States citizens. At the age of 102, a survivor of the tragedy, Mrs Jane Lewis, recalled the sinking of *Lusitania*:

"The sea was calm; if the water had not been like that, there would have been many more lost. It happened about lunchtime. All in the daylight. The most vivid scene of all was when it first started, when the explosion came. We were in the dining room. Everybody was frightened then – they panicked. Had we not been by a door we would never have got out, because a stream of people came down from the dining room, there were others following at the back, and people were being stepped on, walked on. That was the most terrible thing – they just couldn't help themselves, the crowd was too strong. And when they were going down the staircase towards the boats someone fell on top of me – I would never have survived if my husband hadn't got hold of me and had the strength to pull me out."

MRS JANE LEWIS, SURVIVOR, *LUSITANIA*

The Germans claimed that the *Lusitania* was carrying large amounts of war material. And there is evidence to suggest that on her last voyage her hold contained millions of rounds of ammunition and explosives. Nevertheless, the sinking of the *Lusitania* was a gift to Allied propaganda, an example of German "frightfulness". At this stage in the war, however, U-boat commanders were reluctant to use torpedoes against merchantmen, which often sailed alone and unarmed. Torpedoes were expensive items in short supply and it was easier and more economical to surface and board the vessel to open its scuttles, or to use the U-boat's gun with its ample supply of cheap ammunition.

REMEMBER THE 'LUSITANIA'

THE JURY'S VERDICT SAYS:

"We find that the said deceased died from their prolonged immersion and exhaustion in the sea eight miles south-south-west of the Old Head of Kinsale on Friday, May 7th, 1915, owing to the sinking of the R.M.S. 'Lusitania' by a torpedo fired without warning from a German submarine."

"That this appalling crime was contrary to international law and the conventions of all civilized nations, and we therefore charge the officers of the said submarine and the Emperor and Government of Germany, under whose orders they acted, with the crime of wilful and wholesale murder before the tribunal of the civilized world."

IT IS YOUR DUTY

TO TAKE UP THE SWORD OF JUSTICE
TO AVENGE THIS DEVIL'S WORK

ENLIST TO-DAY

In September 1915, the German Navy announced the end of its submarine campaign in the Western Approaches, a largely cosmetic gesture which enabled it to redirect its submarines to the Mediterranean and avoid embarrassment in the American shipping routes. In 1915, U-boats sank nearly 750,000 tons of shipping, convincing the naval high command that a campaign of unrestricted submarine warfare could knock the British out of the war.

There followed a tug-of-war between the German military and its civilian government, which was opposed to the idea of unrestricted submarine warfare. At the beginning of April 1916, a restricted campaign in British home waters was authorised but it was abandoned after US protests. The German government then ordered that Prize Regulations – the stopping and warning of ships before sinking them – should be observed.

Q-ships

One Allied answer to the U-boats was the Q-ship, a well-armed ship disguised as a merchantman which would tempt an enemy submarine into making a surface attack. The Q-ships were a smart idea but only a limited success. U-boat commanders could use the existence of the Q-ships as an excuse for sinking all unarmed merchantmen without warning. Nevertheless, the Q-ships recorded some notable successes. On 30 November 1916, Q7, formerly the steamship *Penshurst*, sank UB-19 off Portland Bill.

UB-19 had surfaced and loosed off a number of warning shots at Q7, before approaching the vessel, whose crew made a good job of appearing to abandon ship. As the U-boat drew nearer, Q7's captain, Commander Francis Grenfell, signalled "open fire":

"Inside ten seconds the 3-pounder got off its first shot, which carried a man clean off the conning tower; the second immediately afterwards went through her engine room. The 6-pounder and the 12-pounder took up the game almost at once, and the shells began to burst all over the sub. We hit her mostly in the conning tower and after part. Shells burst all along her waterline and the 12-pounder lyddite did grand work. Most of the conning tower was blown clean away, and one shell blew a great sheet of deck plating spinning into the air.

We could see the men running on to her deck, and falling or diving overboard. A knot gathered at the fore end where the shells were less numerous. It was a grand sight … All this time the sub was going slowly ahead towards our boats, and we learned afterwards that our second shot, besides preventing her from submerging, also prevented them from stopping the engines. The submarine was now partly shrouded by the smoke of bursting shells, and a shout went up that the men on her were waving in token of surrender. I stopped the firing, but saw nothing of this myself, and as the submarine continued to go ahead, and as I was mindful of Admiral Colville's injunction to me when we were commissioned not to take any chances, but to go on firing until the sub sank, I commenced firing again. A very little more, however, convinced me that all was up with her."

After the Battle of Jutland, the argument within the German high command was renewed. Since 1914, the U-boat fleet had doubled in size and the new German Chief of Naval Staff, Admiral Henning von Holtzendorff, managed to persuade the Kaiser that the only answer to the Allied naval blockade of Germany was to starve Britain out of the war. Holtzendorff's "best case scenario" was that the sinking (by an enlarged U-boat fleet of 105 vessels) of 600,000 tons of Allied shipping a month, and the deterring of some 40 per cent of neutral ships from entering British ports, would bring Britain to its knees within five months. However, Holtzendorff discounted the risk of America entering the war within five months and also the likelihood that the introduction of improved Allied defensive

War artist Charles Pears' painting of the fight in the Bay of Biscay on 8 August 1917 between the Q-ship HMS Dunraven *and the German submarine UC-71.* Dunraven *was commanded by Q-ship ace Captain (later Rear-Admiral) Gordon Campbell, who had won the Victoria Cross in February 1917 for the sinking of U-83. After a lengthy battle, the Q-ship was abandoned and the crew picked up by the destroyer* Christoper. Dunraven *sank two days later. Subsequently, two of* Dunraven's *crew were awarded VCs by ballot.*

measures would prevent the U-boats from meeting their targets.

Germany's new military leaders, Hindenburg and Ludendorff, also bought Holtzendorff's argument. They were convinced that Germany had to achieve victory in 1917. Germany could not endure another winter of war and the British could be defeated before the Americans could intervene on the battlefields of Europe. On 31 January 1917 the Germans announced that all shipping, including neutral vessels, would be sunk on sight in the war zone of the eastern Atlantic.

A close-run thing

The U-boat campaign acted as a spur to the development by the Allies of new defensive measures, although this was not achieved without ruffling a few venerable feathers in the British and American naval establishments (the United States joined the war in April 1917).

Admirals were notably reluctant to allocate adequate resources, particularly destroyers, to guard shipping and hunt U-boats and to implement a universal convoy system. When a scientific approach was urged, the admirals relied on intuition and dug in their heels. It was only in 1917 that the Royal Navy established a staff college (the Americans had founded one in 1884). The Admiralty did not have a statistical branch with which to analyse with any accuracy the precise nature of the U-boat problem.

Another fly in the ointment was Admiral Jellicoe, now sailing a desk as First Sea Lord. Jellicoe argued that the organisation of shipping into convoys would be a vast and unmanageable undertaking. He wanted to husband his destroyers against the possibility of another fleet action the size of Jutland.

Key to Britain's survival in the first Battle of the Atlantic. A convoy steams safely home.

Jellicoe's stubborn resistance was undermined with the help of the statistical analysis, by Commander Reginald Henderson, of Ministry of Shipping records. There were some 140 weekly ocean-going sailings. The vessels which were normally escorted – warships, colliers and troop transports – suffered very few losses because, as Henderson demonstrated, submerged U-boats under threat were unable to fire their torpedoes accurately. In the end the argument was won when Henderson went over Jellicoe's head to the British prime minister Lloyd George to urge the establishment of a convoy system.

It came not a moment too soon. In April 1917 the U-boats had sunk nearly a million tons of shipping. In May, when the convoys were introduced, the figure fell to just under 700,000 tons. As the convoy system was refined, the figures continued to fall. In the vastness of the Atlantic, 100 ships sailing in convoy were as difficult for a U-boat to locate as a ship sailing alone and unprotected.

The convoy was not the only key to Britain's survival. In the early months of 1917, the numbers of neutral ships sailing to British ports fell sharply. Thanks, however, to financial inducements offered by the United States, and the naturally mercantile instincts of the neutrals, by July the volume of neutral shipping sailing to British ports had climbed back up 80 per cent of the January figure.

The convoy system was also proving its worth. One statistic is instructive. Between 2 July and 10 October 1917, 115 wheat ships set out to cross the Atlantic from the United States. Of 18 which sailed independently, four were sunk. Of the 97 which sailed in convoy, one was sunk, having been separated from the rest. By November 1917, the convoy system had become fully operational. Mines and patrols in the Straits of Dover also claimed many U-boats and forced them to sail to and from their hunting grounds around the north of Scotland. By 1918 the life expectancy of a U-boat based on the coast of Flanders was only six voyages.

How to Make a Ship Disappear

One of the most striking sights of the war at sea was that of naval and merchant vessels sporting geometric patterns to mislead predatory U-boats

The remarkable dazzle-paint designs borne by merchantmen and warships in the latter part of the First World War were, in the words of artist Norman Wilkinson, the man who pioneered their colour schemes, intended to confuse the captains of German U-boats as they looked through their periscopes. Wilkinson noted that the dazzle produced "an effect by paint in such a way that all accepted forms of a ship can be broken up by means of strong, contrasted colours, consequently making it a matter of difficulty for a submarine to decide on the exact course of the vessel to be attacked". The principal colours used by Wilkinson and his teams of "camoufleurs" were black, white, blue and green. Vertical lines were largely avoided; sloping lines, curves and stripes were preferred to confer the maximum amount of distortion. The merchantman SS *Industry* was the first ship to be dazzle painted by Wilkinson, and in August 1917 HMS *Alsatian* became the Royal Navy's first ship to receive a treatment that journalists quickly likened to the methods used by the Cubist painters. The morale effect of dazzle-painting was considerable, and convoys of merchantmen painted with composite patterns of geometric shapes in contrasting colours provided one of the most striking sights of the war at sea.

Dazzled Ships Leave Boulogne, *by Charles Bryant.*

163

5 FROM EUROPEAN WAR TO WORLD WAR

"The soldiers in the advanced guard will have a very trying time, embarking in picket boats, pinnaces, cutters etc, about one in the morning, in pitch darkness and silence, then steaming about two hours in the cold and silence, to a shore it will be impossible to be sure of, to splash ashore and then, wet, chilled and cramped from their long sitting in the boats to advance against an invisible enemy ..."

SURGEON DUNCAN LORIMER, RNVR, BEFORE THE
LANDINGS ON THE GALLIPOLI PENINSULA, APRIL 1915

Previous page *The city of Salonika, in north-east Greece, seen from an Allied battleship.*
Opposite *The Empire strikes back. Indian cavalry of the 20th Deccan Horse photographed in mid-July 1916, shortly before an unsuccessful attack at High Wood during the Battle of the Somme. Until the summer of 1918, the Western Front was no place for cavalry.*

The Great War had begun as a European war but became a global conflict because the principal combatants were imperial powers and called on the manpower and resources of their colonies and dependencies across the globe. Algerian spahi cavalry and Senegalese infantry served with the French Army on the Western Front; Australians fought in the Dardanelles campaign and in France; Indians served in Africa, the Middle East and with the BEF on the Western Front. By 1918 the Indian Army, half a million men strong, formed Britain's imperial strategic reserve.

In 1914, Japan seized (former) German possessions in China and the central Pacific and later in the war its ships escorted Allied convoys in the Mediterranean. After the United States joined the conflict in April 1917, American diplomacy brought the satellite Central American states into the war. By the autumn of 1918, the Central Powers (Germany, Austria-Hungary, Turkey and Bulgaria) were opposed by 22 Allied nations.

Everybody was affected by the Great War. Neutrality was a curse for countries like Denmark and Holland, which were forced to agree to trade with Germany on punitive terms. Danish milk went to feed German families and Sweden had to introduce food rationing. The Argentine economy, which had expanded rapidly in the last years of the nineteenth century, slid into recession after 1914 when European investment dried up.

Dardanelles disaster

The fighting spilled far beyond the Eastern and Western Fronts in Europe. The Allied war against Turkey embraced the Gallipoli campaign of 1915, the Russian campaign in the Caucasus and the British defence of Egypt against the Turks and the campaigns in Palestine and Mesopotamia. In October 1914, Turkey had entered the war as an ally of the Central Powers. Turkey's opening moves were ambitious but singularly unsuccessful: a mid-winter offensive in the Caucasus was rolled back by the Russians; and a thrust towards the Suez Canal early in 1915 was brushed aside by the British.

In Britain, operations against the Turks were considered necessary both to safeguard the Suez Canal and to relieve the pressure on the Russians by opening up a supply and communications route to them through the Dardanelles straits, the passage from the Aegean to the Sea of Marmara and the gateway to the Black Sea. Securing a foothold on the Gallipoli peninsula, on the northern side of the straits, would threaten Constantinople (Istanbul), forcing the Germans to withdraw troops from the Western Front. This was the argument advanced by the so-called

"Easterners", notably Winston Churchill, First Lord of the Admiralty.

From the outset, however, the Allied adventure in the Dardanelles was marred by muddled, even wishful, thinking. Churchill had convinced himself that the passage into the Sea of Marmara could be opened up by a purely naval operation. First, the straits would be cleared of mines; the Turkish forts defending them would then be battered into submission at long range by the main armament of capital ships; and after several days of bombardment, the forts would be secured by landing parties. Naval intelligence considered that "it may generally be considered that the defences [in the Dardanelles] are too dispersed and not strong enough at the critical point". The British high command also had a low opinion of the fighting qualities of the Turkish soldier. Kitchener, the Secretary of State for War, was of the opinion that the systematic destruction by naval gunnery of the forts "will exert great moral effect on the Turk". When confronted with this early example of "shock and awe" tactics, "Johnny Turk" would think again and meekly throw in the sponge. What the high command left out of their equation was the fact that the Turks were fighting on their own soil and had been well schooled by German military advisers. The commander of the Turkish troops holding the Gallipoli pensinsula, General Liman von Sanders, was a German who had arrived in Turkey at the head of a military mission in December 1913.

Moreover, the British had already shown their hand on 4 November 1914, before hostilities with Turkey had begun in earnest, when Royal Navy warships bombarded the entrance to the Dardanelles. On 13 December, the submarine B11 had sunk a Turkish patrol vessel on the Asian side of the straits. The Turks immediately began strengthening their defences, and by March 1915 had sown nearly 350 mines in the straits and had also sited torpedo tubes at their narrowest point.

Churchill was reportedly confronted by the Third Sea Lord, Admiral Frederick Tudor, who asked him what he would do if the forcing of the Dardanelles could not be accomplished by ships alone. Churchill breezily brushed Tudor aside with the assurance that "Oh yes, we will." However, the First Lord was less confident when discussing the Dardanelles with Commodore Roger Keyes, the naval chief of staff during the campaign, shortly before the operation began. Keyes commented that Churchill was, understandably, nervous as this was "the biggest coup he [Churchill] had ever played for".

At the end of February the British and French took the naval route in an attempt to silence the Turkish guns. However, the Turks deployed many concealed and mobile batteries which made life very difficult for the Allied minesweepers – most of which were converted trawlers

– and prevented the larger warships, notably the brand-new Dreadnought *Queen Elizabeth*, from getting to grips with the forts guarding the straits.

Meanwhile in London, the politicians had hatched a plan to assemble a large force – eventually some 75,000 men – to mount a full-scale amphibious operation to deal with the Turkish guns. Thus at the end of February there were at least three wholly uncoordinated plans simultaneously moving forward: Churchill's "ships alone" policy; a joint Army–Navy operation; and a plan to take the Dardanelles with a full-scale landing by ground forces.

On 18 March the "ships alone" policy was given one more chance. No fewer than 16 Allied battleships took part, most of them obsolete pre-Dreadnoughts. It was late in the morning when they began firing. Watching from the town of Chanak Kale, on the Asian side, was the Associated Press reporter George Schreiner: "The heavy shells hit the town in pairs. Not merely fragments of the houses struck but whole floors sailed up high in the air. It began to literally rain roof tiles, bricks, rocks and timbers. Shells exploding in front of the old breakwater remains sent a vicious hail of steel fragments broadcast and the fumes of the explosions began to make breathing a difficult task."

It was now nearly 2pm, and the Turkish gunners were beginning to find their range. As the Allied warships moved closer to the shore, they became vulnerable to uncleared mines. The French pre-Dreadnought battleship *Bouvet* struck one of them. Schreiner saw "a sheaf of fire" erupt from *Bouvet*, then "a large black column of smoke

General Sir Ian Hamilton (centre-right) takes leave of his staff on 17 October 1915. A veteran of the Boer War and a pre-war commander-in-chief of forces in the Mediterranean, Hamilton was an obvious choice for the Gallipoli campaigh. However, his command ended after journalists leaked the truth about the scale of the Dardanelles disaster. He never again held a senior military position.

rose and for several seconds the ship took a heavy list. It soon righted itself, however … The next moment brought the beginning of a drama. Slowly the vessel settled astern, then listed to port. Already the aft deck was awash … The forward part of the ship, too, sagged a little. It rose again the next instant, the vessel righted a little … And then came the final plunge. The vessel for an instant showed her sharp prow clear against the sunlit water like a black triangle and then this too disappeared. The *Bouvet* had sunk. It was exactly 2 o' clock."

It proved to be a good day for Turkish mines and a bad day for Allied battleships. *Irresistible* and *Ocean* fell foul of them and also went to the bottom. *Suffren* and *Charlemagne* were crippled by the Turkish guns and the battlecruiser *Inflexible*, the victor of the Battle of the Falklands, was so badly damaged by the shore batteries that it had to be towed to Malta for extensive repairs.

The baton now passed to the Army and the expeditionary force gathered on the Greek island of Lemnos under the command of General Sir Ian Hamilton. It comprised men of the Australian and New Zealand Army Corps (ANZAC), the Royal Naval Division, the British 29th Division and a single French colonial division. However, the troops could not be landed without the help of the Navy, whose commanders still hankered after another crack at the Dardanelles forts, an ambition which was now to remain unrealised.

The initiative still lay with the Allies as the Turks were obliged to disperse their forces in order to cover several possible landing sites. When the landings went in on 25 April, the Turks were taken by surprise but the Allies failed to press home their advantage. Some 15,000 Anzacs were put ashore on the European, north-west coast of the peninsula, but were landed about a mile to the north of the intended beaches on a narrow strip of shore dominated by forbidding hills cut with gulleys and ravines. The resulting confusion prevented them from moving speedily inland to seize the dominating heights of the Sari Bair ridge and allowed elements of the Turkish 19th Division, commanded by an ardent nationalist, Mustafa Kemal, to move up and occupy them. Having been checked and then confined to a very narrow beachhead, effectively clinging to a cliff edge under intense Turkish artillery and sniper fire, the Anzac forces were denied permission to conduct an evacuation. Instead they were ordered by Hamilton to "dig, dig, dig, until you are safe".

The British 29th Division, made up of regular soldiers, veterans of garrison duty throughout the British Empire, landed at the tip of the Gallipoli peninsula, Cape Helles, on five beaches, designated Y, X, W, V and S. They were carried in rowing boats towed by steam launches,

two of them commanded by midshipmen aged just 13. On the heavily defended V Beach, a converted collier, SS *River Clyde*, was to follow the tows in. The aim was to provide the 2,000 troops aboard the collier with some protection and to use the *River Clyde* as a depot ship after the landings. However, the collier ran aground short of the beach and in spite of heroic efforts to provide the troops with a bridge to the beach improvised from wooden lighters, they emerged into a hail of fire from the Turkish defenders. Many men drowned under the 250-pound weight of their equipment, and the sea ran red with blood up to 50 yards from the shore.

Men of the Lancashire Fusiliers before disembarking at Gallipoli, May 1915, where on "W" beach they famously won "six VCs before breakfast".

171

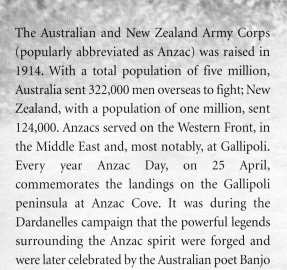

Anzacs

Troops from Australia and New Zealand made a massive contribution
to the Allied war effort

The Australian and New Zealand Army Corps (popularly abbreviated as Anzac) was raised in 1914. With a total population of five million, Australia sent 322,000 men overseas to fight; New Zealand, with a population of one million, sent 124,000. Anzacs served on the Western Front, in the Middle East and, most notably, at Gallipoli. Every year Anzac Day, on 25 April, commemorates the landings on the Gallipoli peninsula at Anzac Cove. It was during the Dardanelles campaign that the powerful legends surrounding the Anzac spirit were forged and were later celebrated by the Australian poet Banjo Paterson:

The mettle that a race can show
Is proved with shot and steel,
And now we know what nations know
And feel what nations feel.

At Gallipoli the Anzacs displayed great courage, endurance, initiative and, a quintesssentially Anzac quality, "mateship". In both world wars, Anzacs also acquired a reputation for being intolerant of the more nit-picking aspects of military discipline, an attitude which was celebrated in the First World War by Australia's official war historian Charles Bean. Hardy and physically toughened by agricultural life in the outback, the Australians were generally free of the class-consciousness and deferential attitudes which bedevilled their British comrades in arms. They fought in many of the crucial campaigns on the Western Front, including the Battles of the Somme (1916), Messines Ridge (1917), Passchendaele (1917) and Hamel (1918). In 1918 the Australian Corps, which contained all five Australian divisions, was the strongest Allied corps on the Western Front.

An Australian bringing in a wounded comrade, a graphic example of the "mateship" so prized by Anzac troops in the Dardanelles campaign, in the Middle East and on the Western Front.

Nevertheless, by nightfall footholds on all five beaches had been secured, and forces from Y Beach had moved some two miles inland before being forced back to the beach by the Turkish defenders. The next day Y Beach was abandoned. To the south the British managed to establish a continuous front but an offensive launched on 28 April was halted as more Turkish forces were fed into the battle.

The British, the French and the Anzacs were to be pinned down by the Turks for the next eight months. Trench warfare ensued in conditions as bad as those on the Western Front. Hamilton's troops held no secure rear, only beaches exposed to Turkish shellfire. Everything – even water – had to be landed by night. In May the Turks launched a series of immensely costly attacks in an attempt to drive the Allies back to the shore. On 19 May a series of suicidal assaults were made on the Anzac lines. By noon over 3,000 dead lay in no man's land. The stench was almost unbearable and a truce was arranged for 24 May.

For nine hours men from both sides dug graves. In scenes reminiscent of the unofficial Christmas truce on the Western Front in 1914, some exchanged gifts with the enemy and snatched brief conversations. Later in the campaign there were several entirely unofficial occasions on which small numbers of troops from both sides adopted a "live and let live" attitude. In one incident in December, a Turk and an Irishman fought each other to a standstill in a hand-to-hand battle in no man's land after a Turkish attack. A witness to the tussle recalled, "we moved forward to collect our man and the Turks did likewise. We were within arm's length of each other

Australians and men of the Royal Naval Division share a trench. The soldier on the left is observing the enemy with a trench periscope, similar to those used in France. The man on the right is using a "sniperscope", a periscope rifle.

but no one spoke … Both parties turned and walked slowly away to their respective trenches. Not a shot was fired from either line even though there were at last a dozen men ambling about at point-blank range." As the campaign wore on, the Allied troops gained a grudging respect for the Turks as soldiers. However, Turkish snipers got short shrift and, if captured, were usually shot out of hand. For their part, the Turks often looked after wounded prisoners of war but, if anecdotal evidence is to be believed, were less scrupulous about preserving the lives of those prisoners who were unwounded.

A pattern was set for the summer. Costly attacks were followed by equally ruinous counter-attacks with little or no change in the front line. At the end of August, Francis Twistleton of the Otago Rifles was on duty in a fire trench for 36 hours near a captured Turkish position on Hill 60: "In many places the parapet and parados … was built up of dead men. Turks of course; the stench was appalling … I felt as though I could scrape the smell of dead men out of my mouth and throat and stomach in chunks."

The Turks were dogged trench fighters and Allied commanders were often cavalier with their men's lives. Major H Mynors, a staff captain with 86th Brigade, recalled the summer fighting:

"When I was there, in every case, attacks were ordered rather lightheartedly and carried out without method. The men on the spot were not listened to when they pointed out steps to be taken before entering on a special task. The Turks had sited their trenches very cleverly, and it was often useless to attack one set before another had been taken. The Turks dig like moles and prepare line after line for defence; seven or eight close behind the other. The great difficulty is in making attacks and supporting them. The trenches become congested; the telephone wires get cut by shrapnel; and the whole show gets out of control."

MAJOR H MYNORS, 86TH BRIGADE

In the pitiless summer heat, diarrhoea and dysentery took their toll. Clouds of flies swarmed, feeding off faeces and corpses. In the line men, horses and mules relieved themselves where they could. Latrines were dug, but they only fostered more flies. Latrines could also be deathtraps. One soldier was hit by shrapnel while seated on the latrine, and "the poor beggar fell back into the pit and was quite dead when pulled out a few minutes after". It was not until September that improvements were made with the introduction of biscuit tins inside close-fitting wooden boxes, the lid of which served as a seat. Once a week the contents were doused in kerosene and burned in a deep pit.

Frost-bitten troops at Suvla Bay take shelter a shelter made of store boxes after a blizzard in November 1915.

To diarrhoea and dysentery was added typhus. At Anzac Cove, the Australian and New Zealand beachhead, huge barges capable of carrying up to 450 sick men left the beach at 10.30am and 3.30pm every day. Horses and mules suffered terribly under the blazing sun, their wounds often undressed. A New Zealander, Lottie LeGallais, working as a nurse on the hospital ship *Maheno*, lying off Anzac Cove, wrote, " …we all had awful wounds [to treat]. It was dreadful, and what with fleas and crawlers at present my skin is nearly raw, but we all scratch, scratch – except the men patients poor devils, they are used to them." It is hardly surprising that only 30 per cent of Allied casualties at Gallipoli were sustained in battle.

In London the politicians were faced with a stark choice – reinforce or evacuate. The short summer nights made the latter option technically impossible. The decision was taken to taken to reinforce and renew the offensive with a further landing, north of Anzac Cove at Suvla Bay, timed to coincide with a drive launched from the Cove towards the heights at Sari Bair.

IX Corps was put ashore at Suvla Bay on 6 August. The landing met little or no resistance, but the troops milled around on the Suvla

Plain while their commanders dithered over what to do next. Lacking adequate water supplies, the men returned to their landing beaches while their superiors on the shore waited for artillery reinforcements. In contrast, the advance on Sari Bair had got off to an encouraging start. The Anzacs, reinforced by one and a half divisions of British and Indian troops, were well briefed and confident but were betrayed by their night-time advance over unfamiliar ground. Most of them became lost. The few who reached the vital high ground, the crest of the ridge at Chunuk Bair, were bundled back after the Turks put in determined counter-attacks directed by Mustafa Kemal. The moment had passed.

The charming but ineffectual Hamilton was removed from his command on 16 October. His replacement was General Sir Charles Monro, a soldier who had the unnerving habit of slapping interlocutors heartily on the arm while bellowing "Ja!" in agreement. Monro was a convinced "Westerner", a man who believed that the war could only be won where Germany was strongest, on the Western Front. Monro arrived at Gallipoli, inspected the three fronts in a day and on the following day recommended withdrawal. Kitchener had other ideas, visited the theatre himself, sacked Monro and replaced him with Lieutenant-General William Birdwood, who was diplomat enough to assure Kitchener that he could hang on at Gallipoli but enough of a realist to oppose any suggestions of further offensives.

Kitchener had convinced himself that a withdrawal could not be accomplished without heavy loss of men and guns. It took three weeks to persuade him to agree to the evacuation of Suvla and Anzac Bays but not the beachheads at Cape Helles in the south. Monro was reinstated as overall commander in the Mediterranean (with the exception of Egypt) and Birdwood remained in control of operations at Gallipoli.

Winter had arrived at Gallipoli and frostbite replaced typhus and dysentery as the principal medical concern. One two-day blizzard caused 16,000 cases of frostbite and exposure and 300 deaths. In London the Cabinet gave the go-ahead for an evacuation from all three bridgeheads on 7 December. At Suvla Bay and Anzac Cove there were some 83,000 men and 5,000 horses and mules. Troops were taken off night after night, leaving a rearguard of about 20,000 men to convince the Turks that all was normal. These men were taken off on the night of 19–20 December. Rifles were rigged up in the trenches to fire automatically when water or candle devices ran down. The last man left Anzac Cove at 4am on 20 December. It was long thought that the Turks remained unaware of the evacuation, but it seems that they had a pretty good idea of what was going on. In any event, it was not in their interest to block the Allies' line of retreat or to incur needless losses in attempting to do so.

The procedure was repeated at Helles three weeks later. In order to sustain morale the commander there, Lieutenant-General Francis Davies, organised a football competition. The Turks used to watch the footballers from the high ground but never opened fire because, so it was said, they were betting on the outcome of the matches. As they had been at Suvla, the Turks were in no mind to attack, and when they launched a raid on 7 January, on the eve of the evacuation, it was a half-hearted affair. By 4am on 8 January the last boat had left Helles.

The campaign in the Dardanelles had cost the Allies half a million casualties, mainly British, and cost the Turks half that number. The fighting had forged the identities not only of Australia and New Zealand, whose Anzacs will forever be associated with this ill-starred operation, but also that of twentieth-century Turkey, the nation which emerged from the Great War under the leadership of a Turkish hero, Mustafa Kemal. He had played a vital role in rallying the defenders of the peninsula in April and August 1915 and was to play an even more significant part in Turkey's post-war history. In 1934, as President of Turkey and now bearing the name Kemal Attaturk, he spoke of the fallen at Gallipoli in the National Assembly:

"Those heroes who shed their blood and lost their lives … You are now lying in the soil of a friendly country. Therefore rest in peace. There is no difference between the Johnnies (Allied soldiers) and the Mehmets (Turkish soldiers) to us where they lie side by side here in this country of ours … You, the mothers, who sent their sons from far away countries, wipe away your tears, your sons are now lying in our bosom and are in peace. After having lost their lives on this land they have become our sons as well."

KEMAL ATTATURK

The Siege of Kut

Gallipoli was not the only theatre of war in which British forces were blocked by the Turks. The debacle at Gallipoli led to another fiasco, this time in Mesopotamia, the ancient region of south-west Asia, between the Euphrates and Tigris rivers, most of which lies in modern Iraq. In 1914 it was part of the Ottoman Empire.

The Allied debate about the evacuation from Gallipoli was coloured by the ripple effect it might cause, not so much in Turkey

but in the wider Muslim world. The government of India provided many of the Allied troops in the Middle East. There was also a substantial Muslim population in India. A victory over the Turks in Mesopotamia might settle Muslim discontent in the subcontinent, a sentiment which grew stronger as the news from the Dardanelles grew worse. By the same token, of course, another setback at the hands of the Turks might deal a mortal blow to British prestige in the Islamic world. Britain had good reason to take this problem seriously; during the Great War, Germany made several unsuccessful attempts to encourage Muslims to wage jihad (holy war) against the British Empire, and even despatched an expedition to Persia to persuade the Shah to raise an army for the invasion of India. Germany's diplomats in the United States purchased arms for shipment to India, and its intelligence agents penetrated nationalist movements in Central Asia and North Africa. During the rest of the twentieth century, nationalism proved more important than Islam. In 2008, the boot seemed to be on the other foot.

As with the Dardanelles, the advocates of action overruled the counsels of caution. There was another consideration: safeguarding the oil pipeline from neutral Persia. On the outbreak of war the British, wary of the Turks and anxious to protect their oil interests, moved troops to Bahrein (Bahrain) in the Persian Gulf. When, two months later, Turkey entered the war, the troops advanced to the Shatt al-Arab, the channel formed by the confluence of the Tigris and Euphrates, which the Turks claimed as their territorial waters.

Indian troops in Kut, manning an improvised anti-aircraft gun precariously perched on a barrel.

179

Turkish pipers at the head of a column. At Gallipoli and in the Middle East, British and Emoire troops afforded Turkish troops grudging respect.

However, Turkish forces in the region were thin and scattered – in the winter of 1915–1916, the Turkish 6th Army in the theatre fielded some 25,000 men, had poor communications with Baghdad, which was five weeks' march away, and deployed no heavy artillery.

The British commander in Mesopotamia, General Sir John Nixon, was anxious that Turkish success at Gallipoli could release substantial reinforcements for the 6th Army. In the autumn of 1915, the British and Indian troops under his command outnumbered the Turks by two to one, and he was given orders to occupy the entire province of Basra, in the Shatt al-Arab delta.

He despatched a force, little stronger than a division and commanded by General Sir Charles Townshend, up the Tigris to seize the town of Kut al-Amara. Townshend's success in taking Kut at the end of September encouraged Nixon, with the backing of the politicians in London, to press on to Baghdad. Townshend's force moved north, partly on land and partly by boat up the Tigris. By 22 November he had reached Ctesiphon (Selman Pak), the ancient capital of the Parthians and Sassanids, and was now only 20 miles from Baghdad. This was the limit of Townshend's advance. He was checked by the Turks in a three-day battle and decided to withdraw. His lines of communication had been stretched to breaking point, his ramshackle medical services had collapsed, and half his British officers were sick or wounded. Townshend's jellied nerve had cracked.

Townshend retreated to flyblown Kut, where his troops dug themselves in behind a bend in the Tigris. The river, swollen by winter rain, had broken its banks and turned the surrounding countryside into a swamp. The Turks arrived hard on the heels of Townshend's command and built earthworks which surrounded Kut and initiated a siege which lasted until the end of April 1916.

Townshend had made his name in 1895 when he had been besieged in Chitral on the Indian North-West Frontier. He decided to sit tight and await the arrival of a relief force, but there was no happy ending to the siege of Kut. At first life continued much as normal. One of Townshend's staff officers, Major E G Dunn, noted in his diary the meal on Christmas Day: "A very good dinner today – what price this menu – mutton scotch broth; salmon mayonnaise: chicken conflets; roast duck and green peas; plum pudding (A and N tinned) [Army & Navy Stores]; pear tart; Italian eggs; chocolate, and of course we all toasted our dear ones at home."

By the end of January, however, Dunn was sampling the dubious delights of horse flesh (the Indian troops refused to eat it). The relief force was now only 20 miles south of Kut but was bedevilled by lack of supplies, ammunition and water, and the quagmire on the banks of the Tigris, on which they depended for most of their transport. General Nixon had been relieved of his command, but by February Townshend's officers were eating starlings, and in early March the tea and cheese ration ended.

By the end of March, German aircraft were flying regular bombing raids against Kut while the relief force strove to break through to the embattled defenders. One of its junior officers, Second Lieutenant Cuthbert Aston, who had served on the Western Front and at Gallipoli, noted: "The Turks hold their line with a good many machine guns and are well equipped with Very lights. We have superiority in guns and numbers and it's just those infernal machine guns that make one man as good as a battalion on this level coverless country. If it weren't for those forever damned machine guns we'd be in Kut now!"

The relief force made four unsuccessful attempts to break the Turkish ring, incurring some 23,000 casualties, twice the strength of the embattled British garrison, which was now facing an outbreak of cholera. They surrendered on 29 April. Townshend and his officers were well treated – Townshend sat out the war in the comfort of a villa in Constantinople, but the 12,000 British and Indian troops, who were already in poor health, were marched 1,200 miles to labour camps in Anatolia, where more than a third of them died.

Palestine

Baghdad was not taken until March 1917. Greater success was achieved in Palestine, where on 28 June 1917 General Sir Edmund Allenby arrived to replace General Murray as commander of the British forces. A veteran of the Boer War and an accomplished commander on the Western Front, Allenby seemed like a conventional cavalry officer of the old school. This was deceptive. He also had an unconventional streak and could work with unorthodox figures inclined to irregular warfare, as his relations with T E Lawrence and the Arabs were to demonstrate.

Allenby was issued with instructions by the British prime minister Lloyd George to "take Jerusalem by Christmas". He was also supported by General Sir William Robertson, the Chief of the Imperial General Staff and the middleman between the Cabinet and the Army, who had declared that Palestine was "no sideshow, because as long as we keep up a good show there, India and Persia will be more or less all right".

At the beginning of November, after the war's heaviest artillery bombardment outside Europe, Allenby's Egyptian Expeditionary Force (EEF) broke the Gaza-Beersheba line held by the Turks. This was a war in which cavalry still had a role to play. A cavalryman recalled: "Though most of us laughed when the first shells screamed

Arab forces co-ordinated by T E Lawrence relied on camels and horses. This photograph was taken by Lawrence near Yenbo in December 1916.

Lawrence of Arabia

The legendary figure of T E Lawrence still has the power sharply to divide opinion long after his death

Legend and military history combine in the enigmatic, robed figure of Thomas Edward Lawrence, universally known as Lawrence of Arabia. Lawrence first travelled to the Middle East as an archaeologist after graduating from Oxford, immersing himself in its peoples and their languages. Early in 1914 he was a member of a reconnaissance party in northern Syria operating under the cover of a scientific expedition. On the outbreak of war, he became an intelligence officer in Cairo. In the autumn of 1916 he persuaded his superiors to aid local sheikhs, among them Hussein Ibn Ali, founder of the modern Hashemite dynasty, against Turkey and acted as their liaison officer. Lawrence quickly became the brains behind the so-called Arab Revolt. He organised raiding parties attacking the Hejaz railway and isolated the city of Medina, the second-holiest city in the Islamic world, forcing the Turks to divert 25,000 troops. In July 1917 he played a part in the capture of the port of Aqaba, on the north-eastern tip of the Red Sea, by Hussein's third son Feisal. Lawrence then turned his attention to Palestine, raiding Turkish railways with the help of Feisal. In 1918 he persuaded Feisal to support the British advance on Damascus. At the Paris Peace Conference, Lawrence acted as Feisal's adviser and saw the placing of Syria under a French mandate as a particular betrayal. He subsequently wrote a number of wartime memoirs, the most famous of which was *The Seven Pillars of Wisdom* (1925). Lawrence died in a motorcycle accident in 1935. In 1955 a biography by Richard Aldington sparked a long-running controversy over the authenticity of Lawrence's own account of his wartime exploits. The great hero is now seen as a more ambivalent figure than he appeared in the immediate aftermath of the Great War.

Hero, charlatan or, perhaps, both? Lawrence poses in his Arab robes and dagger.

towards us, other men smoked as we broke into a thundering canter holding back in the saddles to prevent the horses from breaking into a mad gallop."

The way to Jerusalem now lay open. With Lawrence and the Arabs forming a detached flanking force, Allenby pushed out rapidly beyond Gaza, taking thousands of prisoners on the way, and by the morning of 9 December was on the outskirts of Jerusalem. Both sides were under orders to spare the Holy City from fighting, and the Turks had taken the opportunity to withdraw during the night. Allenby made his official entry to the city through the Jaffa Gate on 11 December, ending centuries of Ottoman rule. Lloyd George had his Christmas present.

Thereafter the Middle East became a dormant front for much of the last ten months of the war. Allenby's freedom of manoeuvre was limited by the fact that in March 1918 he was obliged to transfer five of his divisions to the Western Front to help stem the tide of the Ludendorff offensive. He was compensated by receiving Indian cavalry from France, where they were to all intents and purposes useless, and more Indian units from the subcontinent and Mesopotamia. It took most of the summer to train these formations.

In contrast, the Turkish forces in the Middle East were close to a state of collapse. They had been neglected while their high command, encouraged by the disintegration of Russia, had vainly pursued territorial ambitions in the Caucasus and Central Asia. In Palestine the British now enjoyed a significant numerical superiority and unchallenged aerial supremacy in the build-up to Allenby's renewed offensive in September 1918, the drive to Damascus.

Allenby had at his disposal 35,000 infantry, 9,000 cavalry and 400 guns. He was faced by the Turkish Fourth, Seventh and Eighth Armies, each of which was no bigger than a single division, under the overall command of the veteran of Gallipoli, Liman von Sanders. On 19 September Allenby employed a classic manoeuvre at the Battle of Megiddo. He directed a feint up the Jordan valley and then used his cavalry, screened by air power, to break through the Turkish line and race up the coast. It was a rare example of surprise and mobility in a war dominated by barbed wire and machine-gun bullets. Damascus was occupied at the beginning of October. Turkey capitulated at the end of the month and its representatives signed the instrument of surrender on board a British Dreadnought lying off the island of Lemnos in the Aegean. It was, perhaps, a significant location as Lemnos had been an Allied forward base in the ill-fated campaign to control the Dardanelles.

Africa

Germany had been a late arrival at the colonial scramble for a "place in the sun" and in 1914 its colonies were, in the main, to be found in places of little interest to other European powers – Cameroon, Togoland, East Africa and German South-West Africa. Each covered a vast area but was thinly populated and could boast few resources.

The war in Africa was fought mainly by African and some Indian troops. Only in German South-West Africa (modern Namibia) were the Allies heavily represented by white South Africans and Rhodesians, many of whom did not support the war in Europe and were principally concerned with the maintenance of white rule in Africa. The Africans had no say in the matter and effectively were conscripts in all but name.

Most of the Africans who were pressed into service performed their duties as auxiliaries rather than as soldiers. For the campaign in East Africa, the British pressed more than a million Africans into service. In sub-Saharan Africa, there were few roads and railways and pack animals were preyed on by tsetse flies. Human beings, often undernourished and vulnerable to disease, were the beasts of burden.

A battalion of Nigerian troops entrain at Lagos on 6 August 1914. They played a part in achieving a swift victory over German forces in Togoland and the Cameroons.

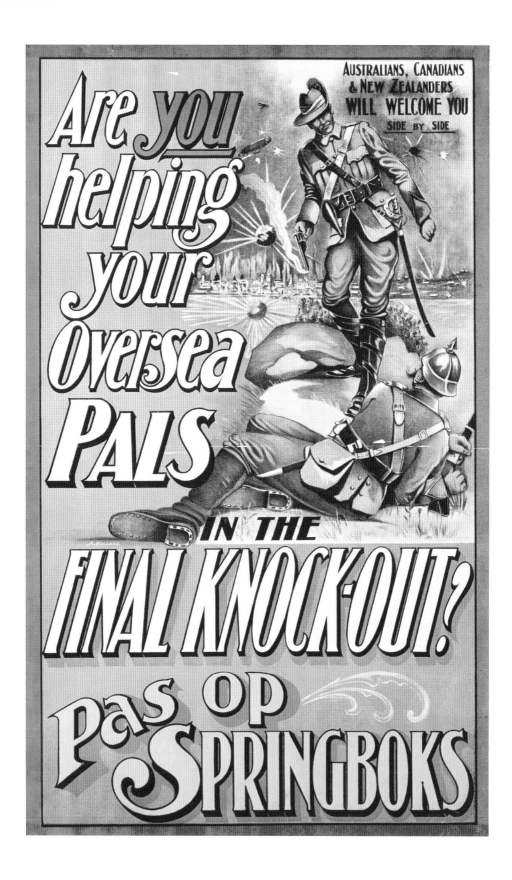

Every soldier required up to three carriers. One in five African carriers died during the Great War, a higher mortality rate than that suffered on the Western Front.

Germany's African colonies were surrounded by British, French, Belgian and Portuguese possessions, and Allied command of the sea prevented their re-supply. To survive, they had to become self-sufficient. By March 1916, however, all but one had been knocked out of the war. The exception, and the most significant of all the colonial "sideshows", was German East Africa, which went on fighting up to and beyond the end of hostilities in Europe. By 1918, the British fielded more than 100,00 troops in the region, most of them African and Indian, and enjoyed complete command of the sea. The German forces numbered only 15,000, predominantly local askaris. The reason they had stayed so long in the field was because of their exceptional commander, Colonel Paul von Lettow-Vorbeck, a master of bush warfare.

A Rhinelander, Lettow-Vorbeck had the mind of a Prussian officer, and was imbued with all the preconceptions of that military caste. He was in no way an advocate of guerrilla warfare in the modern sense. His instinct was to give battle, but caution, the desire to husband the lives of his irreplaceable German officers and NCOs, and the incompetence of his enemies, enabled him to disperse his forces and strike swiftly and boldly at the points where his adversary was weakest. He was always ready to improvise. His field artillery was provided by the guns salvaged from the commerce raider *Königsberg*, which had been sunk in the Rufiji delta by two British shallow-draught monitors

Left *A stern Jan Smuts inspects an African labour battalion.* Opposite *A South African recruiting poster.*

in July 1915. For good measure, *Königsberg's* crew came with them.

Lettow-Vorbeck saw his sole task as that of commanding his tiny army in the field and consistently declined to engage in political warfare. Thus he did not exploit the very real hatred which Africans harboured against the colonial powers, particularly the Belgians and Portuguese. First and foremost, Lettow-Vorbeck's forces were there to draw British troops from the Western Front. Ultimately this proved a vain hope as the British, unlike the French, never used their African troops in France.

Early in the war the British gained control of Lake Victoria and Lake Tanganyika but at the beginning of November 1914 they suffered a setback when an expeditionary force landed at Tanga. Its arrival was intended to be the first step in the seizure of the coastline of German East Africa but Expeditionary Force B was ill-prepared for its mission; its Indian troops were of low quality and their officers were elderly fossils. They had been at sea for a month and had no training in bush warfare.

Against them Lettow-Vorbeck concentrated nine companies of askaris – in Africa, he observed, a company was the equivalent of a division in Europe. The outcome of the battle was sealed by a string of British blunders. Naval gunfire was beginning to exert considerable pressure on the German forces and some of Lettow-Vorbeck's company commanders ordered bugles to sound the recall to enable the men to regroup. However, on the German side this was mistaken as an order to retreat. The jumpy British force, which had been very roughly handled up to this point, were equally mistaken and thought that the bugle blasts were an order to charge. Their commander decided to withdraw. In these highly unpromising circumstances, a legend was born.

For the next year, Lettow-Vorbeck was left to his own devices as the British focused their attention on other parts of the continent. Early in 1916, with the conclusion of the war in South-West Africa, the task of dealing with German East Africa was given to a South African soldier and statesman, the Afrikaner Jan Christian Smuts, whom Lettow-Vorbeck had met in friendlier circumstances before the war.

Smuts was careful with the lives of his men, particularly his fellow South Africans – he did not want to go down in history as "Butcher Smuts" – and most reluctant to use Africans as fighting soldiers. He was also completely at sea in the unfamiliar conditions of East Africa. In South-West Africa, mounted infantry had been the pivot of manoeuvre and the key to success; East Africa's tsetse flies ensured a monthly equine wastage rate of 100 per cent. Humans were equally vulnerable to dysentery and malaria, which relentlessly sapped Smuts' strength. The Second Rhodesia Regiment, for example, was normally 800 strong, but in East Africa it was often reduced to 100 men.

Smuts was unable to draw Lettow-Vorbeck into a decisive battle in which he could make his greater strength tell. The German may have been weaker in numbers but he manipulated with great skill all the advantages of an equatorial climate and a vast and trackless region – partly mountainous and covered with dense bush and forest – to foil his enemy. In the driving rains of December, Smuts briefly had his hands around his opponent's windpipe, but in January 1917 he was called away to London to represent South Africa in the Imperial War Cabinet. Lettow-Vorbeck lived to fight another day.

In 1917 Lettow-Vorbeck was brought to battle by another Afrikaner commander, "Jaap" van Deventer, in a series of bruising encounters on the East African coastal plain. These broke his force as a battle-ready formation. After the Battle of Mahiwa (15–19 October) Lettow-Vorbeck crossed into Portuguese East Africa (Mozambique) with 300 Europeans and 1,700 askaris, and the last of the *Königsberg*'s guns was destroyed.

He carried on marching and fighting for another year. His column, a self-contained community accommodating 3,000 women, children and carriers, ran rings round the brutal and incompetent Portuguese. At the beginning of July 1918, at Namakura, he secured vital booty – food, rifles, ammunition and ten machine guns. He was soon on the move again and had reached Northern Rhodesia (Zambia) where the last battle of the Great War was fought on 12 November between his askaris and 750 men of the King's African Rifles. The next day Lettow-Vorbeck was told of the Armistice, and he formally surrendered on 25 November.

In 1964, the year of his death, the West German Bundestag voted to honour the back pay of any of Lettow-Vorbeck's askaris who were still alive. A temporary office was established on the shore of Lake Victoria to disburse the money. Some 350 elderly men turned up but few retained the certificate which their commander had given them in 1918. Some brought fragments of uniform as proof of identity. The German banker had a solution. As each claimant stepped up, he was handed a broom and told to present arms. They all passed the test.

A line of motor ambulances with their VAD drivers at Etaples, 15 miles south of Boulogne, June 1917.

6 HOME FIRES: WOMEN AND WAR

"Sometimes the trains were packed, so of course, the porters knew that we were all munitions kids; and they'd say, 'Go on girl, 'op in' and they would open the first class carriages. And there'd be officers sitting there and some of them would look at us as if we were insects."

CAROLINE RENNLES, MUNITIONS WORKER

In the autumn of 1914, there was a widespread belief in Britain that in spite of the war, life on the home front would continue much as usual. During the next four years, however, the demands imposed by the conflict brought significant social changes.

The massive exodus of men from Britain's factories and mines to join Kitchener's New Armies, and the subsequent introduction of universal male conscription in May 1916, left Britain's industry severely short of skilled labour. Their places were filled by women. A soldier returning to "Blighty" on leave from the front would have been struck by the sight of women working on the railways as porters and guards, busy on trams as clippies (bus conductors), and operating lathes in factories.

Above A Thetford woman takes over her father's job as Official Bill Poster and Town Crier. Below: *Women cleaning an express engine of the Lancashire and Yorkshire Railway, 1917.* Opposite *The conventional view – men march away to war while their women wait.*

Nowhere was this phenomenon more marked than in the industries dedicated to the production of war material. Women's entry into the industrial mass production of armaments was caused by a series of setbacks in March 1915, when the British Expeditionary Force in France launched its first attempt to break the German line at Neuve Chapelle, in Artois. It achieved an initial breakthrough before

Above A poster for a
fete draws women into
the war effort.
Opposite The reality of
war work – women
operating cranes in the
Chilwell shell-filling factory.

communications broke down, ammunition ran out and the advance stuttered to a halt – the pattern for future battles on the Western Front.

The shortage of shells led to the formal establishment in the summer of 1915 of a Ministry of Munitions, headed by the Liberal politician David Lloyd George. The ministry assumed direct control of a number of factories devoted exclusively to war production and also began to build state-owned factories, complete with accommodation for workers. In addition, it retained a high degree of control over plants which were not wholly dedicated to armaments production. In these sectors, the government could enforce the suspension of trade union practices, which were frequently a barrier to the employment of women, and could actively encourage their absorption into the workforce.

In the drive for increased war production, Lloyd George also enlisted the support of the suffragette leader Emmeline Pankhurst, who before 1914 had led the militant Women's Social and Political Union (WSPU) in the battle for the vote. He gave Mrs Pankhurst a £2,000 grant to organise a demonstration on the theme of "Women's Right to Serve". This was to be linked with a demand for the "vigorous prosecution of the war so that all danger of a compromise peace may be averted and the Allies be in a position to impose on Germany and the nations who have helped to commit criminal and murderous assault upon Europe, a victorious and therefore a permanent peace". At the demonstration, held in driving rain on 17 July 1915, Lloyd George delivered a speech which included the exhortation: "Without women victory will tarry, and the victory which tarries means a victory whose footprints are footprints of blood."

Thereafter, the support of Mrs Pankhurst was less important in the integration of women into war production than the relentless expansion of the Ministry of Munitions itself, and the increasing sophistication of the regulations it brought to bear on the female workforce, often to their disadvantage. In the munitions industry, women who replaced fully skilled tradesmen were, on the face of it, entitled to equal remuneration

Women's Land Army

When the men marched to war it was often up to their women to step up and
fill the breach. The results were soon to be seen in Britain's factories and fields

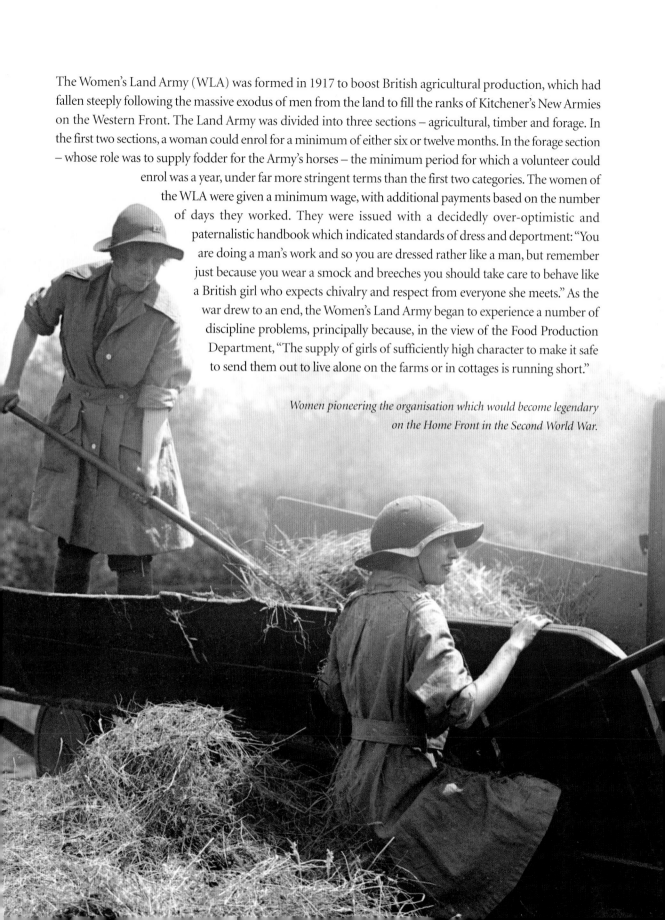

The Women's Land Army (WLA) was formed in 1917 to boost British agricultural production, which had fallen steeply following the massive exodus of men from the land to fill the ranks of Kitchener's New Armies on the Western Front. The Land Army was divided into three sections – agricultural, timber and forage. In the first two sections, a woman could enrol for a minimum of either six or twelve months. In the forage section – whose role was to supply fodder for the Army's horses – the minimum period for which a volunteer could enrol was a year, under far more stringent terms than the first two categories. The women of the WLA were given a minimum wage, with additional payments based on the number of days they worked. They were issued with a decidedly over-optimistic and paternalistic handbook which indicated standards of dress and deportment: "You are doing a man's work and so you are dressed rather like a man, but remember just because you wear a smock and breeches you should take care to behave like a British girl who expects chivalry and respect from everyone she meets." As the war drew to an end, the Women's Land Army began to experience a number of discipline problems, principally because, in the view of the Food Production Department, "The supply of girls of sufficiently high character to make it safe to send them out to live alone on the farms or in cottages is running short."

Women pioneering the organisation which would become legendary on the Home Front in the Second World War.

Miss Joan Williams at her lathe in 1916.

but were in fact paid less because of a let-out clause which ensured that they remained in a permanent state of supervision. Many male trade unionists also remained hostile to the large-scale employment of women, claiming that their presence – in some munitions plants they outnumbered the male workforce by two to one – would lower men's wages. Nor did women readily join trade unions themselves. By January 1916 fewer than 12 per cent of the female munitions workers in the Manchester area, an industrial centre, had joined a union.

One woman who resisted the siren call of trade unionism was Joan Williams, who worked as a lathe operator at Messrs Gwynne's factory in West London. She was not impressed with the female union representative: "I only came across her in the canteen where she was very free with her 'damns' and fond of airing explosive views such as not minding taking German money as long as she got it somehow, with a good deal of explosive stuff to impress the ignorant. She and a few others tried hard to engineer a strike of union women against non-union ones and used to threaten the timid with being turned out of the factory if they didn't join. After some excitement, in the end it all came to nothing."

In some factories, the female labour force was more militant. Gabrielle West, who worked for the Women's Police Service in a factory in South Wales, recalled a lively passage of industrial relations in the late summer of 1917:

"A great and terrible strike, as usual for more pay and less work. The girls stormed around, yelled and shrieked, threw mud and so on. Then they discovered a wretched little creature who had dared to come to work; being a timekeeper's clerk and not in the sheds at all, she really had known nothing about the strike. She was well reared though. They chased her from one of the factory to another and she fled for protection to the WP [Women's Police] office. The strikers threw water at and knocked down a police woman who prevented them from getting at the 'blackleg'. The men police eventually came out and helped drive them away. Then they went to the main office and broke all the windows, demanding to see the manager. He said he wouldn't see them until they were quiet. Major Dobson, CO of the Home Defence, got out the fire hose and began to squirt the strikers, but it burst. Eventually they were tired out and went home, and appeared now to have forgotten all about it".

GABRIELLE WEST, WOMEN'S POLICE SERVICE, SOUTH WALES

In the First World War there was no conscription of women, but in both voluntary and government-sponsored schemes they were required to go through a form of "enlistment" in which they signed a contract agreeing to either six or twelve months' service. Munitions workers were bound to serve in a single factory by a system of "leaving certificates", which had to be obtained from their employer if they wished to work in another plant (the same system applied to male workers). In a conscious echo of the word "suffragette", the women in war factories were often called "munitionettes".

Long hours and tough conditions were the lot of many of the women working in the munitions industry. In 1976, Mrs H A Felstead, who had been in domestic service before the war, told the Imperial War Museum about her experiences:

"I started on hand cutting shell fuses at the converted war works at … Thames Ditton, Surrey. It entailed the finishing off by hand dies of the machine-cut thread on the fuses that held the powder for the big shells, so it had to be very accurate so that the cap fitted perfectly. We worked 12 hours a day apart from the journey morning and night to Kingston-upon-Thames. Believe me, we were very ready for bed in those days, and as for wages I thought I was very well off earning £5 a week. While at the works I remember a Zeppelin got as far as London. We all had to go below ground in an old wood store. We were more afraid of the rats – big water ones – the works being alongside the River Thames near Hampton Court, than the Zeppelin."

Women working with highly toxic explosive TNT could suffer serious side-effects, including nausea, vomiting, giddiness, diarrhoea,

Women workers in a munitions factory being supervised by Women's Legion stalwart Lilian Barker. She was appointed Lady Superintendant at Woolwich Arsenal, where she was eventually responsible for the working conditions and welfare of nearly 30,000 female workers.

loss of memory and impaired vision. The women performing this potentially dangerous task sometimes jokingly referred to themselves as "canaries" because of the yellow mottling of the skin which indicated TNT poisoning. Regulations were introduced to provide the TNT workers with adequate protective clothing and ventilation, and to limit the hours during which they were exposed to TNT. However, the medical journal the *Lancet*, in what seems a typical case of peeved male chauvinism, placed the blame squarely on the women workers: "It is so often the case that it is the neglect on the part of the worker to follow such simple precautions which leads to a disturbance of health. They are offered authoritative help but refuse to help themselves; and the observance of such regulations can be made with little inconvenience and still be consistent with the maximum output of munitions."

One of the "canaries", Caroline Rennles, recalled that when travelling to and from the factory the women workers encountered a wide range of reactions from the public, by no means all of them favourable:

"Sometimes the trains were packed, so of course, the porters knew that we were all munitions kids, and they'd say, 'Go on girl, 'op in there', and they would open the first-class carriages. And there'd be officers sitting there and some of them would look at us as if we were insects. And others used to mutter, 'Well, they're doing their bit'. Some people were quite nice and others used to treat us as if we were the scum of the earth. We couldn't wear good clothes because the powder used to seep into them. You couldn't wear anything posh there really."

CAROLINE RENNLES, "CANARY"

The largest concentration of women workers was at the new national cordite factory at Gretna in Scotland, where 11,000 were employed, the majority housed in purpose-built hostels scattered throughout the area. The plant was notable for its segregated recreation facilities for men and women – the women were provided with a reading and writing room, a library and a "dainty lounge supplied with several sewing machines, and a games room that possesses a piano and a very large gramophone".

The most serious accident at Gretna occurred early in 1917 when a building housing several tons of nitroglycerine was torn apart in a sheet of flame. One woman was killed and many were injured. There were other serious accidents, notably the explosion which killed 12 women at a munitions plant in Silvertown, in London's docklands. During the war, over 200 women lost their lives working in Britain's munitions industry.

Opposite *A young woman working in the largest shell-filling factory in Britain at Chilwell in Nottinghamshire.*

A VAD nurse attends to a German prisoner in France under the watchful eyes of an armed sentry.

In July 1914, some 212,000 women had been employed in Britain's metal and engineering industries. During the Great War, this sector of industry became the one most closely associated with the war effort. The impact of universal male conscription ensured that in this area, by 1918, the figure for female workers had risen to just under one million. In industry as a whole, the total employment of women had increased from just over two million in 1914 to just under three million by war's end.

Healing hands

In 1914 there were several uniformed services in Britain which were open to women: Queen Alexandra's Imperial Military Nursing Service, the Territorial Force Nursing Service, the First Aid Nursing Yeomanry and the Voluntary Aid Detachments (VADs), the last a voluntary and unpaid service which had been formed in 1910 to provide medical assistance in time of war.

Initially the VADs were open to men and women but as the organisation's principal work was in nursing, the volunteers were predominantly female. One single Women's Voluntary Aid Detachment or VAD normally consisted of 23 women, but eventually the initials came to stand for each individual member (a VAD). At first the membership came principally from the middle and upper classes, and there was a stringent vetting procedure for applicants.

The VAD had been established to operate in Britain under the umbrella of the Territorial Forces in the event of invasion, and had not been intended for service overseas. However, at the beginning of 1914, a list was drawn up of individual VADs who were "willing and qualified to take service abroad in case of emergency". By the outbreak of war there were over 2,500 Voluntary Aid Detachments in the United Kingdom staffed by over 47,000 individual VADs, two-thirds of whom were women. Basic first aid and nursing training was provided by the St John Ambulance Association. The VADs were enthusiastic, but as yet unskilled. A schoolboy wrote to his mother, "I spend my time being bandaged and unbandaged by the girls who want to be VADs. If some of them ever manage to get into a hospital, heaven help their patients." It was not long before the VADs were introduced to the realities of modern war. In 1914 the 24-year-old Catherine Cathcart-Smith had volunteered to drive an ambulance. Nothing could have prepared her for what she later found:

"We had to meet the troop trains at the big London railway stations – Waterloo and Victoria. The trains had hundreds of wounded soldiers packed on them. Their wounds were frightful. Young men with no arms or legs. Many had been gassed. Others blinded. I had two nurses with me and we made a good team. One day I saw this young man on a stretcher. It was my brother, so I said to the soldiers who were carrying him: 'Put him in my ambulance, I am his sister'. When he died the next day I was with him, holding his hand."

CATHERINE CATHCART-SMITH, VOLUNTEER AMBULANCE DRIVER

Initially the British War Office was unwilling to allow VADs to serve in theatres of war, but the scale of casualties on the Western Front meant that in 1915 the restriction was removed. Women volunteers over the age of 23 and with more than three months' experience were allowed to serve overseas, not only in France but also in the Middle East and on the Eastern Front.

At home the VAD had to fight a succession of turf wars with rival agencies whose responsibilities overlapped or conflicted with its own. It had to operate under the management of the British Red Cross

Society and the Order of St John of Jerusalem, both of which were international bodies established to undertake unqualified works of mercy, an anomaly in the bitterly nationalistic atmosphere of the Great War. From 1915, VADs received a salary of £20 a year, rising to £30 a year for nurses working in military hospitals. Payment by the War Office compromised the status of the VAD under the Red Cross, which led to the proposal – never implemented – that the VAD be merged with another voluntary agency, the Women's Legion. The position of the VAD was not made easier by the fact that the central committee overseeing its activities was composed entirely of men.

By September 1916, there were some 8,000 VADs serving in military hospitals. Most of them were working under the "General Service Scheme", introduced in June 1916, under which the military authorities made direct payment to VADs who were employed not only on nursing duties but were also tasked with cooking, storekeeping, dispensing and clerical work. The inexperience of some of the well-born VADs inevitably resulted in friction with their professional nursing counterparts. In her 1975 autobiography *All Change Here*, Naomi Mitchison confessed: "Of course I made awful mistakes. I had never done real manual household work; I had never used mops and polishes and disinfectants. I was very willing but clumsy. I was told to make tea but had not realised that tea must be made with boiling water. All that had been left to the servants." Almost as troublesome was the seven-piece VAD uniform, owing much to the influence of Florence Nightingale, which proved a formidable barrier to the maintenance of regulation standards of cleanliness.

In 1917 the Commandant of the VAD, Dame Katherine Furse, was embroiled in a controversy caused by her pressing for the creation of an over-arching body, under the nominal leadership of Queen Mary, which would unify and direct all the different groups which represented women's contribution to the British war effort. She was eventually eased out from the VAD, but its work continued unabated. In the spring of 1918, during the Ludendorff offensive in France, the writer Vera Brittain was working as a VAD sister in a field hospital in Etaples on the Channel coast. *In Testament of Youth* (1936) she recalled: "The picture came back to me of myself standing alone in a newly created circle of hell during the 'emergency' of 22 March 1918, gazing half-hypnotised at the dishevelled beds, the stretchers on the floor, the scattered boots and piles of muddy clothing, the brown blankets turned back from smashed limbs bound to splints by filthy bloodstained bandages. Beneath each stinking wad of sodden wool and gauze an obscene horror waited for me, and all the equipment

David Wilson's 1915 poster poses a loaded question. This time the German "frightfulness" is perpetrated by a nursing sister.

that I had for attacking it in this ex-medical ward was one pair of forceps standing in a potted-meat glass half full of methylated spirit."

For many VADs, the war proved a life-changing experience, their new-found personal freedom coinciding with the almost unimaginable total of about a million fatal casualties sustained by the British Empire. Vera Brittain wrote of post-war Britain: "Already this was a different world from the one I had known during four life-long years … and in that alien world I would have no part. All those with whom I had been really intimate had gone … The War was over, a new age was beginning, but the dead were dead and would never return."

Elsie Inglis

One of the heroines of wartime medicine was Elsie Inglis, the daughter of an official in the Indian Civil Service, who had attended the Edinburgh School of Medicine for Women. She studied under Dr Sophia Jex-Blake, the first woman physician in Scotland, before moving to the University of Glasgow to promote a rival women's faculty and win the right to read medicine alongside men.

In 1892 Inglis had qualified as a licentiate of all the Scottish medical schools. She then moved to London, where she was horrified by the shoddy standards of care endured by many female patients. In 1894 she returned to Edinburgh   and with another female doctor, Jessie MacGregor, established Scotland's only maternity centre run by women. She travelled widely, visiting clinics in Europe and the United States, including the Mayo Clinic in Minnesota. She also became politically active and was one of the founders of the Scottish Women's Suffragette Federation. A philanthropist, Inglis frequently waived her fees and personally funded the convalescence of poor patients.

On the outbreak of the Great War, Inglis offered to provide the British Army with fully staffed Scottish Women's Hospital (SWH) medical units, only to be told by a War Office official, "My good lady, go home and sit still." However, the French took Inglis seriously, despatching two of her units to France and a third, headed by Inglis herself, to Serbia. She dealt with a typhus epidemic before she and the members of her unit became prisoners of the Austrians, who overran Serbia in the autumn and winter offensives of 1915. Thereafter Inglis and her team tended both Serb and Austrian wounded in military hospitals in Krusevac.

Repatriated in February 1916, Inglis immediately organised and accompanied an SWH medical team which was despatched by sea to Russia. She also ensured the establishment of an SWH hospital at Salonika, in north-east Greece, where an Anglo-French expeditionary force, and the rebuilt Serbian Army, had been bottled up since the spring of 1916.

By 1917, Inglis had organised 14 medical units for the Belgian, French, Russian and Serbian armies. When she sailed back to England from Russia in November 1917, she was exhausted and stricken with cancer. With a huge effort, she said farewell to her Serbian staff and, after the ship docked, managed to walk ashore. She died the next day.

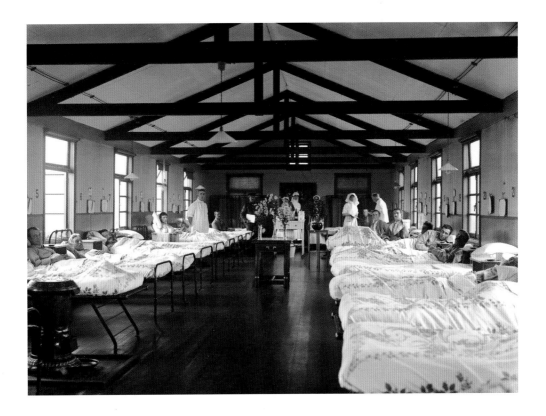

The Heroines of Pervyse

In August 1914, Dr Hector Munro, a Scotsman, organised a flying ambulance unit to work with the Belgian Army. Munro was a feminist and included four women in the unit: an American, Helen Gleason, two English women, Lady Dorothea Fielding and Elsie Knocker, and the 18-year-old Mairi Chisholm, a fellow-Scot.

Elsie Knocker was a widow who had some nursing experience and, like Chisholm, was a keen motorcyclist. After two months of operating with the ambulance corps in Belgium, Knocker decided to establish a first-aid post immediately behind the front line. In November 1914, Knocker and Chisholm established themselves in a cellar in the Belgian town of Pervyse, which had been levelled by German shelling and lay just behind the front-line trenches. Such proximity to the front line was in contravention of British regulations and until 1918 the two women worked with Belgian drivers and orderlies. By early 1915, British newspapers had dubbed them "The Heroines of Pervyse", and King Albert of the Belgians had personally pinned on their tunics the Order of Leopold.

As Mairi Chisholm confided to her diary, the motor ambulance

The surgical ward at No. 13 Stationary Hospital. Stationary hospitals were larger versions of field hospitals. As some of them were mobile, this inevitably made the term somewhat confusing.

drive to the rear was fraught with difficulty and danger: "Taking wounded to hospital 15 miles back at night was a very real strain – no lights, shell-pocked, mud-covered, often under fire, men and guns coming up to relieve the trenches, total darkness, yells to mind one's self and get out of the way, meaning a sickening slide off the pavé [road] into deep mud – screams from the stretchers behind one and thumps in the back through the canvas – then an appeal to passing soldiers to shoulder the ambulance back on the pavé. Two or three of these journeys by night and one's eyes were on stalks, bloodshot and strained. No windscreen, no protection, no self-starters or electric lights to switch on when out of reach of the lines – climb out to light with a match, if possible, the carbide lamps."

After heavy shelling destroyed their first post, the two women moved into the ruins of a house and, after a fund-raising tour in Britain, found a new home in a concrete structure swathed in sandbags and hidden inside the ruins of another house. In this desolate landscape of flooded shell craters and rotting corpses, Elsie Knocker was married to an aristocratic Belgian airman, who had been brought down in no man's land near the post, and became the Baroness de T'Serclaes. Amid the carnage, Mairi Chisholm still had time to see beauty. One of her diary entries comments, "The ruins by moonlight were strangely beautiful and when it reigned over the trenches it was hard to believe that life was at a premium."

In 1917, the two women of Pervyse were awarded the Military Medal, which had been created in 1916 and was open to women (the first woman to receive the award had been their colleague from the flying ambulance days, Lady Dorothea Fielding). Early in 1918 both women were badly injured in a German gas attack and their post was subsequently closed down.

Women soldiers

On 8 December 1916, the War Office instructed Lieutenant-General H M Lawson to prepare a report on the numbers and condition of the British troops employed in France. A month later Lawson made his report, which contained a recommendation that women should be employed on the Western Front.

Lawson's report arrived in the middle of an ongoing debate about the use of women in the British Army. In March 1917, the British commander-in-chief in the field, Field Marshal Sir Douglas Haig, told the War Office that he accepted the proposal in principle, although he had a long list of "objections and difficulties".

By then, however, the wheels were already in motion, and a recruiting programme had been launched through the office of the Director-General of National Service. On 7 July 1917, the Army Council's instruction 1069 became the formal basis of the Women's Auxiliary Army Corps (WAAC) which was led by a Chief Controller, Mrs Chalmers Watson, a distinguished medical woman from Edinburgh and the sister of the Director-General of National Service, Sir Auckland Geddes. Because a commission from the Crown could only be held by male subjects, the WAAC had no military ranks: "controllers" and "administrators" took the place of officers, NCO equivalents were called "forewomen" and privates were "workers". As with the VAD, the intention was to restrict the WAAC, as far as it was possible, to middle- and upper-class women, but the majority of the rank and file consisted of women from the working class. They messed separately from the controllers and administrators.

Members of the WAAC who remained in Britain could live at home, provided that this did not interfere with the efficient performance of their duties, which did not include work as cooks (the authorities feared that they would pilfer food supplies). Many of the working-class recruits joined the WAAC with no warm underclothing and a surfeit of head lice. As a result, Mrs Chalmers Watson issued a decidedly optimistic list of recommended items for each member of the WAAC to assemble before she joined an active unit:

The poster conveys the message succinctly. In spite of Field Marshal Haig's list of "objections and difficulties", the scene was set for the employment of women within Britain's military structure.

1 pair strong shoes or boots (this of course being
in addition to the free issue)
1 pr low-heeled shoes for housewear
2 prs khaki stockings (this of course being
in addition to the free issue)
2 prs at least warm combinations
2 prs dark coloured Knickers with washable linings
2 warm Vests of loosely woven Shetland wool
1 doz khaki Handkerchiefs
2prs Pyjamas or 2 strong Nightdresses
Burning Sanitary Towels
It is advisable if possible to bring as well,
a Jersey or Golf Jacket [sic] which should be worn
under the frock coat in cold weather.

Opposite *"The girl behind the man behind the gun".*

The WAAC claimed that the women in its ranks "do all kinds of work which a woman can do as well as a man, and some which she can do better". The aim, however, was for each member of the WAAC to release a man for combat duty, just as it would be for the ATS and other auxiliary services in the Second World War. Most of the duties undertaken by the WAAC lay in the traditional area of female chores – cooking and catering, telephony and clerical work – but its members also worked on lines of communication, as printers and as motor mechanics.

In April 1918, the WAAC was renamed Queen Mary's Army Auxiliary Corps, but the new title was not generally adopted and its members remained WAACs. By the following month there were just under 7,000 WAAC officers and other ranks serving in France, some of them with the American Expeditionary Force. They were restricted to the Communications Zone, which meant that with the exception of air attacks, they were always out of the firing line. To minimise external sex differences, the salute and other forms of military comportment were introduced, along with strict rules of dress and behaviour. For example, the women's uniforms were subtly defeminised by removing the breast pocket, a measure which was thought to de-emphasise the bust.

Elsie Cooper was a WAAC shorthand typist stationed in northern France, where she became used to being bombed by the Germans. After a series of heavy raids, the WAACs exchanged their slit trenches for a shelter improvised in a nearby system of caves:

"We were allocated one part and the French villagers had access to another part. The caves were situated on the banks of the River Canche and were alleged to be where Napoleon sheltered his troops. The white chalk of the caves, lit here and there by a solitary candle, presented a weird appearance. As the bombing grew worse it was decided that one third of the camp should sleep there each night, taking it in turns to avoid confusion on the alarm being given. Each girl was advised to take a blanket and settle down for the night. The firing of the gun nearby sounded the alarm and it was a work of art for the other two thirds of the girls to pick their way through the sleepers and find a suitable spot. Needless to say, the chalk floor was no substitute for even the army beds, but as we were young we were able to cope. The raids took place mostly at night, the approach in the daytime bring too risky. Occasionally there would be fights between the planes within a short distance of the camp. The girls did not appreciate the danger and invariably went outside to watch, much to the consternation of the officers who insisted on our taking cover."

ELSIE COOPER, WAAC TYPIST

WRNS

In the Great War a new field of opportunities for women opened up. In the Women's Royal Naval Service they filled a wide variety of roles, from cookery to codebreaking

During the Great War, the Royal Navy realised that one solution to its growing manpower problem was the recruitment of women to free men for service at sea. In November 1917, King George V approved the scheme and the Women's Royal Navy Service (WRNS) came into being. Its first director was Katharine (later Dame Katharine) Furse, who soon after the outbreak of war had led the first VAD detachments to France. The recruitment of ratings was undertaken by local employment exchanges while a board interviewed officer candidates. Recruitment was carefully monitored. Women were now moving into a man's world, and dedication, determination and discipline were required to break down the inevitable prejudice against them. Initially, the Wrens (as they soon became known) were restricted to a domestic role, replacing naval cooks and stewards, but the opportunities open to them rapidly widened. Eventually, the trades they could enter covered a wide spectrum, from book-keeping to

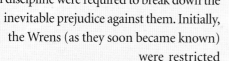

telephony, from driving motor cars to maintaining searchlights, hydrophones and anti-submarine nets. Ratings were at first recruited in the United Kingdom's great navy towns, where their homes were near their work, but soon "mobile" ratings were being recruited and accommodation found for them. The final WRNS division to be established was that for the Mediterranean, and officers and ratings were based in Malta, Gibraltar and Genoa, working principally in the encryption and decryption of cyphers. The WRNS ceased to exist in 1919 but was revived in the Second World War. In 1918 some 5,000 ratings and 4,000 officers served in the WRNS.

Above A WRNS motor driver smiles readily for the camera in an open-topped-car in the port of Lowestoft.
Left A WRNS officer recruit practising with a revolver at Crystal Place in London.
Right A WRNS officer instructs ratings in the use of anti-gas respirators in Lowestoft. She is wearing a tailored uniform and the ratings wear serge jackets and skirts.

In spite of the application of strict rules of fraternisation, the presence of several thousand WAACs in France encouraged rumours of promiscuity which led in February 1918 to the appointment of an all-women Commission of Inquiry, which reported: "We can find no justification of any kind for the vague accusations of immoral conduct on a large scale which have been circulated about the WAAC. The chief difficulty of our task has lain in the very vague nature of the damaging charges we were requested to negotiate. It is common knowledge that fantastic tales have passed from mouth to mouth of the numbers of WAAC women returned to England for misconduct of the gravest character."

The official figures revealed that in March 1918, when there were some 6,000 WAACs in France, there had been 21 cases of pregnancy (0.3 per cent of the total) and 12 of venereal disease. Two of the pregnant women were married and most of the others had conceived children before coming to France. Early in 1918 it was decided that WAACs believed to be pregnant were required to appear before a medical board and, if the pregnancy was confirmed, they were to be discharged "on medical grounds". The same rules applied to cases of venereal disease.

Fighting women

An iron ring worn by Adele Frankl, an Austrian woman, who exchanged gold jewellery for it in 1914. The inscription reads: Gold gab ich fur eisen *[I gave gold for iron].*

In the First World War, the front-line trenches in Belgium and France were places where women were never seen, but Dorothy Lawrence spent nearly two weeks in this hostile landscape disguised as a man.

Lawrence was living in Paris when the war broke out, and tried without success to travel to the front as a war correspondent. She later befriended two English soldiers in a café, and persuaded them to provide her with a uniform. She bound her chest, padded her figure to add extra "muscle", learned how to drill, cropped her hair and darkened her skin with furniture polish. In this disguise, and carrying forged papers, she bicycled to the front.

Remarkably, she was helped by a friendly former coalminer, Tom Dunn, to find work as a sapper in 179th Tunnelling Company, 51st Division. In the stalemate of trench warfare, engineers on both sides ran tunnels from their lines into no man's land, burrowing deep under the enemy's positions, where they would set massive charges to be detonated at the start of a big attack. This subterranean war was punishing and dangerous work.

According to her own account, Dunn found Lawrence accommodation in an abandoned cottage in the Senlis Forest close to the sappers' positions. She returned to it each night after laying surface mines in no man's land by day, frequently coming under fire. Lawrence persisted with the deception for ten days before, chilled and exhausted, she revealed her identity to a non-commissioned officer who promptly placed her under arrest.

Lawrence was taken to the rear of the lines and underwent a succession of interrogations at which her own ignorance of military terminology, and her interrogators' bafflement at her enterprise, initially raised the suspicion that she was a spy. This was replaced by the Army's acute fear of embarrassment if it came out that a woman had tricked her way to the front. She was sent back to London after she had given an undertaking not to speak or write about her experiences. In 1919 she broke her promise and published an account of her time in the trenches, *Sapper Lawrence: the Only English Woman Soldier, Late Royal Engineers 51st Division 179th Tunnelling Company BEF*. In 1925, not yet thirty years of age, she was committed to an insane asylum, where she languished until her death.

The remarkable Flora Sandes saw a great deal more action in the Balkans than Lawrence had seen in France. The daughter of a Suffolk clergyman, Sandes had worked as a secretary in London before 1914 and also received elementary medical training in the First Aid Nursing Yeomanry and the St John Ambulance Association. In August 1914, along with 36 other nurses, she sailed from London, bound for Serbia, then at war with Austria-Hungary.

Initially attached to the Serbian Red Cross and then to an infantry formation, she soon exchanged a nurse's uniform for the khaki and puttees of a front-line soldier in a war in which the Serbs were fighting Austro-German forces and their Bulgarian ally. In November 1915 Sandes, now enlisted in the Serbian Army, joined the "Great Retreat" across the mountains of Albania to the island of Corfu in the Adriatic.

Buxom, open-faced and immensely tough, Sandes relished the military life and was idolised by her Serbian comrades. She quickly adapted to trench warfare, explaining that she derived particular satisfaction from the passages of fighting in which the explosion of her grenades was followed by "a few groans, then silence", since a "tremendous hullabaloo" indicated that she had

The redoubtable Flora Sandes, resplendent in military uniform, with a Serbian officer. Tough, resourceful and uncomplaining, she loved life in the trenches.

Members of the Russian Battalion of Death. They sport shaven heads and bear a shorter version of the standard Russian service Moisin Nagant 7.62mm (0.3in) rifle with bayonets fixed in the Russian fashion. Following the November Revolution of 1917, the Battalion of Death was disbanded by the Bolsheviks.

inflicted "only a few scratches, or the top of someone's finger … taken off." She always insisted that her wartime experience – with its mixture of discomfort and boredom, interspersed with moments of terrible savagery – bestowed upon her a freedom which had been previously unimaginable.

In 1916 she was badly wounded in hand-to-hand fighting and reluctantly returned to nursing and, briefly, to England. She noted that it was like "losing everything at one fell swoop and trying to find bearings again in another life and in an entirely different world".

At the end of the Great War, Sandes decided to throw in her lot with the Serbians. In June 1919, the Serbian Parliament passed legislation enabling her to become the first woman to be commissioned in the Serbian Army. Sandes rose to the rank of captain and retired with her adopted country's highest decoration, the Karageorge Star. In 1927 she married a Russian émigré, Yuri Yudenich, and lived in France and Belgrade, where she was interned by the Germans in the Second World War. Her husband died in 1941, and at the end of the war Sandes returned to Suffolk, where her remarkable journey had begun.

Another redoubtable front-line female combatant of the Great War was the Russian Mariya Bochkareva. Born in Tomsk in 1869, she was the daughter of a serf and in her teens had become a child prostitute and the mistress of a succession of men. In 1914, after surviving an attempt on her life by her husband, she became an ultra-patriot, enlisting as a soldier, winning a chestful of medals and rising to the rank of sergeant.

In May 1917, a low point for Russia in the war, Bochkareva persuaded Alexander Kerensky, the war minister in Russia's newly installed provisional government, to agree to the formation of a women's battalion – the so-called "Battalion of Death" – a shock force with shaven heads which would challenge the prevailing mood of defeatism. In an emotional speech at St Isaac's Cathedral in Petrograd in June 1917, where the battalion's banners were blessed, Bochkareva declared, "Come with us in the name of your fallen heroes! Come with us to dry the tears and heal the wounds of Russia. Protect her with your lives. We women are turning into tigresses to protect our children from a shameful yoke – to protect the freedom of our country."

Despite her own chequered past, Bochkareva set her standards of recruitment high. "Our mother [Russia] is perishing!" she declared. "I want help to save her. I want women whose hearts are pure crystal, whose souls are pure, whose impulses are lofty." That night, 1,500 women enlisted and another 500 the following day. Styling herself 'Yashka', she welcomed them all. Bochkareva's vision and enthusiasm proved contagious, and similar units were organised all over Russia. The formation of the Battalion of Death was much applauded by the English feminist and suffragette leader Emmeline Pankhurst, who was visiting Russia at the time and took their salute.

Of the initial intake, several hundred members of the Battalion of Death – most of them peasants – were sent to the Kovno sector, in Lithuania, under the overall command of General Anton Denikin, where they went into action supported by a battalion of male troops. (Accounts of the Battalion's deployment vary, some stating that they were sent into action to the south against the Austrians.) After three weeks of fighting, the Battalion of Death had suffered losses of 350 killed and 70 wounded, among the latter Bochkareva herself. In his memoirs, Denikin attested to the women's bravery but observed that they were "quite unfit to be soldiers", and claimed that they had to be locked up at night to prevent them from being raped by the men under his command.

Some 200 members of the Battalion of Death continued to serve at the front, but their position was undermined by Bochkareva's autocratic style of command, which was so unpredictable and tyrannical that she drove her remaining supporters away. The Battalion also incurred the hostility of the Bolsheviks, who in October 1917 had swept away Kerensky's government. On 21 November 1917, the Bolshevik Revolutionary Committee disbanded her formation and subsequently sentenced her to death. In 1918 she escaped to the United States via Vladivostok, disguised as a nurse, and dictated a colourful but unreliable book about her wartime experiences

Bochkareva was subsequently introduced to President Woodrow Wilson and unsuccessfully attempted to persuade him to step up aid to the White Russian counter-revolutionaries, among whom her former commander Denikin was a leading figure. She then turned up in England, where she unavailingly petitioned King George V with a similar message. Undaunted and still battling on, she was back in Archangel, the port on Russia's White Sea, in the autumn of 1918 attempting to raise another Battalion of Death to fight the Bolsheviks.

She was sent packing by the commander of the British Expeditionary Force on the spot, General Ironside, who gave her 500 roubles and a ticket back to Omsk, where she was arrested by the Bolsheviks and executed on 16 May 1920.

Another bold mould-breaker was the American war reporter Peggy Hull, who began her journalistic career at the age of 16 as a typesetter for a small-town newspaper in her native Kansas. She gained her first taste of military life, if not action, when in 1916 she travelled to the Texas-Mexico border for the *Cleveland Plain Dealer* to cover the US Army's attempts to deal with the cross-border raids by the Mexican revolutionary, Pancho Villa. She went on a 15-mile route march with an infantry company and, in her own words, emerged a "hardened veteran". In a contemporary photograph, Hull (later Peggy Hull Deuell) posed in a uniform borrowed from the Ohio National Guard, snapping off a salute and looking like an endearingly perky heroine of a Charlie Chaplin movie.

On 6 April 1917, the United States declared war on Germany. The first American troops arrived in London in the following August, although it would be many months before they saw any fighting on the Western Front. Nevertheless, Hull began to press her new employer, the *El Paso Morning Times*, to send her to France as a war correspondent. Her entreaties were initially rejected as being "perfectly ridiculous", principally on the grounds that Deuell was a woman. However, she persisted and in the summer of 1917 established herself in Paris as a roving reporter, supplying the *Morning Times* with "human interest" stories on the American troops in France.

Hull never made it to the front line, but her lively copy on conditions in American training camps created something of a sensation and her reports were taken up by the *Chicago Tribune*'s newspaper for the US troops in Europe, which described her as a "typical young American woman" full of "grit and energy". The grit proved an irritant to the male reporters in France, who ungallantly pointed out that Hull had not received proper accreditation.

She returned to Texas and mid-1918 found her in Washington, working for a news syndicate and lobbying hard for permission to cover the American military expedition which had been despatched to Siberia to extract the Czech Legion from the chaotic aftermath of the Russian Revolution and aid its transfer to the Western Front. In spite of the US War Department's initial reluctance to accede to her request, Hull arrived in Siberia in the autumn of 1918 as the first accredited female American war correspondent.

Raids

In the winter of 1914 the German High Seas Fleet made two attempts to lure the British Grand Fleet, or a significant part of it, to within range of its submarines and minefields and on to the guns of its battleships. On 3 November the bait was a force of battlecruisers which bombarded Great Yarmouth. The High Seas Fleet repeated the exercise on 16 December when it despatched four fast battlecruisers, a heavy cruiser and a number of smaller ships to bombard three more ports on England's eastern coast.

Soon after dawn, the battlecruisers sailed out of a swirling fog to fire over 2,000 shells at the towns of Scarborough, Whitby and Hartlepool. In 30 minutes of shelling, some 150 people were killed, the youngest a 14-month-old baby, hundreds were injured and many buildings were flattened. A Whitby schoolgirl recalled running for shelter with "the deafening noise in our ears, the echo even ringing when the actual firing stopped for a moment". A thick, yellow cloud of smoke shrouded the towns under attack. The raids marked the first occasions since the seventeenth century on which civilians on mainland Britain had come under hostile fire.

The Admiralty's Room 40, where intercepted German wireless traffic was read, had given warning of the raid but in the bad weather conditions Admiral Beatty's battlecruiser squadron and supporting battleships failed to engage the enemy. The overall effect of the raid was to boost recruitment to the British armed services and to provide

Territorials cleaning up after the Zeppelin raid on King's Lynn on 19 January 1915. The Times *commemorated the raid by declaring that it brought to an end the "age-long immunity of the heart of the British Empire from the sight of a foe and the sound of an enemy missile". An English diarist, F A Robinson, noted that the raid "was a great failure; they succeeded in killing four inoffensive people, and destroying property to the value of a few thousand pounds".*

the British press with a propaganda coup. The men of the German High Seas Fleet were dubbed the "babykillers of Scarborough".

The territorial integrity of the British Isles was also to be threatened from another and entirely new quarter – the air – when Zeppelins of the German Army and Navy mounted expeditions against English targets from their bases on the Continent of Europe. The raids began on 19 January 1915 but it was not until 3 September 1916 that a German airship was shot down over England when Lieutenant William Leefe Robinson destroyed the German Army's SL11 in the skies above North London. Cuffley, where the blazing wreckage of the SL11 came to earth, drew thousands of gleeful sightseers, although not all Londoners drew equal comfort from Leefe Robinson's victory. Many years later, a witness of the airship's fiery end, Sybil Morrison, recalled her reactions:

"To me, well to anyone I would think, it was what I would call an awful sight. It was like a big cigar I suppose and all of the bag part had caught fire – the gas part. I mean – it was roaring flames; blue, red, purple. And it seemed to come down slowly instead of falling down with a bang. And we knew that there were about sixty people in it – we'd always been told there was a crew of about sixty – and that they were being roasted to death. Of course, you weren't supposed to feel any pity for your enemies, nevertheless I was appalled to see the kind, good-hearted British people dancing about in the streets at the sight of sixty people being burned alive – clapping and singing and cheering. And my own friends – delighted. When I said I was appalled that anyone could be pleased to see such a terrible sight they said, 'But they're Germans; they're the enemy' – not human beings. And it was like a flash to me that that was what war did; it created this utter inhumanity in perfectly decent nice, gentle kindly people. I just turned my back on it then; I suddenly though it's not right, it is wrong and I can't have any further part in it."

SYBIL MORRISON

In the final analysis the airship raids claimed few lives and inflicted little damage. In 51 raids they dropped just under 200 tons of bombs, killing 557 people and injuring 1,358. The German heavier-than-air machines – Gothas and Staakens – which flew against England in the First World War killed 835 Britons and injured nearly 2,000. Not figures to set beside the losses on the Somme or at Passchendaele, but perhaps that would be to miss the point. The commander of the German Naval Airship Division, Peter Strasser, observed at the end of 1917, "It is not upon the direct material damage that the value of the airship depends but rather on the general result of the German

onslaught upon England's insularity, otherwise undisturbed by war." In this Strasser succeeded. The Zeppelins and their successors, the Gothas and Staakens, had tied down in England large numbers of men and substantial amounts of equipment which otherwise would have been deployed in France. The British Official History of the First World War noted of the airships: "The threat of their raiding potentialities compelled us to set up at home a formidable organisation which diverted men, guns and aeroplanes from more important theatres of war. By the end of 1916 there were specially retained in Great Britain for home anti-aircraft defence, 17,341 officers and men. There were 12 RFC squadrons, comprising approximately 200 officers, 2,000 men and 110 aeroplanes. The anti-aircraft guns and searchlights were served by 12,000 officers and men who would have found a ready place, with continuous work, in France or in other war theatres."

The ugly face of the Home Front. Rioting crowds ransack a German-owned shop after a Zeppelin raid.

Queuing for food

The great majority of Britons were spared visitations by German bombing raids, but few housewives could remain unaffected by the steady rise in the price of staple foods as the war dragged on. In

223

1914–1915, the price of meat rose by 40 per cent and that of sugar by nearly 70 per cent. In the autumn of 1916 the Board of Trade estimated that since the outbreak of war, the retail price of fish and eggs had risen by over 100 per cent while those of milk, granulated sugar and bread had risen, respectively, by 39, 166 and 58 per cent.

By the beginning of 1918, queues for food were growing longer and discontent was growing sharper. On 22 January 1918, Mrs Mary Graham wrote to an officer friend serving in the Middle East about the situation in her home town of Newton Abbot:

"There is only one subject of conversation in this country, and that is the want of food. No one has had any cheese for a long time; butter is very hard to get and even margarine is not to be had. A small grocer's shop here was 'rushed' a few days ago –¬ I found a huge crowd when I passed – the women and children were packed in tight mass right out into the road. I made them let me pass through on the path, and I asked a woman what was going on. 'Oh, margarine', said she. When I came back about half an hour later, the police were there, they had just finished turning the people out. I heard later that the shop was regularly looted; the boys crammed their pockets with sweets and things; and all his dried fish was stolen, and a quantity of jam and biscuits … He shut his shop up for the rest of the day. It appeared that someone reported that he had margarine, and the whole contents of Newton's slums etc ran for supplies. He said he had none, and they would not believe him, and one woman slapped his face!!! At any rate they took all they could before he could get the police up. All the butcher's shops are shut up for two days a week and I should think if things don't improve there will be a general shut up all round. They say London is going to be rationed immediately, but I do not see how that will help us."

MRS MARY GRAHAM

Opposite *A message which was later to be rammed home relentlessly in the Second World War. Wholesale rationing was never introduced in Britain during the Great War, although the measures which were taken in 1918 proved a useful template for the 1939-1945 conflict.*

The Ministry of Food was teetering on the edge of a precipice at the bottom of which lay the introduction of a comprehensive policy of food rationing. At the end of January, a number of tentative measures were introduced to regulate the running of restaurants – introducing "meatless days", obliging customers to supply their own sugar and cutting the consumption of bread – but it could not delay the inevitable. On 25 February the Ministry of Food introduced a rationing system in London for meat, butter and margarine, and in the spring a nationwide rationing system for meat, butter, margarine, sugar and lard was established. The system worked well, and there were no food riots in market towns like Newton Abbot. A template was thus created for the more rigorous rationing system introduced in the Second World War.

A sergeant and two privates of
12th Division near Epéhy on
18 September 1918.

7 VICTORY — AND THE PRICE OF PEACE

"The Cavalry were now going forward in large numbers, and we have lived to see the day of the cavalry in action. Every moment of the last few days has been wonderful."

CAPTAIN LIONEL FERGUSON, 13TH BATTALION,
CHESHIRE REGIMENT, 24 AUGUST 1918

Above Over the Top *by John Nash, who served in France before being appointed as a war artist in 1918. The painting depicts an action in which he participated in December 1917*

Below Nash's paintbox.

On 24 July 1918, General Ferdinand Foch, the Allied Supreme Commander on the Western Front since April, assembled the three Allied Commanders-in-Chief, Haig, Pétain and Pershing, at his headquarters. He told them, "The moment has come to abandon the general defensive attitude forced on us until now by numerical inferiority and pass on to the offensive".

The last great German attempt to break the deadlock had blown itself out. To overhaul military doctrine in the middle of an all-out war is a daunting task, but in 1917 the German Army had risen to meet the challenge. In the winter of 1916-1917, the German high command adopted the concept of "elastic defence in depth" on the Western Front. Manpower was reduced in the front line, while its defensive positions were simultaneously strengthened and deepened. This allowed for a more mobile defence and offered the possibility of the tactical surrender of territory. Special counter-attack divisions were held behind the new defensive positions, the Hindenburg Line, to which the Germans retired in February-March 1917.

At the same time new infantry tactics were developed. The

German high command understood that frontal attacks in extended lines were horribly wasteful of human lives. Now it trained stormtroopers (Stosstruppen) in new all-arms tactics, a concept which the Germans referred to as "coordination". These tactics, combined with the abandonment of a prolonged preliminary bombardment, and its substitution by a short, ferocious and very accurate concentration of fire on the precise point of attack, proved successful on the Eastern Front in September 1917 during the capture of Riga by General Oskar von Hutier. They were employed in the German counter-offensive at Cambrai in the following November, and were to play a major role in the German spring offensive in 1918.

Another winter landscape, south of Arras, January 1918. On the trench firestep, an Artillery Forward Observation Officer identifies likely targets before conveying the information to his battery. At his side stands his linesman, to convey the information by field telephone.

Ludendorff's last throw

The collapse of Russia in the autumn of 1917 had released some 400,000 German troops for employment on the Western Front. Towards the end of March 1918, Germany launched what it hoped would be a knock-out blow against the Allies on the Western Front. The situation was crisply summarised on 11 November 1917 by Germany's First Quartermaster-General, Erich Ludendorff: "The situation in Russian and Italy makes it possible to deliver a blow on the Western Front in the New Year. Our general situation requires that we should strike at the earliest possible moment before the Americans can throw strong forces in."

The German high command hoped to drive a wedge between the French and the British, the former concentrating on defending Paris, the latter keen to protect their communications with the Channel ports. The attack – spearheaded by stormtroops and often referred to as "the Kaiser's battle" – was launched in thick fog on 21 March 1918.

In the initial assault, the German infantry was supported by nearly 6,500 guns – almost half the number of German guns on the Western Front – supported by over 3,500 mortars and 750 aircraft.

The British Commander-in-Chief, Field Marshal Sir Douglas Haig, had correctly anticipated the offensive but had deployed most of his reserves in the north, risking the security of the thinly-spread British Fifth Army – against which the main German blow was aimed on the Somme – in order to insure against a less probable risk to the Channel ports.

The commander of Fifth Army, General Gough, noted the intensity of the German bombardment "… so sustained and steady that it at once gave me the impression of some crushing, smashing power". By noon, the Fifth Army was in headlong retreat, and by the end of the day, the Germans had secured nearly 100 square miles of territory; it had taken the British no less than 140 days to achieve the same result on the Somme in 1916.

Paris came under fire from long-range guns on 23 March. On 26 March Foch was appointed Allied Supreme Commander. A week later, with the first German thrust running out of steam and ammunition, Ludendorff aimed a second blow against the British in Flanders. On 11 April, Haig issued a famous proclamation which included the words: "With our backs to the wall and believing in the justice of our cause, each one us must fight to the end."

The second German blow came close to breaking the British, who had at first been denied help by Foch. Nevertheless, by the end of April the Germans had been halted at a cost to the British Army of 240,000 casualties in 40 days of fighting. German overall losses since the start of the operation were close on 350,000. The stormtrooper battalions were fast being burned out. Their orders had been to push on at all costs, stopping for nothing. They were to bypass enemy positions which still held out and keep on advancing regardless of what was happening behind them or on their flanks. However, once they passed out of the range of their own artillery, having abandoned many of their own heavy weapons on the way, they stalled in front of stiffening British defences which they could not overcome. Ludendorff reflected that the thoughts of his troops were turning "with horror to fresh defensive fighting".

Ludendorff was now running out of cards but he reshuffled his hand. He launched an offensive against the French Sixth Army in Champagne which began on 27 May when 17 divisions stormed the Chemin de Dames ridge in the Aisne sector. This was to be a diversion before the principal blow fell on the British. The Germans broke through and by 3 June were once against on the River Marne, near Château-Thierry, only 56 miles from Paris.

It was here that the Americans made their first significant intervention on the Western Front. American troops were now flooding into France, and by November 1918 would rival in numbers those of the British and French. The US 3rd and 2nd Divisions were rushed into action on the Marne, while 50 miles to the north-west, at Cantigny, the 1st Division was thrown into the US Army's first offensive action of the war. For three days the Americans blocked the German advance at Château-Thierry and then, with the French, counter-attacked in mid-June after the Germans had been fought to a halt.

Ominous cracks were now appearing in the cohesion of the German Army. Each of its offensives in 1918 had been marked by widespread looting and drunkenness. Stern measures had been introduced to deal with desertion, and the growing influenza pandemic was now affecting German formations on the Western Front. Ludendorff persisted, launching an offensive either side of Reims and across the Marne, the preliminary to another blow in Flanders. When it opened on 15 July, the Allies were ready, waiting and defending in depth. This time the German gains were modest and the offensive had ground to a halt by 16 July. Ludendorff's all-or-nothing gamble had failed.

Opposite *Photograph of George James Palmer who served in the Machine Gun Corps. He picked the poppy from the trenches in 1917 during the Battle of Passchendaele (Third Ypres). Machine-gun crews operating Lewis Guns had a badge on their sleeves, a laurel wreath with LG for Lewis Gun in the middle. The crew laconically referred to it as a "suicide badge". If they were captured, they might be shot out of hand. The tasks of a five-man Lewis gun crew were as follows: one man carried the 30lb gun and another the spare parts, weighing almost as much; the other three men carried up to 200lb of ammunition in panniers strapped to their backs.*

Influenza Pandemic

After four years of war, a new and deadly enemy lurked in the wings to claim millions of victims worldwide

In the spring of 1918, large numbers of troops on the Western Front fell ill, complaining of sore throat, headaches and loss of appetite. Although highly infectious, recovery was rapid and the epidemic was dubbed the "three-day fever". Doctors identified a new type of influenza, which the soldiers in the trenches called "Spanish flu", although the origins of the outbreak were not to be found in the Iberian peninsula. Some claimed that the influenza originated in the Middle East but recent studies have suggested that the disease was brought to Europe by a group of American troops from Kansas. In the summer of 1918, however, the effects of the influenza became much more serious. Twenty per cent of its victims developed bronchial pneumonia or septicaemic blood poisoning. The skin of others became bluish, a condition which doctors termed heliotrope cyanosis. Over 95 per cent of patients in the last category died within a few days. By the end of the war, some 43,000 American servicemen had succumbed to influenza. The writer and critic Edmund Wilson, who served in a US Army hospital, noted: "Before I had left Vittel, the flu epidemic of 1918 had taken, I think, as heavy a toll of our troops as any battle with the Germans had done."

The first cases of influenza appeared in Britain in May 1918 and during the following months the virus killed some 230,000 people. The end of the war and the large-scale celebrations of peace were a public health catastrophe and stoked the rapid spread of the influenza. Most of the recommended preventive measures, which included spraying the streets with chemicals, eating large amounts of porridge and smoking cigarettes, proved wholly ineffective. In Britain the epidemic had the highest mortality rate since the cholera outbreak of 1849. In the United States, by the beginning of December, the pandemic had claimed approximately 450,000 lives, many of them from the ranks of the young and fit rather than the elderly and frail. The Great War, with its mass movements of troops in ships, aided the worldwide spread of the disease. In Spain it killed 170,000; in India the death toll rose to 12.5 million. In Germany, where the British naval blockade had resulted in serious malnutrition, over 400,000 succumbed. In all, the 1918 pandemic claimed as many as 40 million lives and later outbreaks claimed millions more.

I had a little bird
Its name was Enza,
I opened the window
And in-flu-enza
Children's skipping rhyme, 1918

A hospital ward in Wimereux staffed by members of Queen Mary's Auxiliary Army Corps.

The Allied counterblow

The riposte came on 18 July when the Americans and the French opened a campaign to recapture the Marne salient from the Germans. They crossed the river on 21 July and took Soissons on 1 August, forcing the Germans to conduct a general withdrawal from the salient. By 4 August the Allies had advanced 30 miles and had taken 25,000 German prisoners.

On 8 August, the British attacked on the Somme. This was not 1916, however, and their preparations had been concealed from the Germans with considerable skill. Learning the lessons of Cambrai, the British avoided a protracted preliminary bombardment and supported the attack with 464 tanks. The Ulster artilleryman Aubrey Wade saw them moving up in the small hours: "Lumbering grey shapes loomed up. The caterpillar flanges bit deep into the road as they advanced. They were the biggest of all their tribe – with machine guns fore and aft, tractor-belts propelling them like ships with squat conning towers. One by one they rolled past towards the trenches, tank succeeding tank as I stood and marvelled at their number."

Wade watched as the attack went in: " … never before had such a barrage been fired in the Amiens sector. It was colossal. North and south the line was aflame with gunfire. Under cover of a travelling wall of shell bursts the Fifth Australian Division, whom we were to follow,

The assault on the Hindenburg Line. Mk V tanks and New Zealand and British infantry advance after the capture of Grevillers. Note the captured guns in the background.

stormed the line. The army of tanks arose slowly from its hiding places behind the front-line trench and heaved itself over, to the terror and confusion of the enemy front".

Fog masked the initial British thrust, which within 24 hours had driven seven miles into the German lines. Ludendorff stigmatised 8 August as the "black day" of the German Army and three days later tendered his resignation to the Kaiser, who refused it but nevertheless observed, "I see that we must strike a balance. We have nearly reached the limit of our powers of resistance. The war must be ended".

On 8 August, the British had taken 13,000 prisoners and 400 guns. But the Germans recovered their balance and within 48 hours, when only 67 of the British tanks remained in service, the offensive was brought to an end. The pattern was now set for the closing months of the war. The Allied armies were to conduct an unrelenting succession of coordinated offensives, which had limited aims and were subordinated to the strategy of eliminating the gains which the Germans had made in the spring of 1918. Their effect was twofold: they took Allied forces deep into the German rear areas and, in so doing, broke the enemy's will to resist.

In spite of the Kaiser's prophetic words, the war continued. At the beginning of September, Aubrey Wade and his comrades entered the town of Peronne, on the River Somme south of Bapaume and investigated an abandoned German field hospital in a large tent: "Pushing aside the canvas flaps we found the place consisted of one long ward, down the sides of which ran a double row of camp beds. In each of the first dozen beds was a dead man, dressed in a white crinkly-paper affair like a nightgown and laid out neatly with folded arms. It was rather a mortuary than a hospital. Fourteen more corpses lay in their paper shrouds on the other side of the ward. Each one, as well as those opposite, was tricked out with a red paper bow at the neck. White sheets covered them. The effect of the whole thing, seen in a dim light, was eerie in the extreme".

The final assault on the Hindenburg Line began at the end of September after a preliminary American operation against the St Mihiel salient, which had posed a threat to Allied movements in Champagne since 1914. Foch gave the task to the US First Army. It was the first independent action undertaken by the Americans in the war. The attack was launched against the two sides of the salient on 12 September, combined with an assault against the centre by French troops. The Germans were caught in the act of leisurely retirement and were bundled out by the Americans in the space of 36 hours.

The clearing of the St Mihiel salient was followed by the decisive

Above Burial party near Monchy-le-Preux, August 1918. Private Archie Surfleet wrote of a similar scene, "I am still amazed at the casual way we piled those bodies, like so many huge logs, without any horror at such a gruesome task; which seemed to show we must be getting hardened".

Opposite The capture of Cambrai, October 1918. The men of the Loyal North Lancashire Regiment have their equipment in full marching configuration Note the mess tin carried by the soldier on the rear right.

.

Allied offensive of the war, the centrepiece of which was the breaking of the Hindenburg Line with a drive by French and American troops along the Meuse valley towards Mézières and a British thrust east of the Somme. Aubrey Wade crossed a section of the Hindenburg Line after it had been taken by the British 3rd Infantry Brigade. On the approaches, Wade had seen "more dead men on the advance than we, as artillerymen not concerned with the fighting in its special sense, had ever seen. At the bridges and crossroads they lay in two ands threes and sometimes dozens where the shells had caught them in the moment of escape. The frequent presence of corpses round the gun positions or observation posts made us utterly callous. They were merely souvenir dumps. We cut off badges and buttons and searched their pockets as a matter of routine. Once two of us had a great find – a set of gold false teeth in a Fritz officer's head. The teeth, immediately extracted with the aid of a bayonet, brought us seventy francs from an Engineer sergeant".

By mid-October, after hard fighting in which the Americans suffered heavy losses in the Argonne Forest, the German Army was hanging on by a thread. On 4 October, Germany requested discussions for an armistice along the lines laid out by President Wilson to the US Congress in January 1918 as the foundation for a lasting peace, a theme to which he returned in a speech delivered in New York on 27 September.

End game

Wilson's underlying preoccupation was that of national self-determination. The state of Belgium was to be restored and the French territory occupied by the Germans in the Great War was to be handed back, along with Alsace-Lorraine, which had been annexed by Germany in 1871. Wilson anticipated that the Habsburg and Ottoman empires would not survive the end of the war, enabling new states to emerge in central and eastern Europe, among them an independent Poland with full access to the Baltic Sea. Wilson also urged the democracies of Western Europe to welcome Russia "back into the society of free nations under institutions of her own choosing", and looked forward to the "mutual guarantees of political independence and territorial integrity" to all states.

In October, Wilson also listed a series of demands to Germany: the withdrawal of German forces from all occupied territories; an end to the U-boat campaign; and a recognition that the peace could not be concluded with the existing imperial and military authorities. The German high command was thus manoeuvred into a corner and obliged to conduct an irreversible surrender piecemeal, and also tied the armistice and future peace treaty to Wilson's Fourteen Points.

Fighting continued almost to the very end. Lieutenant Alex Wilkinson of the 2nd Battalion The Coldstream Guards was in the thick of it. On 6 November he wrote to his father with a vivid glee which many a grizzled veteran of the trenches, and even "Old Bill" himself, would have eyed askance. The fighting in which he had been was:

" … the best I have ever had and I would not have missed it for anything … We were right on top of the Huns before he could get his MG [machine gun] and we got a nice few prisoners and MGs straight away. And a nice few Huns were killed there too. I had sworn to shoot the first one I saw, but I could not bring myself to do it. I am a sentimental ass. Having sent the prisoners back, on we went at a tremendous pace. The men were perfectly splendid and showed amazing skill in their use of Lewis Guns and rifles … But what I call the battle discipline left a great deal to be desired. The men got out of their formation unless carefully watched and were inclined to lose direction and too much time was wasted searching prisoners not only for arms but also for souvenirs. Even so it was most amusing to see practically every man smoking a cigar after we had passed the first objective."

LIEUTENANT ALEX WILKINSON, 2ND BATTALION, THE COLDSTREAM GUARDS

The men who served in the 1918 British Army were very different troops to the professionals who had fought at Mons in 1914 during the "race to the sea". Only the ghosts of that original army, and those of Kitchener's New Armies, remained, the latter blooded on the Somme in 1916. For more than two years, the Army's recruits had been conscripts, many of whom had been mere lads in 1914.

Their morale was high as they pushed eastwards. In Germany morale was plummeting. Ludendorff called on the army to ignore the German government's negotiations with Wilson, and was dismissed by the Kaiser. In Wilhelmshaven, Kiel and Lübeck, sailors and stokers of the High Seas Fleet, inactive since the Battle of Jutland, mutinied rather than obey orders to steam into the North Sea in a final "death ride" against the Royal Navy.

The key to the railway carriage where the Armistice was signed in Compiègne.

On 5 November, Wilson informed the German government that negotiations should proceed on the basis of the Fourteen Points and that an armistice would have to be secured with the Allied military led by its Supreme Commander, Marshal Foch. A German delegation arrived at Foch's headquarters, in the Forest of Compiègne, where on the morning of 8 November it was obliged to ask formally for terms. Without access to wireless communications and denied the right of transit for 24 hours, they were unable to relay the terms to German headquarters until 10 November.

On the previous day Germany had gained a new chancellor, the socialist Friedrich Ebert. It was also on the point of losing its Kaiser, Wilhelm II who abdicated on 9 November and then the next day took refuge in neutral Holland while his family remained in Berlin. The Armistice was signed in a carriage of Marshal Foch's command train a few minutes after five on the morning of the 11 November and was effective from 11am.

At 10.45am, Lieutenant A S Gregory had written to his mother from his battery near Mons, where the men of the BEF had stood their ground on August 1914:

"My Dear Mother

A quarter of an hour more War! Cumulative rumours have been crowned by an official intimation. This is my last letter ON ACTIVE SERVICE. Never again, I hope, shall I wear tin hat and box respirator. We were expecting to go up into action early this morning, but – didn't. I am 6 miles S. of MONS. Well, that's enough for one letter. The church bells are ringing now. TE DEUM LAUDEAMUS.

Arthur"

All Quiet on the Western Front

The terms of the armistice recognised the territorial stipulations outlined by President Wilson in his Fourteen Points. In addition, German troops were to withdraw into Germany to a point 25 miles east of the Rhine, leaving all installations intact. The treaties of Brest-Litovsk and Bucharest, signed in 1918 with Russia and Romania respectively, were to be annulled and Germany was to relinquish the territories it had gained in Eastern Europe. The Allies were to be given access to Polish territories through Danzig on the Baltic Sea. The German troops were also to lay down their arms in East Africa.

In addition Germany was to surrender colossal quantities of materiel: all its artillery, machine guns and mortars, 5,000 locomotives, 150, 000 railway wagons and 5,000 lorries (all with spare parts for maintenance). The Allies reserved the right to enforce further requisitions, all of which would be paid for by the German government.

The entire German air service was to be surrendered to the Allies and the High Seas Fleet was to be interned. The process began when, at the end of November, 114 U-boats were escorted into Harwich harbour. Simultaneously, Germany's battleships and battlecruisers sailed to surrender at Scapa Flow. Admiral Beatty drew grim comfort from the scene:

"We never expected that the last time we should see them as a great force would be when they were being shepherded, like a flock of sheep, by the Grand Fleet. It was a pitiable sight, in fact I should say it was a horrible sight, to see those great ships that we have been looking forward so long to seeing, expecting them to have the same courage that we expect from men whose work lies on great waters – we did expect them to do something for the honour of their country – and I think it was a pitiable sight to see them come in, led by a British light cruiser, with their old antagonists, the battlecruisers gazing at them."

ADMIRAL BEATTY

All Allied prisoners of war were to be handed over by the Germans, and Allied nationals in occupied territories were to be repatriated. The Allies did not indicate whether this arrangement would be reciprocated. The Allied naval blockade of Germany's ports, which was causing immense hardship, would stay in place, with the proviso that the Allies would, if appropriate, consider providing food supplies.

In London and New York, church bells pealed and crowds thronged the streets to celebrate "Victory Day". Winston Churchill,

who had spent some months on the Western Front in 1917 as a colonel commanding the 6th Battalion, Royal Scots Fusliers, remembered the scene in London as it unfolded below his office in the Ministry of Munitions: "I looked into the street. It was deserted. Then from all sides men and women came into the streets. The bells began to clash. Thousands rushing in a frantic manner, shouting, screaming. Flags appeared … London streets were in pandemonium".

In spite of the outpouring of joy, there was a melancholy undercurrent running just below the surface even as the flags of the Allies were unfurled against the dull autumn skies. The war which many thought would have been over by Christmas 1914 had lasted so long, and so many had died.

There was grim reminder of the cost of victory at the start of the great victory parade held in Paris eight months later, on 14 July 1919. At the head of thousands of marching Allied troops were three young men, representatives of the tens of thousands of "grands mutilés de la guerre", horribly crippled but in uniform and trundled along, like delinquent and mute children, in bath chairs by their nurses. Behind

Above The end at last. *Celebrations in London greet the Armistice on "Victory Day".*
Opposite What now little *men? German prisoners at Abbeville, October 1918.*

War Poets

The Western Front was, paradoxically, an environment
conducive to poetry. Soldier-poets soon found themselves
in the thick of battle

For many of the young men who donned uniform
in 1914, war seemed like an adventure and their
role in it akin to that of the knights of the Middle
Ages. This studied approach to the conflict was
embodied by Rupert Brooke, the "golden warrior",
who wrote in "The Dead", part of a sonnet
sequence of 1914:

These hearts were woven of
*   human joys and cares,*
Washed marvellously with sorrow,
*   swift to mirth.*
The years had given them kindness.
Dawn was theirs,
And sunset and other colours
*   of the earth.*

Gassed: In Arduis Fidelis *by Gilbert Rogers, 1919.*

Such effusions could not survive the clammy grip of the trenches on the Western Front, where the living soon learned to survive alongside the dead. Brooke saw little combat in the war, and died of blood poisoning in the Aegean in April 1915. It was left to other poets, among them Edmund Blunden, Wilfred Owen, David Jones, Isaac Rosenberg, Siegfried Sassoon and Robert Graves, to evoke the desolate landscapes of murdered nature in which they served. Blunden, who served with the Royal Sussex Regiment, and won a Military Cross at the Battle of the Somme (1916), struck a sardonic note in *Third Ypres*:

> They're done, they've all died
>   on the entanglements,
> The wire stood up like an unplashed
>   hedge and thorned
> With giant spikes – and there they've
>   paid the bill.

Siegfried Sassoon, who served with the Royal Welch Fusiliers, earned the nickname "Mad Jack" for his courage on the Western Front. In "Counter-Attack", he blended breathless action with stomach-churning horror:

> The place was rotten with dead;
>   green clumsy legs
> High-booted, sprawled and grovelled
>   along the saps
> And trunks face downwards,
>   in the sucking mud,
> Wallowed like trodden sand-bags
>   loosely filled;
> And naked sodden buttocks,
>   mats of hair,
> Bulged, clotted heads slept in
>   plastering slime.
> And then the rain began – the jolly
>   old rain!

Sassoon was awarded the Military Cross in 1916 and was later wounded. Whilst recovering in a military hospital, Sassoon met fellow patient Wilfred Owen, who returned to the trenches and died a week before the signing of the Armistice. "In Dulce et Decorum Est", Owen caught the panic of a gas attack:

> Gas! GAS! Quick boys! – An ecstasy
>   of fumbling,
> Fitting the clumsy helmets just in time;
> But someone still was yelling out
>   and stumbling,
> And flound'ring like a man in fire
>   or lime …
> Dim, through the misty panes and
>   thick green light,
> As under a green sea I saw
>   him drowning.

Isaac Rosenberg also died in 1918, on a night patrol. "In Break of Day in the Trenches", he froze a moment of time on the firestep:

> The darkness crumbles away –
> It is the same old Druid Time as ever.
> Only a live thing leaps my hand –
> A queer sardonic rat –
> As I pull the parapet's poppy
>   to stick behind my ear.
> Droll rat, they would shoot you
>   if they knew
> Your cosmopolitan sympathies.
> Now you have touched this English hand
> You will do the same to a German –
> Soon, no doubt, if it be your pleasure
> To cross the sleeping green between.

them came hundreds of their wounded comrades, all bearing the scars of war and marching with no semblance of military order. It was only after they had passed by the silent crowds, and occupied the stands reserved for them, that the parade snapped into the spit and polish celebration of French military might.

Only in Belgium, which had suffered under harsh German occupation, was joy unconfined. The Germans had stripped the country of its industrial plants and raw materials and press-ganged 120,000 workers to the Reich. The Belgian soldiers who advanced into Belgium at the end of the Great War, returning home after four years of exile, were greeted as liberators in scenes of wild rejoicing.

In Germany, rocked by revolutionary unrest, ravaged by influenza and malnutrition, and dismayed by the abdication of the Kaiser, there was a numb bewilderment. Ordinary German civilians had been unaware of the dramatic course of events, both military and diplomatic, since July 1918. They could not comprehend why the armistice had been signed while the German Army still occupied parts of France and Belgium. A feeling grew that they had been "stabbed in the back". This sentiment was held by all the political classes. In November 1918, returning troops were greeted by the citizens of Berlin with flowers and laurel leaves, and a speech from the new Chancellor Friedrich Ebert, in which he declared, "I salute you who return unvanquished from the field of battle".

Top Keep smiling through. *Two British amputees put on a cheerful face for the camera. The brutal but honest French expression for such men was* "grands mutilées de la guerre". *Above* A prosthetic hand.

Peace and its problems

The feeling of betrayal felt by many Germans grew when the victorious Allies met in Paris to redraw the map of Europe and much of the world beyond, a task made all the more urgent by the collapse of the Russian, Austro-Hungarian and Ottoman empires. The principal treaty, signed by the Allies and Germany, was concluded at the Palace of Versailles on 28 June 1919.

A famous painting by Sir William Orpen captures the moment of signature by the German delegates. In the centre of the frame are the Big Three – the US President Woodrow Wilson, and Prime Ministers Lloyd George of the United Kingdom and Georges Clemenceau of

To the victors the spoils? Wilson, Clemenceau and Lloyd George in Orpen's painting of the German signature of the principal treaty at Versailles.

France, all of them serene and exquisitely suited, the victors of the Great War. Clemenceau later observed that Orpen had pictured him sitting between a would-be Napoleon (Lloyd George) and a would-be Jesus Christ (Woodrow Wilson).

On this occasion, at least, Clemenceau got the better of Jesus Christ, although in the long run it did neither him nor France little good. Josef Stalin would later muse, "How many divisions has the Pope?". France, although grievously mauled by four years of war, still had the divisions. If the war had continued into 1919 and beyond, which many believed it would until the sudden German collapse in the autumn of 1918, then the balance of military power would have swung inexorably towards the Americans. However, just as the German military believed that they had been "stabbed in the back" by the armistice, so the French high command was convinced that the German collapse had denied them the crushing victory in the field that in 1918 was rightly theirs. They would achieve it by other means at Versailles.

Lloyd George felt a premonition of the disaster which lay ahead during the discussion of armistice terms. He observed then, "if peace were made now, in twenty years' time the Germans would say what Carthage had said about the First Punic War, namely that they had made this mistake and that mistake, and by better preparation and organisation they would be able to bring about victory next time".

Nearly all the peace terms imposed at Versailles –¬ this was not a conference between victor and vanquished, the Germans were required merely to turn up and sign on the dotted line – had been anticipated at the time of the armistice. It was a matter of dotting "i's" and crossing "t's". Control of coal mines in the Saar was given to the French for fifteen years, in compensation for the German wrecking of the mines in north-east France; the east bank of the Rhine was demilitarised to a depth of 30 miles and was occupied by the Allies, also for 15 years, with Germany paying the cost of the occupation; conscription in Germany was abolished and the size of the German army was limited to 100,000 men; Germany was stripped of her colonies and denied membership of the League of Nations. The League had been the last of Wilson's Fourteen Points, and was established in 1920 to adjudicate international problems. It started promisingly by organising population transfers in the Balkans, (a problem which persists to the present day), but by 1939 had declined into irrelevance: when the Second World War broke out, the delegates were debating the standardisation of level crossings. Nevertheless, the League laid the foundations for international collaboration which have become, for better or worse, the hallmarks of its successor body, the United Nations which was established in 1945.

In 1919, what really stuck in the craw of Germans of all political persuasions was the Allies' demand, led by the French, for massive reparations to pay for war damage and the costs of occupation. Germany was to be "squeezed until the pips squeak", according to popular demands at the time. In December 1918, the French Minister of Finance, Louis-Lucien Klotz (according to Clemenceau, "the only Jew who knows nothing about money") had made it clear that he expected France's budgetary deficits to be redeemed then and in the future by reparations. At Versailles, France claimed that its total war damages ran to 209,000 million gold francs, and the overall claims of the Allies amounted to approximately 400,000 million francs.

Armed Spartacists in Berlin in January 1919. They believed that Germany was ripe for a Communist revolution.

However, sceptical experts at the British Treasury thought that the most that could be squeezed from Germany would be 75,000 million francs. Eventually the sum to be paid by Germany was left for future negotiations and in 1932 they were written off.

By then the damage had been done. In 1923 Germany defaulted on the payments and, in an effort to force payment, French and Belgian troops occupied the Ruhr. Many ardent French nationalists hoped that the occupation would prove permanent. The British looked the other way, the German mark collapsed and, down in Bavaria, an obscure Austrian-born German nationalist, Adolf Hitler, acquired his first heady taste of revolutionary notoriety. After the Great War, Germany had not been irrevocably crushed but Germans had been irrevocably humiliated. Reparations caused a lasting legacy of hatred in Germany which was among the most important factors behind Hitler's and the Nazis' rise to power in the early 1930s and their repudiation of Versailles, reparations and all.

Tying up loose ends

Separate treaties dealing with the each of the Central Powers were modelled on the Treaty of Versailles. For modern eyes, the settlement in the Middle East, in the territories which had made up the Ottoman empire, is of particular interest. In a plan submitted by T E Lawrence in 1918, "Irak" was broken into separate Kurdish and Arab states, foreshadowing what is happening on the ground in 2008. However, Lawrence's plan, which attempted to take account of regional characteristics, was ignored as the British and French tried to carve the region into separate spheres of influence, a process which had begun in secret by 1916. Old colonial habits died hard.

Following an agreement at San Remo in 1920, Lebanon and Syria were run by the French under a League of Nations mandate, and Iraq and Palestine (the future state of Israel) by the British. This was scant reward for the Arabs who had looked for more substantial rewards after their help in defeating the Ottoman Turks. Lawrence wryly observed that while in the years before 1914 Turkey had run Iraq with 14,000 locally raised troops, after 1918 the British needed 100,000 men, plus tanks and aircraft, to maintain a semblance of order.

Turkey emerged from the wreckage of the Ottoman empire in its modern form at the Treaty of Lausanne (1923). Under the leadership of Mustafa Kemal (Kemal Attaturk), it had beaten off an invasion by the Greeks, aided by the Armenians which had the tacit support of

Above *The Allied Victory Medal 1914–1919 (British version).*
Opposite *Vision of the future. Members of the of the SA (Sturmabteilung) branch of the Nazi Party prepare for the unsuccessful Munich putsch in November 1923. Its failure nevertheless launched Hitler on a march to power which was reached in 1933 and was brought to an end on 30 April 1945 after another global bloodletting.*

the British and French. It was now the task of Kemal Attaturk to drag his country into the twentieth century.

The Great War was supposed to have been a "war to end all wars", but its aftermath was hardly a time of peace. Russia descended into civil war, and the victorious Bolsheviks confidently expected a red tide of revolution to sweep across Europe. It did not happen, but much blood was shed: in Hungary a murderous Communist regime led by Bela Kun briefly held power in 1919; in April 1920, Poland invaded the Ukraine; in Berlin in January 1919, there was a short-lived and unsuccessful revolution by the Communist Spartacists; in 1920 their mirror image, right-wing paramilitaries, the Freikorps, attempted to seize power, ushering in several years of simmering violence.

The First World War had been fought by generals who had cut their military teeth in the colonial wars of the latter part of the nineteenth century. It began with cavalry charges and infantry in red trousers advancing in open order, and ended with all-arms battles in which tanks, aircraft and infantry cooperated in tactics which anticipated the Blitzkrieg battles of 1940. In 1914, the arbiters of seapower were the Dreadnought battleships of the Grand and High Seas Fleets. By 1918 their days of supremacy were over and the torch was handed to the submarine and the aircraft carrier. The combatant nations had mobilised millions for the war effort and in the process strengthened the sinews of the modern state.

In the Great War, the weapons of the future had been forged, even if the implications for their future employment had not been fully grasped. In 1919, Allied stubbornness created the casus belli of the Second World War, during which the Versailles settlement was overturned. Rather late in the day, President Wilson's 1918 plea to welcome Russia back into the international fold was answered when the Soviet Union joined the Western Allies after the German invasion of European Russia in the summer of 1941. During the course of the Second World War, an initially victorious Germany and then a resurgent Red Army overran many of the states created by the Treaty of Versailles – Poland, Lithuania, Latvia, Estonia, Czechoslovakia and Hungary. Until the late 1980s, their peoples were locked in the permafrost of the Cold War, fought between the two great victims of 1945 – the United States and the Soviet Union. In a new century they are multi-party democracies, and modern Europe has re-assumed the configuration it assumed in 1919. The Europe of the 1920s which emerged from the First World War is broadly the Europe of the early years of the twenty-first century.

"In Flanders fields the
poppies blow
Between the crosses
row on row
That marks our place:
and in the sky
The larks, still
bravely singing, fly
Scarce heard amid
the guns below."
John McCrae, 1915

The Cenotaph and the Tomb of the Unknown Warrior

In the aftermath of the Great War the stark and simple power of two monuments to the fallen provided a catharsis to a population scarred by four years of sacrifice and loss

The Cenotaph (which means "empty tomb" in Greek) was designed by Sir Edwyn Lutyens to stand in London's Whitehall as a temporary feature to mark the first anniversary of the November 1918 Armistice. Made of wood and plaster, its clean, eloquent lines made such an impression on the British public that the decision was taken to transform it into a permanent memorial fashioned from Portland stone and bearing the inscription "The Glorious Dead". Each year, on the Sunday nearest to 11 November, a Remembrance Service is held at the Cenotaph to commemorate the British and Commonwealth dead of the two World Wars. The man behind the idea to remember the dead of the Great War who had no memorial was a British Army chaplain David Railton, who in 1916 had noticed a grave in Armentières marked with a wooden cross and bearing the inscription "An Unknown British Soldier (of the Black Watch)". In 1920, Railton approached the Dean of Westminster with the suggestion that the corpse of an anonymous British serviceman who had fallen in France should be buried in Westminster Abbey. The idea took wing, receiving the support of David Lloyd George and, after initial resistance, King George V. The bodies of four unidentified

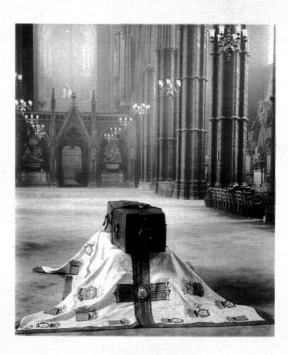

servicemen (some accounts say six) were exhumed from battlefields in France and taken to St Pol, near Arras, where they lay covered in Union flags. On 7 November 1921, one was chosen at random and placed in a plain coffin. The other bodies were re-interred. The coffin was then placed in a larger coffin made of Hampton Court oak, which bore a plaque inscribed "A British Warrior who fell in the

Above The Unknown Warrior at Westminster Abbey, November 1920.
Opposite King George V unveils the permanent Cenotaph in London's Whitehall on 11 November 1920.

Great War 1914–1918 for King and Country". A flag that had been used by Railton as an altar cloth was wrapped around the coffin, and a medieval Crusader's sword, selected by George V from the Royal Collection, was slipped through its encircling iron bands. On 11 November, after an overnight stay in Dover, the coffin was covered by a Union flag and placed on a gun carriage drawn by six black horses. Bearing a steel helmet, side arms and a belt, it was then carried through the streets of London to the newly built Cenotaph, where George V unveiled the memorial and placed a wreath of red roses and bay leaves on the coffin. After a two-minute silence, the coffin was moved to Westminster Abbey, followed by the King and his three sons, other members of the Royal Family and ministers of state. At the Abbey, the coffin was borne to the west end of the nave, escorted by 100 holders of the Victoria Cross and followed by 100 women who had lost husbands and sons in the Great War. The helmet and side arms were removed from the coffin, which was lowered into the tomb as the King scattered some French earth, the last resting place for so many of the war dead.

COUNTING THE COST

It is impossible to calculate with any degree of finality the overall human cost of the war. Some 70 million men of the combatant nations were mobilised, 8.9 million of them from Britain and its Empire, and 8.4 million from the French Empire. Germany mobilised almost 11 million, Austria–Hungary 7.8 million, Turkey 2.8 million, Bulgaria 1.2 million, Russia 12 million and the United States 4.3 million. Losses were on an equally sobering scale. The Austro–Hungarian Empire lost at least 1 million dead and suffered 2 million wounded, but these returns are almost certainly an underestimate. German figures are also uncertain; by their own estimate they suffered some 2 million dead and 5.7 million wounded. The French Empire had total casualties of 5.7 million, of which 1.4 million were military dead or missing. French losses amounted to 34 for every 1,000 head of France's wartime population. The British Empire suffered 3.2 million casualties, of whom nearly a million were dead or missing. Of these some 750,000 came from the United Kingdom. Fighting on a single narrow front (with the exception of small contingents in Salonika and France), the Italians lost 460,000 dead. It is worth noting that this figure represents almost half of the death toll of the entire British Empire on all fronts. The Russians lost 1.8 million military dead and 5 million wounded, plus 2 million civilian dead. The Turks estimated their losses at 2.3 million, combatant and civilian, while the United States armed forces sustained 280,000 casualties, of whom nearly 50,000 were dead and 230,000 wounded or missing.

THE COMMONWEALTH WAR GRAVES COMMISSION

On 17 November 1918, the social reformer Beatrice Webb wrote in her diary, "Every day one meets saddened women, with haggard faces and lethargic movements, and one dares not ask after husband or son". That the dead were not forgotten in the years after the end of the Great War was largely the result of the labours of one man, Major-General Sir Fabian Ware (1869–1949). A 45-year-old educationalist in 1914, Ware joined the Red Cross and served in France, where he assumed personal responsibility for recording where the British Empire dead had been buried. By February 1915, Ware's work had received official recognition and his unit was charged with finding, marking and registering the graves of British officers and men in France. He was given two assistants, the rank of Major and the job of running the newly formed Graves Registration Commission. Ware was subsequently authorised to negotiate with the French the purchase of land, in Britain's name, for the burial of Allied soldiers. The responsibility for the maintenance of these war grave sites was to be undertaken in perpetuity by the British.

By the spring of 1916, the Graves Registration Commission had become the Directorate of Graves Registration and Enquiries and its work was extended to theatres of war beyond France, in Greece, Mesopotamia and Egypt. A horticultural policy was evolved under the aegis of a National Committee, the precursor of the Imperial War Graves Commission (now the Commonwealth War Graves Commission), which came into being in May 1917. One of the Commission's first key decisions was that no distinction would be made between officers and men, a principle which was to become the cornerstone of its philosophy. In the same year Rudyard Kipling, who had lost his son on the first day of the Battle of the Somme, was appointed literary adviser to the Commission. It was Kipling who suggested the wording to be carved on the headstone of an unidentified soldier: "A Soldier of the Great War/ Known unto God".

Also appointed in 1917, as one of the three principal architects engaged in the work of the War Graves Commission in France and Belgium, was Sir Edwin Lutyens (1869–1944). Responsible for the dignified and harmonious overall aspect of the cemeteries was Sir Frederic Kenyon (1863–1952), Director of the British Museum. These men were to play a vital role in shaping the enduring character of the War Graves Commission, whose unwavering principle of extending equality of treatment for all the war dead, irrespective of military or civil rank, race or creed, has guided it since the end of the war in 1918. In that year, Sir Frederic Kenyon wrote, "Those who are interested – and hundreds of thousands must be most deeply and poignantly interested – in the treatment of our dead in France and Belgium may rest assured that no labour is spared, and that nothing that careful thought can provide is wanting to pay the tribute of reverence and honour which is due to those that have fallen for their country."

GLOSSARY

All-big-gun ship a battleship, or battlecruiser, armed exclusively with heavy guns of the same calibre. The perfect examples were the Royal Navy's battleships of the Queen Elizabeth class – *Barham, Valiant, Warspite, Malaya* and *Queen Elizabeth* – which were more heavily armed than any other battleships and almost as fast as the fastest battlecruisers.

Army the highest military grouping. Used only in time of war, it could comprise anything from three to six corps.

Battalion standard unit for British infantry (approximately 36 officers and 1,000 men) subdivided into companies (240 men) platoons (60 men) and specialist sections (machine gun, mortar, pioneers etc). The British infantryman's home, it was rarely at full strength in France.

Battery unit of organisation for artillery. A British battery normally consisted of six guns.

Battlecruiser a ship of battleship size and armament in which armoured protection was sacrificed for speed.

Battleship fleet's largest class of fighting ship, boasting the heaviest guns and armour.

Brigade a formation which in the British Army consisted of four infantry battalions (some 4,000 men).

Capital ship a term now obsolete and first used in 1909, denoting the largest fighting ships in a fleet – battleships and battlecruisers.

Corps a formation usually consisting of two divisions (approximately 40,000 men).

Creeping barrage artillery bombardment intended to land in front of advancing infantry and thus prevent the enemy from re-occupying forward fire positions. First employed in 1916.

Cruiser a fighting ship one step down in size from a battlecruiser or battleship. Often used to scout ahead of the battle fleet. In the Royal Navy there were three types of cruiser – armoured, protected and light. The last was the most effective, being fast enough to play an effective reconnaissance role and carrying sufficiently heavy armament to outgun destroyers.

Defence in depth a German concept, developed after 1916, which eschewed meeting enemy attacks from forward positions in favour of constructing a succession of interlinked defensive positions which stretched several miles to the rear. This network defied seizure in a single attack and, as German firepower increased, inflicted heavy losses on Allied infantry attempting to batter their way through.

Destroyer a term derived from torpedo-boat destroyer and applying to fast, highly manoeuvrable warships smaller than cruisers whose original task was to protect the battle fleet from torpedo boats. In the Great War, destroyers carried torpedoes and anti-submarine equipment.

Division the largest formation in the British Army (usually of three brigades of four battalions each) to hold the same units permanently. At full strength, 17,000 to 20,000 men. On the Western Front, British divisions, where possible, contained battalions of the same type. Thus Regular, Territorial and New Army spirit was reflected in complete divisions.

Dreadnought an all-big-gun battleship or battlecruiser. Named after HMS *Dreadnought*, laid down in 1905 and launched in 1906, the type became obsolescent in 1918.

Pre-Dreadnought battleship built and launched before the dawn of the Dreadnought era in 1905 when the keel of HMS *Dreadnought* was laid. A small number of such battleships were built after the launch of HMS *Dreadnought* in 1906 but only because cancellation of the ships did not make economic sense.

Enfilade firing at the flank of an enemy formation along its length. Troops caught by enfilading fire invariably sustained heavy losses.

Howitzer short-barrelled, high-angle artillery piece, used for smashing fortifications, buildings and trench systems with high-trajectory, high-explosive shells.

Mine explosives planted in tunnels dug under enemy positions. Also explosive devices floated on or just below the surface of the sea.

Mortar high-angle, short-range artillery piece, principally used in the trenches.

Sap a deep and narrow trench used to approach and undermine an enemy position. Also a narrow passage extending some 30 yards from the frontline trench to a small listening post.

Tracer bullet a small arms or machine-gun bullet with illuminant to enable sighting and correction of fire.

BIBLIOGRAPHY

Recent years have seen the publication of a number of excellent single-volume histories of the First World War. One of the best is *The First World War* by Hew Strachan (2003). Shorter and more quirky is *World War One: A Short History* by Norman Stone (2007). A more judicious account of the conflict is *The First World War* by John Keegan (1999). Still immensely readable is A J P Taylor's *The First World War* (1966). Comprehensive and superbly illustrated introductions to the Great War can be found in *World War I* by H P Willmott (2003) and *The Experience of World War I* edited by J M Winter (1989). Still of immense value is *History of the First World War* by Basil Liddell Hart (1970), a soldier who fought in the conflict and foresaw the inevitable aftermath in 1939.

Addressing various aspects of the conflict covered in this volume, the reader will find the following helpful. On the origins of the Great War, an invaluable starting point is *Europe's Last Summer: Who Started the War in 1914?* by David Fromkin (2004). On aspects of the war on the Western Front, particularly from the British soldier's point of view, essential reference books are *Eye-Deep in Hell: Trench Warfare in World War I* by John Ellis (2002) and *Tommy Goes to War* by Malcolm Brown (2001). *War on the Western Front: In the Trenches of World War I*, edited by Dr Gary Sheffield (2007) covers even-handedly the technical and tactical problems faced by all the combatants.

The First Day on the Somme: 1 July 1916 by Martin Middlebrook (1971) is a moving account of the blackest day in the history of the British Army from the soldier's point of view; *The Price of Glory: Verdun 1916* by Alistair Horne (1982) covers a longer but equally terrible passage of arms endured by the French Army in 1916. John Keegan's *The Face of Battle* (2004) also contains an incisive account of the battle of the Somme. A look at the other side of the hill is to be found in *Through German Eyes: The British & the Somme 1916* by Christopher Duffy (2006) and *All the Kaiser's Men: The Life and Death of the German Army on the Western Front 1914-1918* by Ian Passingham (2003). *Band of Brigands: The First Men in Tanks* by Christy Campbell (2007) is an absorbing history of the birth of armoured warfare. The best defence of Field Marshal Haig remains *Douglas Haig, The Educated Soldier* by John Terraine (1963). The Ludendorff offensives are comprehensively covered in *The Kaiser's Battle* by Martin Middlebrook (1978)

A very useful introduction to the Gallipoli campaign is *Gallipoli 1915* by Tim Travers (2001) which deftly contrasts the Anzac and Turkish points of view. On naval aspects of the war, John Keegan provides an excellent description of the Battle of Jutland from both sides in *The Price of Admiralty* (1988), while the standard work on the Royal Navy in the Great War remains *From Dreadnought to Scapa Flow* (Vols I–III) by A J Marder (1961-1966). For naval enthusiasts, another useful volume is *Admiral of the Fleet Earl Beatty* by Captain S W Roskill (1980).

An excellent introduction to the war in the air is *Canadian Airmen in the First World War* by S F Wise (1980). The story of the development of the bomber can be found in *The Bombers: The Illustrated Story of Offensive Strategy and Tactics in the Twentieth Century* by Robin Cross (1987). A lively history of the Zeppelin campaign is given in *Zeppelin: The Battle for Air Supremacy* by RC Rimmell (1984); and the offensive against England undertaken by the Gothas and their successors is covered in *The Sky on Fire: The First Battle of Britain 1917–18* by Major Raymond H Fredette (1991). The career of Manfred von Richthofen is ably chronicled in *Under the Guns of the Red Baron: The Complete Record of von Richthofen's Victories and Victims* by Norman Franks, Hal Giblin, Nigel McCrery and Barry Weekley (2007). The history of the RFC's fighter pilots is chronicled in *Above the Trenches: A Complete Record of the Fighter Aces and Units of the British Empire Air Force 1915–20* by Christopher Shores, Norman L R Franks and Russell Guest (1990).

The social history of the British home front has been covered by Arthur Marwick in *The Deluge: British Society and the First World War* (1991) and *Women at War, 1914–1918* (1977). Insights into many aspects of life in Britain during the First World War can be found in *The Imperial War Museum Book of The First World War* by Malcolm Brown (2002). Other useful books of a general nature on the Great War include *Technology in War: The Impact of Science on Weapon Development and Modern Battle* by Kenneth Macksey (1986) which provides a stimulating canter through the scientific aspects of warfare as it developed between 1914 and 1918, from weaponry to war industry; and *Remembered* by Julie Summers, Brian Harris and Ian Hislop (2007) an exquisitely illustrated history of the work of the Commonwealth War Graves Commission. A brilliant work of literary criticism is provided by *The Great War and Modern Memory* by Paul Fussell (1985). An able account of the peacemaking process in 1918–1919 can be found in *Paris 1919* by Margaret MacMillan (2003).

In the preparation of this book I have relied on a number of vivid personal memoirs of the Great War, among them *Undertones of War* by Edmund Blunden (1987), *Soldier From the Wars Returning* by Charles Carrington (1964), *The War of the Guns* by Aubrey Wade (1936), *Goodbye To All That* by Robert Graves (1929), *The Last Fighting Tommy: The Life of Harry Patch, the Only Surviving Veteran of the Trenches* by Harry Patch with Richard van Emden (2007), *Winged Warfare* by W A Bishop (1938) and the fictional autobiography by Siegfried Sassoon, *Memoirs of an Infantry Officer* (1932).

NOTES

Chapter 2

1. "Old Bill", a moustachioed, indestructible old sweat created by the cartoonist Bruce Bairnsfather, always put the point of view of the battle-hardened British soldier. His Second World War equivalents were the philosophical GIs Willie and Joe created by the American cartoonist Bill Mauldin.

2. The logistical demands of the Western Front placed a considerable strain on Allied manpower. A huge labour pool was required to sustain logistics and transport, and part of this task was undertaken by Chinese labourers. By the end of the war nearly 100,000 Chinese were working for the BEF and 30,000 for the French.

3. "Female" was the designation for a tank which was armed only with machine guns. They were man-killers while "Male" tanks, fitted with machine guns and cut-down naval 6-pounder guns housed in sponsons, were emplacement destroyers. The Mk V tank which appeared in July 1918 had a new Ricardo engine, new transmission and improved gears and had a road speed of 5mph. However, its impressed steel-plate tracks usually wore out after just 20 miles.

Chapter 3

1. In the Great War, the French pioneered the ace system. A French pilot qualified with five victories while the Germans specified 10. The German Manfred von Richthofen, with 80 victories, outstripped everyone. The Allied ace of aces was the Frenchman Rene Fonck, with 75. The RFC pilot Major Edward "Mick" Mannock is credited with 73 victories, making him the top-scoring British fighter ace.

Chapter 7

1. Foch was subsequently appointed a Marshal of France on 6 August 1918

2. This was a "rolling" barrage, first introduced in 1915 in an attempt to break the stalemate of trench warfare. The barrage was indiscriminate, each battery firing down a "lane" (approximately 200 yards of front per battery) to a predetermined barrage line kept 150 yards ahead of the advancing infantry. Once this line had been pulverised for anything from 3 to 10 minutes, the fire was lifted to the next barrage line and then on to the next. The jumps the barrage made were normally 500 to 1,000 yards deep, theoretically enabling the infantry to advance unmolested behind a curtain of high explosive and shrapnel. In any rolling barrage, approximately one-third of the field guns would fire shrapnel ahead of the high explosive. Divisional artillery would add heavy shrapnel shells to their fire which consisted mainly of high explosive. These barrages took time to prepare – it was reckoned that for each 2,500 yards of advance by the infantry at least one day's artillery preparation was required. By 1918, however, some attacks were made without any artillery preparation at all.

PICTURE CREDITS

With the exception of the photograph of "Charlie" May on page 9 (MR4/17/295/5/1), which is reproduced courtesy of Tameside Local Studies and Archives, the map of the Western Front on page 40 (Rodney Paull), the first aid box on page 69 (Shutterstock) and the photograph of *skat* cards on pages 120–21, which was kindly provided by Simon Dunston, all the images were supplied by the Imperial War Museum. Reference numbers for these images are as follows:

Title page Q6893; page 10 Q9534; page 12 Q3014; page 13 Q17390.

Chapter 1: The Origins and Course of the War
pages 18–19 Q 53446; page 20 Q 91840; page 21 Q91848; page 23 IWM/ART 5608; page 26 Q 81852; page 28–29 Q30068 (top) and Q30076 (bottom); page 30 IWM/ART PST 560; page 32 IWM/ART PST 2735; page 34 EPH 5790; page 35 Q 57240; pages 36–37 EPH 3147 (tankard), Q11718 (top), Q50719 (bottom); page 38 EPH 4083; page 43 IWM PST 303; pages 44–45 Q55500; page 47 E AUS 842; page 49 Q20615.

Chapter 2: The Western Front
Pages 50–51 Q4665; page 52 Q 60734; page 54 Q 49104; pages 56–57 E AUS 844; page 58 Q 872; page 59 Q6229; page 60 EPH 8262; page 61 E AUS 572; page 62 CO 2076; page 63 Q635; page 64 EPH 3863; page 67 Q751(top) and Q5101 (bottom); page 68 Q5935; page 69 Q 88580 (top); page 70 WEA 2160; page 72 UNI 12268 (cap); page 73 Q 992; page 75 Q 1581; page 76 Q 1630; page 78 E AUS 1067; pages 80–81 Q754; page 82 Q1142; pages 84–85 Q70168; page 85 Q79501; page 86 Q 4065; page 87 Q3995; pages 88–89 Q 4501; pages 90–91 Q 11586; page 92 CO 2241; page 94 EQU 1654; page 95 Q 690.

Chapter 3: The War in the Air
Pages 96–97 Q12066; page 98 Q67690; page 99 Q 54985; page 103 Q 65969; page 105 Q 33850; page 106 Q8533; page 107 Q11864 ; page108 Q65882; page109 Q 69222; page 110 Q61077 (top) and Q 67780 (bottom); page 111 Q 63124 (top) and Q 42283 (bottom); page112 Q 56012; page 113 EPH 9003; page 114 CO 1751; page 115 Q 50328; page 116 Q 63153; pages 116–17 Q11863; page 118 EPH 9441-9443; page123 IWM ART 3077; page 125 Q 58468; page 127 Q 108846; page 128 HO 98; page 130 Q 11987; page 131 Q 57564.

Chapter 4: The War at Sea
Pages 132–33 Q 39267; page135 Q 55499; page 136 Q 50992; page 139 SP 3129; page 140 Q 22687; page 142 Q 20348; page 143 Q18121; page 145 SP 1706; page 148 SP 1708; page 151 SP 2469 (top) IWM ART 1247 (bottom); page 152 Q21396; page 154 Q 56781; page 155 Q 20762; page 156 UNI 11978; page 158 Q 33149; page159 IWM ART 5130; pages

PICTURE CREDITS

160–61 SP 2143; pages 162–63 IWM ART 1346.

Chapter 5: From European War to World War

Pages164–65 Q 13626; pages166–67 Q823; page169 Q 13550; page 171 Q 13219; pages 172–73 Q 13622; page 174 Q 13426; page 176 Q 13644; page 179 HU 51386; page 180 Q 50358; pages 182–83 Q 58754; page 184 Q 73535; page 187 Q 45771; page 188 PST 355; page 189 Q 5104.

Chapter 6: Home Fires: Women and War

Pages192–93 Q 2441; page194 Q31030 (top) and Q107142 (bottom); page 195 0313; page 196 IWM PST 13169; page 197 Q 30010; pages198–99 Q30687; page 200 HU 59113; page 201 Q 27889; page 202 Q 30031; page 204 Q 2469; page 207 Q71311; page 208 Q68949; page 209 Q 29155; page 211 IWM ART 4881; page 213 IWM ART 13167; page 214 Q18706 (bottom left) and Q19657 (top right); page 215 Q19655; page 216 EPH 4477; page 217 Q 32704; page 218 Q106252; page 221 Q53589; page 223 HU 52451; page 225 PST 4470.

Chapter 7: Victory – and the Price of Peace

Pages 226–27 Q 11326; page 228 IWM ART 1656 (top) and EPH 9425 (bottom); page 229 Q10610; page 230 EPH 3938; pages 232–33 Q 8006; page 234 Q 11262; page 236 Q 23612; page 237 Q 11363; page 239 IWM ART 2722; page 240 EPH 9353; page 242 Q 9353; page 243 Q 47894; page 244 IWM ART 3819; page 246 Q 27815 (top) and SUR 684 (bottom); page 247 IWM ART 2856; page 249 Q 110864; page 250 MH 11397; page 251 OMD 2264; page 253 CO 940; page 254

INDEX

Note: page numbers in **bold** refer to information contained in captions, photographs and illustrations.